Hills of Spices

The Jewish Publication Society is
one of the most respected international
Jewish cultural and educational institutions.
In all of its endeavors, JPS seeks to preserve
and enrich Jewish heritage.

The Society honors the members of its Giving Circles,
whose generosity strengthens
its ability to achieve its multifaceted mission.

Hills of Spices

Poetry from the Bible

Editor
Rena Potok

Introduction by
Andrea L. Weiss

2006 · 5766
The Jewish Publication Society
Philadelphia

The Jewish Publication Society
2100 Arch Street
Philadelphia, PA 19103
www.jewishpub.org

Manufactured in the United States of America

06 07 08 09 10   10 9 8 7 6 5 4 3 2 1

Library of Congress Cataloging-in-Publication Data

Bible. O.T. English. Selections. 2006.
    Hills of spices: poetry from the Bible / edited by Rena Potok; introduction by Andrea Weiss.
        p. cm.
    Poems in Hebrew with English translations on facing pages.
    Includes index.
    ISBN 0-8276-0826-8 (alk. paper)
    Hebrew poetry, Biblical. 2. Hebrew poetry, Biblical—Translations into English.
    I. Potok, Rena. II. Bible. O.T. Hebrew. Selections. 2006. III. Title.

BS1091.P68 2006
21.5'208—dc22
                                                            2006041712

O you who linger in the garden,
A lover is listening;
Let me hear your voice.
"Hurry, my beloved,
Swift as a gazelle or a young stag,
To the hills of spices!"

— The Song of Songs 8:13–14

CONTENTS

PREFACE

The Story of Biblical Poetry

Open the Bible. It is an old book, compiled over hundreds of years, composed in vast deserts and along raging river beds, recited on slate-capped mountain tops and in cities built of white stone gleaming in the hot red Mediterranean sunset. It tells the story of families, deceits and pleasures, of simple men and women, heroes, villains, and kings, terrible battles and astonishing miracles. It paints the portrait of a wrathful, punishing God, a loving, nurturing God. And of God's relationship to individuals – personal, poignant, perplexing. It tells the story of human experience.

Human beings are creatures of habit; one of our most consistent habits is storytelling. How do we tell our stories? Orally, and in writing. The history of written language is rife with myths, legends, tales – and poems. Indeed, one of the oldest forms of storytelling is the poem. It is a compact, compressed form of expression. Every word has a precise weight and measure. The poem, whatever its length, shows an economy of literary expression. It has texture, tone, image, rhythm, meter, and sometimes rhyme.

Open the Bible. Its poems show you the anguish of Lamentations, bewailing the devastation of Jerusalem by Babylon; the playful eroticism and luscious imagery of Solomon in Song of Songs; the humor and wit of the Wisdom Writings; the joy and devotion of praising God in song; the fantastic imagery of kingly dreams and visions; the tender approach of the psalmist to healing, death, parenting, the presence of the divine in day-to-day human life. *Hills of Spices* is not intended as a comprehensive representation of all the poems appearing in the Tanakh texts. Here, you'll find a rich sampling of the lush terrain of this biblical poetry in all its various forms.

The poems included here were selected on the merit of their literary value—evocative phrasing and imagery, compelling themes and variations; their ability to evoke a powerful emotional response; their fanciful wordplay and rhythmic balances. Some will be familiar because they are found in contemporary Jewish liturgy, such as Psalms 113, 114, 115, and 117, which are part of the Hallel service, recited for the new moon, festivals, and Hanukkah. Others are famous or beloved poems, such as the entire text of the Song of Songs, and the 23rd Psalm, recited for the sick, at a funeral, or at the unveiling of a tombstone. Psalms 1, 16, 23, and 103 are psalms of comfort, often recited at funerals, or in a house of mourning. Proverbs 31 is traditionally recited at Sabbath dinner by a husband to his wife, and Psalm 126 is sung at the opening of birkat ha-mazon (grace), after Sabbath or holiday meals.

The poems are organized into nine broad sections to provide a sense of the many poetic genres and topics appearing in the Bible: Blessings, Prayers and Songs of Praise, Poetic Moments (short verses on a variety of topics), Testaments and Pronouncements, Laments, Judgment Oracles, Prophecies of Salvation and Consolation, Wisdom Writings, and Love Songs. There is a scriptural index at the end of the book, to help identify specific poems and their location in this volume.

Cantillation Marks

Hills of Spices has been set to look like a modern bilingual poetry edition. The cantillation marks have been removed from the original Hebrew Bible text to bring the biblical Hebrew into a modern setting. In the Jewish tradition, when biblical poetry is used in prayer–in siddurim and mahzorim (daily, Sabbath, and festival prayer books)–it appears without cantillation, as modern poetry. Leaving these marks in the text would be akin to printing dictionary pronunciation marks in a bilingual edition of poetry by Baudelaire or Rilke.

Translation

All the translations here are from the 1985 New Jewish Publication Society (NJPS) translation, with one exception: the Old Jewish Publication Society (OJPS) translation of the 23rd Psalm, which possesses stronger cadences and poetic meter than the NJPS translation. It is also more familiar; it is the commonly cited version of that famous and oft-used psalm. But to give this psalm a similar feel to the rest of the volume, "Thou" was changed to "You," "wouldst" was changed to "would," and so on.

Acknowledgments

Special thanks must go to two people who put their imprints on this book: Andrea Weiss graciously gave of her time and expertise, offering advice on the content, structure, and organization of this volume. Her lucid, cogent introduction sheds light on the question of how to read and identify biblical poetry and its many literary components. Rebecca Fischman, assistant editor at The Jewish Publication Society, was instrumental in shaping this book from its inception. Her gentle and incisive input was as productive as it is invaluable.

The poems in this volume are as vibrant and vital today as on the day they were created. Read them aloud. Let them rise up to you from the deep, fertile soil of our cultural heritage. Let the magic and power of generations wash over you through these ancient words, for these are the roots of modern civilization. Immerse yourself in the beauty and power of these verses, their abundant joy and quivering terror, their pathos and hubris, the sexual desire and literary passion cascading from the lips of the poet, king, patriarch, warrior. The desolate mother. The ecstatic prophet. Words attributed to the Creator of the Universe. Words of love. Punishing words of disappointment and rage. Words of consolation and acceptance.

Immerse yourself. You can almost hear the beating of timbrels, the gentle plucking of the harp or lyre. You can almost feel the desert heat rising from the earth, smell the tantalizing aroma of spices intoxicating your senses.

Rena Potok
January, 2006

INTRODUCTION
TO BIBLICAL POETRY

Andrea L. Weiss

The Bible preserves several versions of the first plague upon the Egyptians. The account in the Book of Exodus is commonly classified as prose, while the retellings in the psalms are categorized as poetry:

> Moses and Aaron did just as the LORD commanded: he lifted up the rod and struck the water in the Nile in the sight of Pharaoh and his courtiers, and all the water in the Nile was turned into blood and the fish in the Nile died. The Nile stank so that the Egyptians could not drink water from the Nile; and there was blood throughout the land of Egypt. (Exod. 7:20–21)

> He turned their rivers into blood;
> He made their waters undrinkable. (Ps. 78:44)

> He turned their waters into blood
> and killed their fish. (Ps. 105:29)

What qualifies the Exodus passages as "prose" and the psalms passages as "poetry"? What are the distinguishing features of biblical poetry? These questions are not easily answered, partially because of a lack of scholarly consensus about many aspects of biblical poetry and partially because there are not always sharp distinctions between poetry and prose. Nevertheless, in spite of uncertainties in our understanding of this ancient, sacred literature, it is possible to delineate those sections of the Bible widely considered poetry and to outline their key stylistic features.

The Search for Identifiable Indicators of Biblical Poetry

In the classical period, thinkers like Aristotle and Horace penned theories about the nature, mechanics, and effects of poetry. However, in the Bible we do not find definitions of poetry or discussions of how biblical poetry operates. In fact, biblical Hebrew does not have a general term for "poetry," though various terms do seem to signal the presence of a poetic passage. For instance, the passage known as the "Song of Moses" is introduced with the statement: "Then Moses and the Israelites sang this song (*shirah*)" (Exod. 15:1). David's eulogy for Saul and Jonathan is labeled as a "dirge" (*kinah*) (2 Sam. 1:17). Many compositions in the Book of Psalms begin with the word "*mizmor*," which is translated as a "psalm" and likely indicates a song accompanied by a stringed instrument. Such terms suggest that a number of labels were used to classify certain types of compositions; yet these titles are not used consistently throughout the Bible, nor are they affixed to every text that we would consider a poetic passage.

Since these internal indicators do not point conclusively or consistently to the presence of biblical poetry, we might look to visual means in order to identify biblical poetry. When opening selected Hebrew editions or translations of the Bible, one can determine the poetic sections by the distinctive layout of the verses. For example, in the JPS TANAKH, in Genesis 4:23–24, the prose format gives way to poetic verse, signaling a shift in discourse. Yet, in other editions of the Bible no graphic distinction is made between poetry and prose.

The convention of visually distinguishing poetic passages, called stichography, evolved over time. In Qumran texts versification is found sporadically. In talmudic times, spacing was used widely in certain books, but it was not required. The Talmud established special writing for only five sections: Exodus 15:1–18, Deuteronomy 32, and Judges 5, which are poetic texts, as well as Joshua 12:9–24 and Esther 9:7–9, which are lists found in prose passages. Throughout the Middle Ages, Jewish scribes commonly incorporated some type of special spacing, not only for the sections mentioned in talmudic sources, but also for other parts of the Bible, such as Psalms, Proverbs, Job, Lamentations, the Song of Asaph (1 Chron. 16:8–35), and selected lists. After the advent of the printing press, most printed masoretic Bibles abandoned stichographic arrangement of all but those passages mandated by the Talmud. Most modern scholarly editions reversed this trend, employing stichography for everything considered poetry, including many of the prophetic books.

The Presence of Poetry in the Tanakh

Lacking conclusive indicators of the presence of biblical poetry, one must rely on stylistic features to identify it. Though some scholars caution against drawing sharp distinctions between poetry and prose, a general consensus exists about which parts of the Bible contain poetry. Prose dominates, but poetry permeates every part of the Bible, totaling approximately one-third of the corpus.

The Writings contains the most poetic material, including Psalms, Proverbs, Job 3:3–42:6, Song of Songs, and Lamentations, along with scattered poetic selections in Ecclesiastes (e.g., 1:2–9; 3:1–8) and other books (e.g., 1 Chron. 16:8–35). Poetry overshadows prose in the Latter Prophets, for most of the prophetic books contain poetic verse exclusively or predominantly; Jonah and Ezekiel stand out as exceptions. In the Former Prophets, poems punctuate the narrative account of Israel's history in Judges 5 (Song of Deborah), 1 Samuel 2:1–10 (Hannah's Prayer), 2 Samuel 1:19–27 (David's eulogy for Saul and Jonathan), 2 Samuel 22 (David's Song), and 2 Samuel 23:1–7 (David's last words). Some of the smaller poetic passages include the war song quoted by Joshua (Josh. 10:12–13) and Solomon's declaration to God (1 Kings 8:12–13).

The Torah preserves several lengthy poems, including the Testament of Jacob (Gen. 49:2–27), the Song of the Sea (Exod. 15:1–18), the Song of Moses (Deut. 32), and Moses' Blessing (Deut. 33). We also find a number of shorter poetic compositions or fragments, such as the Song of Lamech (Gen. 4:23–24), Miriam's Song at the Sea (Exod. 15:21), the Song of the Ark (Num. 10:35–36) the Song at the Well (Num. 21:17–18), the Victory Song over Moab (Num. 21:27–30), and the Oracles of Balaam (Num. 23:7–10, 18–24; 24:3–9, 15–24). In some instances, often in the course of a dialogue, a few poetic verses interrupt the surrounding prose narrative, as when the man names the woman (Gen. 2:23), God speaks to Cain (Gen. 4:6–7), or Rebekah's family bids her farewell (Gen. 24:60).

In each part of the Bible, the poetic material displays a considerable degree of diversity in content. Note the range of poetic expression in the Writings, with aphorisms in Proverbs, passionate diatribes on human suffering in Job, sensual love songs in the Song of Songs, and mournful laments for the destruction of Jerusalem in Lamentations. Within the Book of Psalms itself, in certain texts the speaker joyfully sings God's praises, while in others, the psalmist cries out in pain and calls upon God's help. Likewise, the poetry of the Prophets contains many passages in which the prophets rail against the people for their moral and religious failings and others in which they exhort their listeners to repent or entice them with visions of a glorious future. The Torah contains a similar poetic panoply, with songs of victory, deathbed blessings, oracles, and other assorted passages. Nevertheless, for all this variety in genre and subject matter, the poetic sections of the Bible exhibit considerable stylistic similarities. Understanding biblical poetry requires a familiarity with the literary devices adeptly wielded by the writers of biblical poetry, namely parallelism, rhythm, terseness, imagery, metaphor, repetition, patterning, and other tropes.

Parallelism

The identification of parallelism as a central defining feature of biblical poetry traces back to the *Lectures on the Sacred Poetry of the Hebrews*, delivered by Bishop Robert Lowth in 1753. Lowth defines parallelism as a certain "equality" or "resemblance" between the members of a poetic unit. He identifies three types of poetic parallelism: synonymous, antithetic, and synthetic. In the most frequent variety, synonymous parallelism, the same sentiment is repeated in different, but equivalent terms, as in Isaiah 60:3:

> And nations shall walk by your light,
> Kings, by your shining radiance.

Antithetic parallelism pairs contrary or opposite terms, as seen in Proverbs 27:6:

> Wounds by a loved one are long lasting;
> The kisses of an enemy are profuse.

The third and rather amorphous category, called synthetic parallelism, consists of everything that does not fit in the other two classifications. Lowth cites Psalm 46:7 as an example:

> Nations rage, kingdoms topple;
> at the sound of His thunder the earth dissolves.

For over 200 years, Lowth's tripartite understanding of parallelism dominated the discussion of biblical poetry. Then, starting the in late 1970s and 1980s, a number of studies were published that challenged Lowth's perception of parallelism and expanded our understanding of the nuances and complexities of biblical verse. In the 1981 book, *The Idea of Biblical Poetry: Parallelism and Its History*, James Kugel contends that the ways of parallelism are numerous and varied, far exceeding Lowth's limited three categories. He observes that the degree of connection between two parallel clauses may range anywhere from no perceivable correspondence to just short of a word-for-word repetition. He insists that the second, "B" clause does not simply restate the first, "A" clause. Instead, the B-line expands upon the A-line in a multitude of different ways: reasserting, supporting, particularizing, defining, completing, or going beyond the first line. In the 1985 work, *The Art of Biblical Poetry*, Robert Alter highlights what he terms the "impulse to intensification" in biblical poetry. He argues that even in lines that appear at first glance to be nearly synonymous, a closer reading often reveals a "dynamic progression" from one half of the line to the next.

In the 1985 study, *The Dynamics of Biblical Parallelism*, Adele Berlin applies the study of linguistics to the topic of parallelism in a way that helps the reader to uncover and appreciate the intricacies of biblical parallelism. She sees parallelism as a multifaceted phenomenon, one that involves grammatical, lexical-semantic, and phonological aspects on the level of individual words, as well as clauses and larger expanses of a text. Instead of drawing a stark contrast between synonymous and antithetical elements, she asserts that parallelism achieves its effectiveness from the interplay of equivalence and contrast along these various aspects and levels.

Isaiah 1:10 provides a good example of the dynamic nature of poetic parallelism:

> Hear the word of the LORD,
> You chieftains of Sodom;
> Give ear to our God's instruction,
> You folk of Gomorrah!

The two lines in this verse, often called "cola," certainly meet Lowth's definition of synonymous parallelism, for the same sentiment appears to be repeated in different, but equivalent terms. However, further investigation reveals varying degrees of equivalence and contrast. Looking first at the lexical aspect of this bi-colon, the correspondence between the words in the two cola may range from exact equivalence to complete contrast. In this case, we find a number of word pairs that exhibit a high degree of semantic similarity. The divine names "LORD" and "God" belong at the far end of the scale, for the two names point to the same referent. The verbs "hear" and "give ear" are frequently paired terms that both call upon the audience to listen, though the first verb is more standard and the second more poetic. Similarly, the nouns "word" and "instruction" are both used to designate God's teaching, though the first term is more general and the second more specific. With the last two words in each cola, we move more toward the contrast side of the scale. The nouns "chieftains" and "folk" cannot be considered synonymous, for the first word refers specifically to the ruling class, whereas the second denotes the population as a whole. The place names "Sodom" and "Gomorrah" identify two different cities, though often the nouns appear as a consecutive, fixed phrase ("Sodom and Gomorrah"); the two cities symbolize a place of debauchery and sin.

Expanding the scope of the examination from the relationships between the individual words to the connections between the two cola as a whole, on a semantic level, the two lines appear fairly synonymous: the second colon echoes the basic sentiment of the first. In both sentences, the prophet calls the intended audience to listen to God's message. By invoking the place names "Sodom" and "Gomorrah" Isaiah metaphorically maligns his listeners, a fitting prelude to the divine diatribe that follows.

Applying the same approach to the grammatical aspects of the verse reveals a similar amalgam of relationships of equivalence and contrast. Syntactically, the two sentences are identical. They both contain a verb, followed by a direct object (a noun and divine name) and then the subject (a noun and place name). However, when we unpack the cola grammatically, we discover a number of contrasting elements. For instance, the masculine noun "*davar*" (word) contrasts with the feminine "*torah*" (instruction), and the plural noun "*ketsinim*" (chieftains) contrasts with the singular "'*am*" (folk).

These various types of grammatical variation stand in opposition to the more pervasive sense of semantic and syntactical similarity. The interplay of equivalence and contrast on these different levels animates the verse. In addition, the grammar reinforces the prophet's message. By addressing both the leaders and the people as a whole, Isaiah implies that all strata of society are guilty and thus fitting recipients of his words. In a more subtle manner, the grammatical contrast supplements this inclusive message: masculine and feminine, singular and plural, all need to heed God's charge to "cease to do evil; learn to do good" (Isa. 1:16–17).

Berlin also contributes to the study of biblical parallelism by introducing the linguistic concepts of paradigmatic and syntagmatic relations to describe the connections between isolated words and entire cola. Compare the relationship between the two cola in Isaiah 1:10 to the two cola in Hosea 14:2:

> Return, O Israel, to the LORD your God,
> For you have fallen because of your sin.

In this case, the two halves of the verse do not mirror each other syntactically or echo each other semantically. Instead, the second colon continues the topic introduced in the first colon, providing a justification for the prophet's call to return. The relationship between the two cola in Hosea 14:2 can be termed "syntagmatic," whereas the connection between the two parts of Isaiah 1:10 can be labeled "paradigmatic"—concepts introduced by the influential linguist Ferdinand de Saussure. "Syntagmatic" refers to the linear relationships between the signs in a sentence, the way the words and sentences connect to one another and form a sequence. "Paradigmatic" refers to the way words and phrases can substitute for one another.

Often, the nature of the relationship is not as clear as in Isaiah 1:10 and Hosea 14:2, or a passage may combine paradigmatic and syntagmatic elements. In some cases, how one views the relationships between isolated words and the cola as a whole can influence how one interprets a given passage. For example, Hosea 14:3 reads:

> Take words with you
> And return to the LORD.

If we consider "taking words" and returning to God as paradigmatic phrases, meaning that the two cola can be substituted for or equated with one another, that implies that repentance involves a verbal confession or declaration of the sort provided by Hosea in the subsequent verses. In contrast, if we understand the two phrases as syntagmatic, or as two parts of a consecutive sequence, that suggests that one must speak words of contrition *before* one can reconcile with God. These examples show how analyzing the various aspects and levels of a poetic passage helps us to gain a keener appreciation of the artistry and interpretative possibilities of involved in biblical parallelism.

Meter and Rhythm

In many types of poetry, meter stands out as a defining feature. The word "meter" derives from the Greek term "measure" and refers to the counting and organization of various aspects of spoken discourse, such as syllables or accents. Over the centuries, scholars have scoured the poetic sections of the Bible, looking for signs of these various forms of meter. One factor that complicates the matter is that, unlike other ancient languages such as Akkadian and Greek, we are not certain as to precisely how biblical Hebrew was pronounced. Largely influenced by contemporary poetic aesthetics—be that Greek, Arabic, Renaissance, or other types of poetry—some ancient, medieval, and modern scholars have insisted on the existence of biblical meter. Throughout these different time periods others have maintained that meter does not exist in the poetry of the Bible. In more recent studies, the consensus has shifted toward the latter perspective. Because biblical poetry does display a certain degree of symmetry and sound patterning, some have suggested shifting the focus of the discussion from meter to the broader notion of rhythm, which refers to various forms of sound repetition and regularity.

Terseness

The rhythm of biblical poetry results in part from the terseness of parallel lines, the fact that the lines of biblical poetry tend to be short and comprised of about the same number of words and stresses. Several trends contribute to the terseness of biblical poetry. First, poetic verses frequently omit certain grammatical particles, such as the definite article (*ha-*), the accusative marker (*'et*), and the relative pronoun (*'asher*). Secondly, biblical poetry abounds with parataxis, meaning that cola often are joined together without conjunctions. In prose, hypotaxis dominates, meaning that dependent clauses are usually linked with conjunctions that specify how one clause relates to the other. Frequently, as in the above example from Hosea 14:3, two cola appear one after another, merely connected by the conjunction "*vav*," which carries a range of meanings (translated in Hosea 14:3 as "and"). The vague nature of this conjunction can produce ambiguity, thus requiring the interpreter to determine the nature of the connection. Does the conjunction indicate that the second line repeats the basic idea of the first: Take with you words and *thus* return to the LORD? Or does it imply a sequence of actions: Take with you words and *then* return to the LORD? In many other cases, two poetic lines are juxtaposed with no grammatical marker specifying the relationship between the statements, as seen in the following passages:

> You turned my lament into dancing,
> you undid my sackcloth and girded me with joy.
> (Ps. 30:12)

A garden locked
Is my own, my bride,
A fountain locked,
A sealed-up spring. (Song 4:12)

Imagery, Metaphor, and Simile

The quotes from Psalm 30 and Song of Songs highlight another defining feature of biblical poetry: the abundant use of imagery. The term "imagery" is a complicated term that often is used to speak about figurative language in general or the more specific figure of speech. In fact, the terms "imagery" and "metaphor" designate two distinct though frequently overlapping literary devices. In Psalm 30:12, the speaker paints a visual picture of a person in mourning who breaks out in dancing. In Song of Songs 4:12, the speaker also evokes a mental image, but in this case the images of the garden, fountain, and spring function as part of a comparison, the key component of a metaphor.

Imagery creates a mental image, which can involve sight, hearing, smell, or other senses. For instance, the prophet Joel depicts a future time of judgment, "the day of the LORD," when "the beasts groan" and "the watercourses are dried up" (Joel 1:18, 20). The first comment involves an auditory element, while the second is primarily visual. Amos also speaks about the day of the LORD, warning that "it shall be darkness, not light" (Amos 5:18). When Isaiah speaks about a very different future, he likewise relies upon imagery, creating a vision of a wolf dwelling with a lamb and a leopard stretching out alongside a young goat (Isa. 11:6).

In these examples, the speaker uses language to take a snapshot: a picture of predators reclining alongside their former prey, a vision of total darkness, a scene of parched streams and groaning beasts. In each case, as the saying goes, one picture is worth a thousand words. Amos does not specify what will happen on the day of the LORD; instead, the image of darkness communicates the general impression that this will be a dreadful time. Similarly, Isaiah paints a series of mental pictures from which his audience can extrapolate the larger point that a glorious future will bring peace and harmony among all creatures. In doing so, he taps into a larger motif that signals a return to Eden. With imagery, the poet goes beyond the straightforward language on the page, delivering a more vivid, but less explicit message. Utilizing the listener's various senses, the writer employs a concrete image to convey a more abstract idea.

While a metaphor also evokes an image, what makes it distinct is the presence of an analogy, a comparison between a hypothetical situation and an actual situation. For example, in the extended metaphor in Isaiah 5:1–7 (the "Song of the Vineyard"), the prophet likens the actual situation, God's displeasure about Israel's immoral behavior, to a hypothetical situation: a gardener's disappointment about the way the vineyard he lovingly tended yielded wild grapes. Applying the frequently used terminology coined by I. A. Richards, the subject under discussion (here, the Israelites) would be considered the "tenor" and that to which the subject is being compared (here, the vineyard) would be called the "vehicle."

In a metaphor, the analogy is implicit, whereas it is explicit in a simile, a closely related figure of speech. Examples of similes abound in biblical poetry, as seen in the following passages from the Book of Hosea. At several points, Hosea favorably compares God to dew or rain in order to send the message that God nourishes Israel and will bring about her revival and success. For instance, in Hosea 14:6, God promises:

> I will be to Israel like dew;
> He shall blossom like the lily.

In this simile, the preposition "*ke-*" (like or as) signals the presence of an analogy.

With a metaphor, the speaker crafts the comparison in a variety of ways. The most obvious type of metaphor takes the form of a predicative statement, as in "the LORD is my shepherd" (Ps. 23:1), "All flesh is grass" (Isa. 40:6), and "Israel is a ravaged vine" (Hos. 10:1). Each of these nominal sentences equates one object with another object, thus creating an anomaly. In other instances, the metaphor is introduced by weaving together words connected with the actual situation and vocabulary associated with the hypothetical situation. For example, in the previous citation from Isaiah 1:10, the prophet compares his audience to the archetypal sinners of Sodom and Gomorrah by linking the second person plural imperative verbs and the nouns "chieftains" and "folk" with the place names "Sodom" and "Gomorrah." The Israelites addressed are not, in fact, residents of Sodom and Gomorrah, but only metaphorically equated with them. In Amos 1:2, the metaphor is more subtle, created by pairing a divine subject with a verb primarily associated with the sound produced by lions:

> The LORD roars from Zion,
> Shouts aloud from Jerusalem.

The combination of "the LORD" and "roars" creates an incongruity that, in part, marks this statement as a metaphor. A metaphor contains both an analogy and an anomaly; in contrast, a simile lacks any sort of anomalous element, for it explicitly compares two entities, without equating them.

Interpreting metaphors and similes involves unpacking the common features that motivate the analogy, called the "associated commonplaces." Imagine a Venn diagram, with "God" in one circle and "dew" in another. What qualities do the two have in common? What characteristics would fit in the overlapping section of the two circles? In the abstract, we might compile a list of various attributes shared by God and dew. However, when interpreting the simile as it appears in Hosea 14:6, the relevant question is: What specific qualities are focused upon in this particular verse? In Hosea 14, the larger context allows the interpreter to decipher the associated commonplaces, for the subsequent verses describe how Israel will flourish like a verdant plant. One can infer from the larger passage that just as dew nourishes trees and flowers, so God will sustain and support Israel so the nation can thrive.

Repetition and Patterning

David's tribute to Saul and Jonathan concludes with two phrases invoked to describe the deceased men:

> How have the mighty fallen,
> The weapons of war perished! (2 Sam. 1:27)

In the first colon, literal language is used to characterize Saul and Jonathan. In the second, David communicates through figurative language, employing the image of abandoned armor to speak of the loss of Israel's military leaders. The phrase "how have the mighty fallen" is repeated two other times in this passage: once at the end of the first verse (v. 19) and again toward the end of the unit (v. 25). When a word or phrase recurs at the beginning and end of a composition, it is called an inclusio, or envelope structure. When a word or phrase repeats a number of times, particularly at marked intervals, it is called a refrain.

Repetition stands out as an important way to convey meaning in the Bible. In poetry as well as prose, repetition of key words allows the author to highlight and emphasize central themes. For instance, in Hosea 14:2–9, the root "*shuv*" (to turn) appears five times. First, the prophet charges his listeners to return to God (vv. 2, 3); then he promises that God will "heal their turning back," for God's anger "has turned away" from them (v. 5; also see v. 8). Additional types of repetition can be found in poetic compositions throughout the Bible. In Isaiah 40–66, reduplication, or the side-by-side repetition of the same word, punctuates numerous passages, including the well-known verse: "Comfort, oh comfort My people" (Isa. 40:1). In certain psalms, the same phrase repeats at the beginning of several consecutive lines, such as "how long" in Psalm 13:2–3 or "bless" in Psalm 115:12–13. Even more prominently, in Psalm150, the phrase "Hallelujah" (*halelu Yah*) (Praise Yah) frames the psalm, functioning as an inclusio; in between, the verb *halelu* (praise) starts each of the subsequent ten lines. In other cases, the repetition appears at the end of the line, as seen in Psalm 136, where the phrase "for His steadfast love is eternal" (*ki le'olam ḥ asdo*) concludes each of the twenty-six verses. As these examples demonstrate, repetition not only conveys meaning, but also serves as a structuring device and enhances the aesthetic quality of the composition.

In biblical poetry, patterns are created through repetition as well as through other means. In various psalms and in the Book of Lamentations, the verses are arranged alphabetically, in what is called an acrostic (Lam. 1–4; Ps. 25; 34; 111; 112; 119; 145). A prominent pattern in the Bible is a chiasm, where elements in a verse or over the larger expanse of a text are arranged in reverse order. Genesis 9:6 provides a good example: "The one who sheds [A] the blood [B] of a human [C], by a human [C'] shall his blood [B'] be shed [A']."

Another form of repetition and patterning involves the use of sound. Alliteration entails the repetition of the same or similar sound; in the Bible, we find many examples of consonance, the more specific category of the repetition of consonants. For instance, listen to the way Amos 5:5 incorporates several recurring sound patterns, which Shalom Paul attempts to capture in his English translation:

> But do not seek Beth–el!
> Nor go to Gilgal!
> Nor cross over to Beer–sheba!
> For Gilgal shall go into galling exile
> > [*ki ha–gilgal galoh yigleh*],
> And Beth–el shall become a nullity.
> > [*uvet 'el yiheyeh le'aven*].

Isaiah 5:7 provides a good example of paranomasia, a play on words using similar sounding words with different meanings:

> And He hoped for justice [*mishpat*],
> But behold, injustice [*mispaḥ*];
> For equity [*tsedakah*],
> But behold, iniquity [*tseʻakah*]!

Other Poetic Devices

Paranomasia is one of a host of literary devices found in biblical poetry. Classical Greek rhetoricians coined much of the terminology that is still used today to label the manifold ways language can be manipulated to produce various rhetorical effects. The few mentioned below reflect some of the more prominent tropes in biblical poetry.

In 2 Samuel 1:27, David speaks of Jonathan and Saul as "weapons of war." He does not compare them to armor, which would constitute a metaphor. Instead, he metonymically speaks of them, using the name of an object with which they are associated. Metonymy involves a connection between two entities related in some sort of a part/whole manner; synecdoche is considered either a subset of metonymy or a distinct trope. Amos creates a metonym when he refers to the ruler of Ashkelon as "sceptered ruler" (Amos 1:8), thus linking the king with an action and object associated with him.

The Book of Amos contains examples of a number of other tropes. Amos employs hyperbole, or emphatic exaggeration, when he expresses the message that God rejects religious rituals if people do not act with justice and morality. The juxtaposition of two verbs in the first half of Amos 5:21 amplifies the tone of the passage:

> I loathe, I spurn your festivals,
> I am not appeased by your solemn assemblies. (Amos 5:21)

Earlier in the book, Amos effectively uses rhetorical questions, constructing a prophecy comprised of nine rhetorical questions. He begins by asking: "Can two walk together without having met?" (Amos 3:3). Then, question after question, he draws his audience in so that they eventually recognize his main point: "My Lord GOD has spoken, who can but prophesy?" (Amos 3:8). Deutero-Isaiah cleverly crafts a rhetorical question in order to respond to the Israelites' feeling of having been abandoned by God:

> Can a woman forget her baby,
> Or disown the child of her womb?
> Though she might forget,
> I never could forget you. (Isa. 49:15)

This rhetorical question forms a metaphor that compares God to a mother in order to reassure the Israelites of God's enduring love and commitment.

This example demonstrates the way poetic devices often operate in conjunction with one another. In many cases, we can identify the specific type of trope found in a poetic passage. In other cases, a writer's creativity defies easy categorization. None of the stylistic features discussed here is restricted to biblical poetry. They all appear in biblical prose, though not with nearly the same degree of frequency and intensity. Appreciating the artistry of biblical poetry and the depth of its meaning requires being a skillful reader, one who can unpack the language, structure, and imagery of a poetic passage and then piece everything back together in a way that gives voice to the ideas conveyed in the elevated discourse of poetry.

Works Cited

Alter, Robert. *The Art of Biblical Poetry.* New York: Basic Books, Inc., 1985.

Berlin, Adele. *The Dynamics of Biblical Parallelism.* Bloomington: Indiana University Press, 1985.

Kugel, James. *The Idea of Biblical Poetry: Parallelism and Its History.* Baltimore: The Johns Hopkins University Press, 1981.

Lowth, Robert. *Lectures on the Sacred Poetry of the Hebrews.* London: S. Chadwick & Co., 1847.

Richards, I. A. *The Philosophy of Rhetoric.* Oxford: Oxford University Press, 1936.

Biblical Poetry

BLESSINGS

Seedtime and Harvest

God's promise to Noah after the flood

So long as the earth endures,
Seedtime and harvest,
Cold and heat,
Summer and winter,
Day and night
Shall not cease.

Genesis 8:22

Lekh Lekha: And You Shall Be a Blessing

God's promise to Abram

Go forth from your native land and from
    your father's house to the land that I will
    show you.
I will make of you a great nation,
And I will bless you;
I will make your name great,
And you shall be a blessing.
I will bless those who bless you
And curse him that curses you;
And all the families of the earth
Shall bless themselves by you.

Genesis 12:1–3

עֹד כָּל־יְמֵי הָאָרֶץ
זֶרַע וְקָצִיר
וְקֹר וָחֹם
וְקַיִץ וָחֹרֶף
וְיוֹם וָלַיְלָה
לֹא יִשְׁבֹּתוּ

לֶךְ־לְךָ
מֵאַרְצְךָ וּמִמּוֹלַדְתְּךָ וּמִבֵּית אָבִיךָ אֶל־
הָאָרֶץ אֲשֶׁר אַרְאֶךָּ
וְאֶעֶשְׂךָ לְגוֹי גָּדוֹל
וַאֲבָרֶכְךָ
וַאֲגַדְּלָה שְׁמֶךָ
וֶהְיֵה בְּרָכָה
וַאֲבָרֲכָה מְבָרְכֶיךָ
וּמְקַלֶּלְךָ אָאֹר
וְנִבְרְכוּ בְךָ
כֹּל מִשְׁפְּחֹת הָאֲדָמָה

El-roi: Hagar's Blessing

*The angel's
promise to Hagar
after she flees
from Sarai into
the wilderness*

And the angel of the Lord said to her,
"I will greatly increase your offspring,
And they shall be too many to count."
The angel of the Lord said to her further,
"Behold, you are with child
And shall bear a son;
You shall call him Ishmael,
For the Lord has paid heed to your suffering.
He shall be a wild ass of a man;
His hand against everyone,
And everyone's hand against him;
He shall dwell alongside of all his kinsmen."

Genesis 16:10–12

Isaac and Jacob

*Isaac gives Jacob
the blessing
intended for his
brother Esau*

May God give you
Of the dew of heaven and the fat of the
    earth,
Abundance of new grain and wine.
Let peoples serve you,
And nations bow to you;
Be master over your brothers,
And let your mother's sons bow to you.
Cursed be they who curse you,
Blessed they who bless you.

Genesis 27:28–29

וַיֹּאמֶר לָהּ מַלְאַךְ
יְהוָה
הַרְבָּה אַרְבֶּה אֶת־זַרְעֵךְ
וְלֹא יִסָּפֵר מֵרֹב׃
וַיֹּאמֶר לָהּ מַלְאַךְ יְהוָה
הִנָּךְ הָרָה
וְיֹלַדְתְּ בֵּן
וְקָרָאת שְׁמוֹ יִשְׁמָעֵאל
כִּי־שָׁמַע יְהוָה אֶל־עָנְיֵךְ
וְהוּא יִהְיֶה פֶּרֶא אָדָם
יָדוֹ בַכֹּל
וְיַד כֹּל בּוֹ
וְעַל־פְּנֵי כָל־אֶחָיו יִשְׁכֹּן

וְיִתֶּן־לְךָ הָאֱלֹהִים
מִטַּל הַשָּׁמַיִם וּמִשְׁמַנֵּי הָאָרֶץ
וְרֹב דָּגָן וְתִירֹשׁ
יַעַבְדוּךָ עַמִּים
וישתחו וְיִשְׁתַּחֲוּוּ לְךָ לְאֻמִּים
הֱוֵה גְבִיר לְאַחֶיךָ
וְיִשְׁתַּחֲוּוּ לְךָ בְּנֵי אִמֶּךָ
אֹרְרֶיךָ אָרוּר
וּמְבָרֲכֶיךָ בָּרוּךְ

El Shaddai:
Jacob's Blessing

God's blessing for
Jacob at Bethel

God appeared again to Jacob on his arrival
    from Paddan-aram,
and He blessed him.
God said to him,
"You whose name is Jacob,
You shall be called Jacob no more,
But Israel shall be your name."
Thus He named him Israel.
And God said to him,
"I am El Shaddai.
Be fertile and increase;
A nation, yea an assembly of nations,
Shall descend from you.
Kings shall issue from your loins.
The land that I assigned to Abraham and
    Isaac
I assign to you;
And to your offspring to come
Will I assign the land."

Genesis 35:9–12

Moses' Blessing

This is the blessing with which Moses, the
    man of God, bade the Israelites farewell
    before he died. He said:

וַיֵּרָא אֱלֹהִים אֶל־יַעֲקֹב עוֹד בְּבֹאוֹ מִפַּדַּן
אֲרָם וַיְבָרֶךְ אֹתוֹ וַיֹּאמֶר־לוֹ אֱלֹהִים
שִׁמְךָ יַעֲקֹב
לֹא־יִקָּרֵא שִׁמְךָ עוֹד יַעֲקֹב
כִּי אִם־יִשְׂרָאֵל יִהְיֶה שְׁמֶךָ
וַיִּקְרָא אֶת־שְׁמוֹ יִשְׂרָאֵל
וַיֹּאמֶר לוֹ אֱלֹהִים
אֲנִי אֵל שַׁדַּי
פְּרֵה וּרְבֵה
גּוֹי וּקְהַל גּוֹיִם
יִהְיֶה מִמֶּךָּ
וּמְלָכִים מֵחֲלָצֶיךָ יֵצֵאוּ
וְאֶת־הָאָרֶץ אֲשֶׁר נָתַתִּי לְאַבְרָהָם
וּלְיִצְחָק
לְךָ אֶתְּנֶנָּה
וּלְזַרְעֲךָ אַחֲרֶיךָ
אֶתֵּן אֶת־הָאָרֶץ

וְזֹאת הַבְּרָכָה אֲשֶׁר בֵּרַךְ מֹשֶׁה
אִישׁ הָאֱלֹהִים אֶת־בְּנֵי יִשְׂרָאֵל לִפְנֵי
מוֹתוֹ וַיֹּאמַר

The Lord came from Sinai;
He shone upon them from Seir;
He appeared from Mount Paran,
And approached from Ribeboth-kodesh,
Lightning flashing at them from His right.
Lover, indeed, of the people,
Their hallowed are all in Your hand.
They followed in Your steps,
Accepting Your pronouncements,
When Moses charged us with the Teaching
As the heritage of the congregation
   of Jacob.
Then He became King in Jeshurun,
When the heads of the people assembled,
The tribes of Israel together.
May Reuben live and not die,
Though few be his numbers.
And this he said of Judah:
Hear, O Lord the voice of Judah
And restore him to his people.
Though his own hands strive for him,
Help him against his foes.
And of Levi he said:
Let Your Thummim and Urim
Be with Your faithful one,
Whom You tested at Massah,
Challenged at the waters of Meribah;
Who said of his father and mother,
"I consider them not."
His brothers he disregarded,
Ignored his own children.
Your precepts alone they observed,
And kept Your covenant.
They shall teach Your laws to Jacob

יְהֹוָה מִסִּינַי בָּא

וְזָרַח מִשֵּׂעִיר לָמוֹ

הוֹפִיעַ מֵהַר פָּארָן

וְאָתָה מֵרִבְבֹת קֹדֶשׁ

מִימִינוֹ אשׁדת אֵשׁ דָּת לָמוֹ

אַף חֹבֵב עַמִּים

כָּל־קְדֹשָׁיו בְּיָדֶךָ

וְהֵם תֻּכּוּ לְרַגְלֶךָ

יִשָּׂא מִדַּבְּרֹתֶיךָ

תּוֹרָה צִוָּה־לָנוּ מֹשֶׁה

מוֹרָשָׁה קְהִלַּת יַעֲקֹב

וַיְהִי בִישֻׁרוּן מֶלֶךְ

בְּהִתְאַסֵּף רָאשֵׁי עָם

יַחַד שִׁבְטֵי יִשְׂרָאֵל

יְחִי רְאוּבֵן וְאַל־יָמֹת

וִיהִי מְתָיו מִסְפָּר

וְזֹאת לִיהוּדָה וַיֹּאמַר

שְׁמַע יְהֹוָה קוֹל יְהוּדָה

וְאֶל־עַמּוֹ תְּבִיאֶנּוּ

יָדָיו רָב לוֹ

וְעֵזֶר מִצָּרָיו תִּהְיֶה

וּלְלֵוִי אָמַר

תֻּמֶּיךָ וְאוּרֶיךָ

לְאִישׁ חֲסִידֶךָ

אֲשֶׁר נִסִּיתוֹ בְּמַסָּה

תְּרִיבֵהוּ עַל־מֵי מְרִיבָה

הָאֹמֵר לְאָבִיו וּלְאִמּוֹ

לֹא רְאִיתִיו

וְאֶת־אֶחָיו לֹא הִכִּיר

וְאֶת־בנו בָּנָיו לֹא יָדָע

כִּי שָׁמְרוּ אִמְרָתֶךָ

וּבְרִיתְךָ יִנְצֹרוּ

יוֹרוּ מִשְׁפָּטֶיךָ לְיַעֲקֹב

And Your instructions to Israel.
They shall offer You incense to savor
And whole-offerings on Your altar.
Bless, O Lord, his substance,
And favor his undertakings.
Smite the loins of his foes;
Let his enemies rise no more.
Of Benjamin he said:
Beloved of the Lord,
He rests securely beside Him;
Ever does He protect him,
As he rests between His shoulders.
And of Joseph he said:
Blessed of the Lord be his land
With the bounty of dew from heaven,
And of the deep that couches below;
With the bounteous yield of the sun,
And the bounteous crop of the moons;
With the best from the ancient mountains,
And the bounty of hills immemorial;
With the bounty of earth
    and its fullness,
And the favor of the Presence in the Bush.
May these rest on the head of Joseph,
On the crown of the elect of his brothers.
Like a firstling bull in his majesty,
He has horns like the horns of the wild-ox;
With them he gores the peoples,
The ends of the earth one and all.
These are the myriads of Ephraim,
Those are the thousands of Manasseh.
And of Zebulun he said:
Rejoice, O Zebulun, on your journeys,
And Issachar, in your tents.

וְתוֹרָתְךָ לְיִשְׂרָאֵל
יָשִׂימוּ קְטוֹרָה בְּאַפֶּךָ
וְכָלִיל עַל־מִזְבְּחֶךָ
בָּרֵךְ יְהוָה חֵילוֹ
וּפֹעַל יָדָיו תִּרְצֶה
מָחַץ מָתְנַיִם קָמָיו
וּמְשַׂנְאָיו מִן־יְקוּמוּן
לְבִנְיָמִן אָמַר
יְדִיד יְהוָה
יִשְׁכֹּן לָבֶטַח עָלָיו
חֹפֵף עָלָיו כָּל־הַיּוֹם
וּבֵין כְּתֵיפָיו שָׁכֵן
וּלְיוֹסֵף אָמַר
מְבֹרֶכֶת יְהוָה אַרְצוֹ
מִמֶּגֶד שָׁמַיִם מִטָּל
וּמִתְּהוֹם רֹבֶצֶת תָּחַת
וּמִמֶּגֶד תְּבוּאֹת שָׁמֶשׁ
וּמִמֶּגֶד גֶּרֶשׁ יְרָחִים
וּמֵרֹאשׁ הַרְרֵי־קֶדֶם
וּמִמֶּגֶד גִּבְעוֹת עוֹלָם
וּמִמֶּגֶד אֶרֶץ וּמְלֹאָהּ
וּרְצוֹן שֹׁכְנִי סְנֶה
תָּבוֹאתָה לְרֹאשׁ יוֹסֵף
וּלְקָדְקֹד נְזִיר אֶחָיו
בְּכוֹר שׁוֹרוֹ הָדָר לוֹ
וְקַרְנֵי רְאֵם קַרְנָיו
בָּהֶם עַמִּים יְנַגַּח
יַחְדָּו אַפְסֵי־אָרֶץ
וְהֵם רִבְבוֹת אֶפְרַיִם
וְהֵם אַלְפֵי מְנַשֶּׁה
וְלִזְבוּלֻן אָמַר
שְׂמַח זְבוּלֻן בְּצֵאתֶךָ
וְיִשָּׂשכָר בְּאֹהָלֶיךָ

They invite their kin to the mountain,
Where they offer sacrifices of success.
For they draw from the riches of the sea
And the hidden hoards of the sand.
And of Gad he said:
Blessed be He who enlarges Gad!
Poised is he like a lion
To tear off arm and scalp.
He chose for himself the best,
For there is the portion of the revered
    chieftain,
Where the heads of the people come.
He executed the Lord's judgments
And His decisions for Israel.
And of Dan he said:
Dan is a lion's whelp
That leaps forth from Bashan.
And of Naphtali he said:
O Naphtali, sated with favor
And full of the Lord's blessing,
Take possession on the west and south.
And of Asher he said:
Most blessed of sons be Asher;
May he be the favorite of his brothers,
May he dip his foot in oil.
May your doorbolts be iron and copper,
And your security last all your days.
O Jeshurun, there is none like God,
Riding through the heavens
    to help you,
Through the skies in His majesty.
The ancient God is a refuge,
A support are the arms everlasting.
He drove out the enemy before you

עַמִּים הַר־יִקְרָאוּ

שָׁם יִזְבְּחוּ זִבְחֵי־צֶדֶק

כִּי שֶׁפַע יַמִּים יִינָקוּ

וּשְׂפֻנֵי טְמוּנֵי חוֹל

וּלְגָד אָמַר

בָּרוּךְ מַרְחִיב גָּד

כְּלָבִיא שָׁכֵן

וְטָרַף זְרוֹעַ אַף־קָדְקֹד

וַיַּרְא רֵאשִׁית לוֹ

כִּי־שָׁם חֶלְקַת מְחֹקֵק סָפוּן

וַיֵּתֵא רָאשֵׁי עָם

צִדְקַת יְהוָה עָשָׂה

וּמִשְׁפָּטָיו עִם־יִשְׂרָאֵל

וּלְדָן אָמַר

דָּן גּוּר אַרְיֵה

יְזַנֵּק מִן־הַבָּשָׁן

וּלְנַפְתָּלִי אָמַר

נַפְתָּלִי שְׂבַע רָצוֹן

וּמָלֵא בִּרְכַּת יְהוָה

יָם וְדָרוֹם יְרָשָׁה

וּלְאָשֵׁר אָמַר

בָּרוּךְ מִבָּנִים אָשֵׁר

יְהִי רְצוּי אֶחָיו

וְטֹבֵל בַּשֶּׁמֶן רַגְלוֹ

בַּרְזֶל וּנְחֹשֶׁת מִנְעָלֶיךָ

וּכְיָמֶיךָ דָּבְאֶךָ

אֵין כָּאֵל יְשֻׁרוּן

רֹכֵב שָׁמַיִם בְּעֶזְרֶךָ

וּבְגַאֲוָתוֹ שְׁחָקִים

מְעֹנָה אֱלֹהֵי קֶדֶם

וּמִתַּחַת זְרֹעֹת עוֹלָם

By His command: Destroy!
Thus Israel dwells in safety,
Untroubled is Jacob's abode,
In a land of grain and wine,
Under heavens dripping dew.
O happy Israel! Who is like you,
A people delivered by the Lord,
Your protecting Shield, your Sword
    triumphant!
Your enemies shall come cringing before you,
And you shall tread on their backs.

Deuteronomy 33:1–29

וַיְגָרֶשׁ מִפָּנֶיךָ אוֹיֵב

וַיֹּאמֶר הַשְׁמֵד

וַיִּשְׁכֹּן יִשְׂרָאֵל בֶּטַח

בָּדָד עֵין יַעֲקֹב

אֶל־אֶרֶץ דָּגָן וְתִירוֹשׁ

אַף־שָׁמָיו יַעַרְפוּ טָל

אַשְׁרֶיךָ יִשְׂרָאֵל מִי כָמוֹךָ

עַם נוֹשַׁע בַּיהוָה

מָגֵן עֶזְרֶךָ וַאֲשֶׁר־חֶרֶב גַּאֲוָתֶךָ

וְיִכָּחֲשׁוּ אֹיְבֶיךָ לָךְ

וְאַתָּה עַל־בָּמוֹתֵימוֹ תִדְרֹךְ

PRAYERS & SONGS OF PRAISE

The Belly of Sheol

The LORD provided a huge fish to swallow
    Jonah; and Jonah remained in the fish's
    belly three days and three nights. Jonah
    prayed to the LORD his God from the belly
    of the fish. He said:
In my trouble I called to the LORD,
And He answered me;
From the belly of Sheol I cried out,
And You heard my voice.
You cast me into the depths,
Into the heart of the sea,
The floods engulfed me;
All Your breakers and billows
Swept over me.
I thought I was driven away
Out of Your sight:
Would I ever gaze again
Upon Your holy Temple?
The waters closed in over me,
The deep engulfed me.
Weeds twined around my head.
I sank to the base of the mountains;
The bars of the earth closed upon me forever.
Yet You brought my life up from the pit,
O LORD my God!
When my life was ebbing away,
I called the LORD to mind;

וַיְמַן יְהוָה דָּג גָּדוֹל לִבְלֹעַ אֶת־יוֹנָה
וַיְהִי יוֹנָה בִּמְעֵי הַדָּג שְׁלֹשָׁה יָמִים
וּשְׁלֹשָׁה לֵילוֹת   וַיִּתְפַּלֵּל יוֹנָה אֶל־יְהוָה
אֱלֹהָיו מִמְּעֵי הַדָּגָה   וַיֹּאמֶר
קָרָאתִי מִצָּרָה לִי אֶל־יְהוָה
וַיַּעֲנֵנִי
מִבֶּטֶן שְׁאוֹל שִׁוַּעְתִּי
שָׁמַעְתָּ קוֹלִי
וַתַּשְׁלִיכֵנִי מְצוּלָה
בִּלְבַב יַמִּים
וְנָהָר יְסֹבְבֵנִי
כָּל־מִשְׁבָּרֶיךָ וְגַלֶּיךָ
עָלַי עָבָרוּ
וַאֲנִי אָמַרְתִּי נִגְרַשְׁתִּי
מִנֶּגֶד עֵינֶיךָ
אַךְ אוֹסִיף לְהַבִּיט
אֶל־הֵיכַל קָדְשֶׁךָ
אֲפָפוּנִי מַיִם עַד־נֶפֶשׁ
תְּהוֹם יְסֹבְבֵנִי
סוּף חָבוּשׁ לְרֹאשִׁי
לְקִצְבֵי הָרִים יָרַדְתִּי
הָאָרֶץ בְּרִחֶיהָ בַעֲדִי לְעוֹלָם
וַתַּעַל מִשַּׁחַת חַיַּי
יְהוָה אֱלֹהָי
בְּהִתְעַטֵּף עָלַי נַפְשִׁי
אֶת־יְהוָה זָכָרְתִּי

17

And my prayer came before You,
Into Your holy Temple.
They who cling to empty folly
Forsake their own welfare,
But I, with loud thanksgiving,
Will sacrifice to You;
What I have vowed I will perform.
Deliverance is the LORD's!
The LORD commanded the fish, and it
   spewed Jonah out upon dry land.

Jonah 2:1–11

Habakkuk's Prayer

O Lord! I have learned of Your renown;
I am awed, O LORD, by Your deeds.
Renew them in these years,
Oh, make them known in these years!
Though angry, may You remember
   compassion.
God is coming from Teman,
The Holy One from Mount Paran. *Selah.*
His majesty covers the skies,
His splendor fills the earth:
It is a brilliant light
Which gives off rays on every side—
And therein His glory is enveloped.
Pestilence marches before Him,
And plague comes forth at His heels.
When He stands, He makes the earth shake;

וַתָּבוֹא אֵלֶיךָ תְּפִלָּתִי

אֶל־הֵיכַל קׇדְשֶׁךָ

מְשַׁמְּרִים הַבְלֵי־שָׁוְא

חַסְדָּם יַעֲזֹבוּ

וַאֲנִי בְּקוֹל תּוֹדָה

אֶזְבְּחָה־לָּךְ

אֲשֶׁר נָדַרְתִּי אֲשַׁלֵּמָה

יְשׁוּעָתָה לַיהוָה

וַיֹּאמֶר יְהוָה לַדָּג וַיָּקֵא אֶת־יוֹנָה אֶל־

הַיַּבָּשָׁה

יְהוָה שָׁמַעְתִּי שִׁמְעֲךָ

יָרֵאתִי יְהוָה פׇּעֳלֶךָ

בְּקֶרֶב שָׁנִים חַיֵּיהוּ

בְּקֶרֶב שָׁנִים תּוֹדִיעַ

בְּרֹגֶז רַחֵם תִּזְכּוֹר

אֱלוֹהַ מִתֵּימָן יָבוֹא

וְקָדוֹשׁ מֵהַר־פָּארָן   סֶלָה

כִּסָּה שָׁמַיִם הוֹדוֹ

וּתְהִלָּתוֹ מָלְאָה הָאָרֶץ

וְנֹגַהּ כָּאוֹר תִּהְיֶה

קַרְנַיִם מִיָּדוֹ לוֹ

וְשָׁם חֶבְיוֹן עֻזֹּה עֻזּוֹ

לְפָנָיו יֵלֶךְ דָּבֶר

וְיֵצֵא רֶשֶׁף לְרַגְלָיו

עָמַד וַיְמֹדֶד אֶרֶץ

רָאָה וַיַּתֵּר גּוֹיִם

19

When He glances, He makes nations
    tremble.
The age-old mountains are shattered,
The primeval hills sink low.
His are the ancient routes:
As a scene of havoc I behold
The tents of Cushan;
Shaken are the pavilions
Of the land of Midian!
Are You wroth, O LORD, with Neharim?
Is Your anger against Neharim,
Your rage against Yam—
That You are driving Your steeds,
Your victorious chariot?
All bared and ready is Your bow.
Sworn are the rods of the word. *Selah.*
You make the earth burst into streams,
The mountains rock at the sight of You,
A torrent of rain comes down;
Loud roars the deep,
The sky returns the echo.
Sun and moon stand still on high
As Your arrows fly in brightness,
Your flashing spear in brilliance.
You tread the earth in rage,
You trample nations in fury.
You have come forth to deliver Your people,
To deliver Your anointed.
You will smash the roof of the villain's
    house,
Raze it from foundation to top. *Selah.*
You will crack his skull with Your bludgeon;
Blown away shall be his warriors,
Whose delight is to crush me suddenly,

וַיִּתְפֹּצְצוּ הַרְרֵי־עַד
שַׁחוּ גִּבְעוֹת עוֹלָם
הֲלִיכוֹת עוֹלָם לוֹ
תַּחַת אָוֶן רָאִיתִי
אָהֳלֵי כוּשָׁן
יִרְגְּזוּן יְרִיעוֹת
אֶרֶץ מִדְיָן
הֲבִנְהָרִים חָרָה יְהוָה
אִם בַּנְּהָרִים אַפֶּךָ
אִם־בַּיָּם עֶבְרָתֶךָ
כִּי תִרְכַּב עַל־סוּסֶיךָ
מַרְכְּבֹתֶיךָ יְשׁוּעָה
עֶרְיָה תֵעוֹר קַשְׁתֶּךָ
שְׁבֻעוֹת מַטּוֹת אֹמֶר   סֶלָה
נְהָרוֹת תְּבַקַּע־אָרֶץ
רָאוּךָ יָחִילוּ הָרִים
זֶרֶם מַיִם עָבָר
נָתַן תְּהוֹם קוֹלוֹ
רוֹם יָדֵיהוּ נָשָׂא
שֶׁמֶשׁ יָרֵחַ עָמַד זְבֻלָה
לְאוֹר חִצֶּיךָ יְהַלֵּכוּ
לְנֹגַהּ בְּרַק חֲנִיתֶךָ
בְּזַעַם תִּצְעַד־אָרֶץ
בְּאַף תָּדוּשׁ גּוֹיִם
יָצָאתָ לְיֵשַׁע עַמֶּךָ
לְיֵשַׁע אֶת־מְשִׁיחֶךָ
מָחַצְתָּ רֹּאשׁ מִבֵּית רָשָׁע
עָרוֹת יְסוֹד עַד־צַוָּאר   סֶלָה
נָקַבְתָּ בְמַטָּיו רֹאשׁ
פְּרָזָו יִסְעֲרוּ
לַהֲפִיצֵנִי עֲלִיצֻתָם

To devour a poor man in an ambush.
You will make Your steeds tread the sea,
Stirring the mighty waters.
I heard and my bowels quaked,
My lips quivered at the sound;
Rot entered into my bone,
I trembled where I stood.
Yet I wait calmly for the day of distress,
For a people to come to attack us.
Though the fig tree does not bud
And no yield is on the vine,
Though the olive crop has failed
And the fields produce no grain,
Though sheep have vanished
   from the fold
And no cattle are in the pen,
Yet will I rejoice in the LORD,
Exult in the God who delivers me.
My Lord GOD is my strength:
He makes my feet like the deer's

And lets me stride upon the heights.
For the leader, with instumental music.

Habakkuk 3:2–19

Song of the Sea

Moses praises God for the deliverance from slavery in Egypt

I will sing to the LORD, for He has triumphed
   gloriously;
Horse and driver He has hurled into the sea.
The LORD is my strength and might;
He is become my deliverance.

כְּמוֹ־לֶאֱכֹל עָנִי בַּמִּסְתָּר

דָּרַכְתָּ בַיָּם סוּסֶיךָ

חֹמֶר מַיִם רַבִּים

שָׁמַעְתִּי וַתִּרְגַּז בִּטְנִי

לְקוֹל צָלֲלוּ שְׂפָתַי

יָבוֹא רָקָב בַּעֲצָמַי

וְתַחְתַּי אֶרְגָּז

אֲשֶׁר אָנוּחַ לְיוֹם צָרָה

לַעֲלוֹת לְעַם יְגוּדֶנּוּ

כִּי־תְאֵנָה לֹא־תִפְרָח

וְאֵין יְבוּל בַּגְּפָנִים

כִּחֵשׁ מַעֲשֵׂה־זַיִת

וּשְׁדֵמוֹת לֹא־עָשָׂה אֹכֶל

גָּזַר מִמִּכְלָה צֹאן

וְאֵין בָּקָר בָּרְפָתִים

וַאֲנִי בַּיהוָה אֶעְלוֹזָה

אָגִילָה בֵּאלֹהֵי יִשְׁעִי

יְהוָה אֲדֹנָי חֵילִי

וַיָּשֶׂם רַגְלַי כָּאַיָּלוֹת

וְעַל בָּמוֹתַי יַדְרִכֵנִי

לַמְנַצֵּחַ בִּנְגִינוֹתָי

אָז יָשִׁיר־מֹשֶׁה וּבְנֵי יִשְׂרָאֵל אֶת־הַשִּׁירָה הַזֹּאת לַיהוָה וַיֹּאמְרוּ

לֵאמֹר   אָשִׁירָה לַיהוָה כִּי־גָאֹה גָּאָה   סוּס

וְרֹכְבוֹ רָמָה בַיָּם   עָזִּי וְזִמְרָת יָהּ וַיְהִי־לִי

This is my God and I will enshrine Him;
The God of my father, and I will exalt Him.
The LORD, the Warrior—
LORD is His name!
Pharaoh's chariots and his army
He has cast into the sea;
And the pick of his officers
Are drowned in the Sea of Reeds.
The deeps covered them;
They went down into the depths like a
    stone.
Your right hand, O LORD, glorious in power,
Your right hand, O LORD, shatters the foe!
In Your great triumph You break Your
    opponents;
You send forth Your fury, it consumes them
    like straw.
At the blast of Your nostrils the waters piled
    up,
The floods stood straight like a wall;
The deeps froze in the heart of the sea.
The foe said,
"I will pursue, I will overtake,
I will divide the spoil;
My desire shall have its fill of them.
I will bare my sword—
My hand shall subdue them."
You made Your wind blow, the sea covered
    them;
They sank like lead in the majestic waters.
Who is like You, O LORD, among the
    celestials;
Who is like You, majestic in holiness,
Awesome in splendor, working wonders!

לִישׁוּעָה   זֶה אֵלִי וְאַנְוֵהוּ   אֱלֹהֵי

אָבִי וַאֲרֹמְמֶנְהוּ   יְהוָה אִישׁ מִלְחָמָה יְהוָה

שְׁמוֹ   מַרְכְּבֹת פַּרְעֹה וְחֵילוֹ יָרָה בַיָּם   וּמִבְחַר

שָׁלִשָׁיו טֻבְּעוּ בְיַם־סוּף   תְּהֹמֹת יְכַסְיֻמוּ יָרְדוּ בִמְצוֹלֹת כְּמוֹ־

אָבֶן   יְמִינְךָ יְהוָה נֶאְדָּרִי בַּכֹּחַ   יְמִינְךָ

יְהוָה תִּרְעַץ אוֹיֵב   וּבְרֹב גְּאוֹנְךָ תַּהֲרֹס

קָמֶיךָ   תְּשַׁלַּח חֲרֹנְךָ יֹאכְלֵמוֹ כַּקַּשׁ   וּבְרוּחַ

אַפֶּיךָ נֶעֶרְמוּ מַיִם   נִצְּבוּ כְמוֹ־נֵד

נֹזְלִים   קָפְאוּ תְהֹמֹת בְּלֶב־יָם   אָמַר

אוֹיֵב אֶרְדֹּף אַשִּׂיג   אֲחַלֵּק שָׁלָל תִּמְלָאֵמוֹ

נַפְשִׁי   אָרִיק חַרְבִּי תּוֹרִישֵׁמוֹ יָדִי   נָשַׁפְתָּ

בְרוּחֲךָ כִּסָּמוֹ יָם   צָלֲלוּ כַּעוֹפֶרֶת בְּמַיִם

אַדִּירִים   מִי־כָמֹכָה בָּאֵלִם יְהוָה   מִי

כָּמֹכָה נֶאְדָּר בַּקֹּדֶשׁ   נוֹרָא תְהִלֹּת עֹשֵׂה

You put out Your right hand,
The earth swallowed them.
In Your love You lead the people You redeemed;
In Your strength You guide them to Your holy
  abode.
The peoples hear, they tremble;
Agony grips the dwellers in Philistia.
Now are the clans of Edom dismayed;
The tribes of Moab—trembling grips them;
All the dwellers in Canaan are aghast.
Terror and dread descend upon them;
Through the might of Your arm they are still as
  stone—
Till Your people cross over, O LORD,
Till Your people cross whom You have
  ransomed.
You will bring them and plant them in Your
  own mountain,
The place You made to dwell in, O LORD,
The sanctuary, O LORD, which Your hands
  established.
The LORD will reign for ever and ever!

Exodus 15:1–18

Miriam's Song

*Miriam and the
Israelite women
dance and sing
to celebrate their
freedom*

Sing to the LORD, for He has triumphed
  gloriously;
Horse and driver He has hurled into the sea.

Exodus 15:21

פֶּלֶא נָטִיתָ יְמִינְךָ תִּבְלָעֵמוֹ אָרֶץ נָחִיתָ

בְחַסְדְּךָ עַם־זוּ גָּאָלְתָּ נֵהַלְתָּ בְעָזְּךָ אֶל־נְוֵה

קָדְשֶׁךָ שָׁמְעוּ עַמִּים יִרְגָּזוּן חִיל

אָחַז יֹשְׁבֵי פְּלָשֶׁת אָז נִבְהֲלוּ אַלּוּפֵי

אֱדוֹם אֵילֵי מוֹאָב יֹאחֲזֵמוֹ רָעַד נָמֹגוּ

כֹּל יֹשְׁבֵי כְנָעַן תִּפֹּל עֲלֵיהֶם אֵימָתָה

וָפַחַד בִּגְדֹל זְרוֹעֲךָ יִדְּמוּ כָּאָבֶן עַד־

יַעֲבֹר עַמְּךָ יְהוָה עַד־יַעֲבֹר עַם־זוּ

קָנִיתָ תְּבִאֵמוֹ וְתִטָּעֵמוֹ בְּהַר נַחֲלָתְךָ מָכוֹן

לְשִׁבְתְּךָ פָּעַלְתָּ יְהוָה מִקְּדָשׁ אֲדֹנָי כּוֹנְנוּ

יָדֶיךָ יְהוָה יִמְלֹךְ לְעֹלָם וָעֶד

שִׁירוּ לַיהוָה כִּי־גָאֹה גָּאָה
סוּס וְרֹכְבוֹ רָמָה בַיָּם

Ha'azinu:
The Song of Moses

*Moses describes
Israel's future
betrayal of God,
and God's
deliverance of
Israel*

Give ear, O heavens, let me speak;
Let the earth hear the words I utter!
May my discourse come down as the rain,
My speech distill as the dew,
Like showers on young growth,
Like droplets on the grass.
For the name of the LORD I proclaim;
Give glory to our God!
The Rock!—His deeds are perfect,
Yea, all His ways are just;
A faithful God, never false,
True and upright is He.
Children unworthy of Him—
That crooked, perverse generation—
Their baseness has played Him false.
Do you thus requite the LORD,
O dull and witless people?
Is not He the Father who created you,
Fashioned you and made you endure!
Remember the days of old,
Consider the years of ages past;
Ask your father, he will inform you,
Your elders, they will tell you:
When the Most High gave nations their homes
And set the divisions of man,
He fixed the boundaries of peoples
In relation to Israel's numbers.
For the Lord's portion is His people,
Jacob His own allotment.

הַאֲזִינוּ הַשָּׁמַיִם וַאֲדַבֵּרָה

וְתִשְׁמַע הָאָרֶץ אִמְרֵי־פִי

יַעֲרֹף כַּמָּטָר לִקְחִי

תִּזַּל כַּטַּל אִמְרָתִי

כִּשְׂעִירִם עֲלֵי־דֶשֶׁא

וְכִרְבִיבִים עֲלֵי־עֵשֶׂב

כִּי שֵׁם יְהוָה אֶקְרָא

הָבוּ גֹדֶל לֵאלֹהֵינוּ

הַצּוּר תָּמִים פָּעֳלוֹ

כִּי כָל־דְּרָכָיו מִשְׁפָּט

אֵל אֱמוּנָה וְאֵין עָוֶל

צַדִּיק וְיָשָׁר הוּא

שִׁחֵת לוֹ לֹא בָּנָיו מוּמָם

דּוֹר עִקֵּשׁ וּפְתַלְתֹּל

הֲ־לַיהוָה תִּגְמְלוּ־זֹאת

עַם נָבָל וְלֹא חָכָם

הֲלוֹא־הוּא אָבִיךָ קָּנֶךָ

הוּא עָשְׂךָ וַיְכֹנְנֶךָ

זְכֹר יְמוֹת עוֹלָם

בִּינוּ שְׁנוֹת דּוֹר־וָדוֹר

שְׁאַל אָבִיךָ וְיַגֵּדְךָ

זְקֵנֶיךָ וְיֹאמְרוּ לָךְ

בְּהַנְחֵל עֶלְיוֹן גּוֹיִם

בְּהַפְרִידוֹ בְּנֵי אָדָם

יַצֵּב גְּבֻלֹת עַמִּים

לְמִסְפַּר בְּנֵי יִשְׂרָאֵל

כִּי חֵלֶק יְהוָה עַמּוֹ

יַעֲקֹב חֶבֶל נַחֲלָתוֹ

He found him in a desert region,
In an empty howling waste.
He engirded him, watched over him,
Guarded him as the pupil of His eye.
Like an eagle who rouses his nestlings,
Gliding down to his young,
So did He spread His wings and take him,
Bear him along on His pinions;
The Lord alone did guide him,
No alien god at His side.
He set him atop the highlands,
To feast on the yield of the earth;
He fed him honey from the crag,
And oil from the flinty rock,
Curd of kine and milk of flocks;
With the best of lambs,
And rams of Bashan, and he-goats;
With the very finest wheat—
And foaming grape-blood was your drink.
So Jeshurun grew fat and kicked—
You grew fat and gross and coarse—
He forsook the God who made him
And spurned the Rock of his support.
They incensed Him with alien things,
Vexed Him with abominations.
They sacrificed to demons, no-gods,
Gods they had never known,
New ones, who came but lately,
Who stirred not your fathers' fears.
You neglected the Rock that begot you,
Forgot the God who brought you forth.
The Lord saw and was vexed
And spurned His sons and His daughters.
He said:

יִמְצָאֵהוּ בְּאֶרֶץ מִדְבָּר
וּבְתֹהוּ יְלֵל יְשִׁמֹן
יְסֹבְבֶנְהוּ יְבוֹנְנֵהוּ
יִצְּרֶנְהוּ כְּאִישׁוֹן עֵינוֹ
כְּנֶשֶׁר יָעִיר קִנּוֹ
עַל־גּוֹזָלָיו יְרַחֵף
יִפְרֹשׂ כְּנָפָיו יִקָּחֵהוּ
יִשָּׂאֵהוּ עַל־אֶבְרָתוֹ
יְהוָה בָּדָד יַנְחֶנּוּ
וְאֵין עִמּוֹ אֵל נֵכָר
יַרְכִּבֵהוּ עַל־במותי בָּמֳתֵי אָרֶץ
וַיֹּאכַל תְּנוּבֹת שָׂדָי
וַיֵּנִקֵהוּ דְבַשׁ מִסֶּלַע
וְשֶׁמֶן מֵחַלְמִישׁ צוּר
חֶמְאַת בָּקָר וַחֲלֵב צֹאן
עִם־חֵלֶב כָּרִים
וְאֵילִים בְּנֵי־בָשָׁן וְעַתּוּדִים
עִם־חֵלֶב כִּלְיוֹת חִטָּה
וְדַם־עֵנָב תִּשְׁתֶּה־חָמֶר
וַיִּשְׁמַן יְשֻׁרוּן וַיִּבְעָט
שָׁמַנְתָּ עָבִיתָ כָּשִׂיתָ
וַיִּטֹּשׁ אֱלוֹהַ עָשָׂהוּ
וַיְנַבֵּל צוּר יְשֻׁעָתוֹ
יַקְנִאֻהוּ בְּזָרִים
בְּתוֹעֵבֹת יַכְעִיסֻהוּ
יִזְבְּחוּ לַשֵּׁדִים לֹא אֱלֹהַּ
אֱלֹהִים לֹא יְדָעוּם
חֲדָשִׁים מִקָּרֹב בָּאוּ
לֹא שְׂעָרוּם אֲבֹתֵיכֶם
צוּר יְלָדְךָ תֶּשִׁי
וַתִּשְׁכַּח אֵל מְחֹלְלֶךָ
וַיַּרְא יְהוָה וַיִּנְאָץ
מִכַּעַס בָּנָיו וּבְנֹתָיו

I will hide My countenance from them,
And see how they fare in the end.
For they are a treacherous breed,
Children with no loyalty in them.
They incensed Me with no-gods,
Vexed Me with their futilities;
I'll incense them with a no-folk,
Vex them with a nation of fools.
For a fire has flared in My wrath
And burned to the bottom of Sheol,
Has consumed the earth and its increase,
Eaten down to the base of the hills.
I will sweep misfortunes on them,
Use up My arrows on them:
Wasting famine, ravaging plague,
Deadly pestilence, and fanged beasts
Will I let loose against them,
With venomous creepers in dust.
The sword shall deal death without,
As shall the terror within,
To youth and maiden alike,
The suckling as well as the aged.
I might have reduced them to naught,
Made their memory cease among men,
But for fear of the taunts of the foe,
Their enemies who might misjudge
And say, "Our own hand has prevailed;
None of this was wrought by the LORD!"
For they are a folk void of sense,
Lacking in all discernment.
Were they wise, they would think upon this,
Gain insight into their future:
"How could one have routed a thousand,
Or two put ten thousand to flight,

וַיֹּאמֶר אַסְתִּירָה פָנַי מֵהֶם
אֶרְאֶה מָה אַחֲרִיתָם
כִּי דוֹר תַּהְפֻּכֹת הֵמָּה
בָּנִים לֹא־אֵמֻן בָּם
הֵם קִנְאוּנִי בְלֹא־אֵל
כִּעֲסוּנִי בְּהַבְלֵיהֶם
וַאֲנִי אַקְנִיאֵם בְּלֹא־עָם
בְּגוֹי נָבָל אַכְעִיסֵם
כִּי־אֵשׁ קָדְחָה בְאַפִּי
וַתִּיקַד עַד־שְׁאוֹל תַּחְתִּית
וַתֹּאכַל אֶרֶץ וִיבֻלָהּ
וַתְּלַהֵט מוֹסְדֵי הָרִים
אַסְפֶּה עָלֵימוֹ רָעוֹת
חִצַּי אֲכַלֶּה־בָּם
מְזֵי רָעָב וּלְחֻמֵי רֶשֶׁף
וְקֶטֶב מְרִירִי
וְשֶׁן־בְּהֵמוֹת אֲשַׁלַּח־בָּם
עִם־חֲמַת זֹחֲלֵי עָפָר
מִחוּץ תְּשַׁכֶּל־חֶרֶב
וּמֵחֲדָרִים אֵימָה
גַּם־בָּחוּר גַּם־בְּתוּלָה
יוֹנֵק עִם־אִישׁ שֵׂיבָה
אָמַרְתִּי אַפְאֵיהֶם
אַשְׁבִּיתָה מֵאֱנוֹשׁ זִכְרָם
לוּלֵי כַּעַס אוֹיֵב אָגוּר
פֶּן־יְנַכְּרוּ צָרֵימוֹ
פֶּן־יֹאמְרוּ יָדֵנוּ רָמָה
וְלֹא יְהוָה פָּעַל כָּל־זֹאת
כִּי־גוֹי אֹבַד עֵצוֹת הֵמָּה
וְאֵין בָּהֶם תְּבוּנָה
לוּ חָכְמוּ יַשְׂכִּילוּ זֹאת
יָבִינוּ לְאַחֲרִיתָם
אֵיכָה יִרְדֹּף אֶחָד אֶלֶף
וּשְׁנַיִם יָנִיסוּ רְבָבָה

33

Unless their Rock had sold them,
The LORD had given them up?"
For their rock is not like our Rock,
In our enemies' own estimation.
Ah! The vine for them is from Sodom,
From the vineyards of Gomorrah;
The grapes for them are poison,
A bitter growth their clusters.
Their wine is the venom of asps,
The pitiless poison of vipers.
Lo, I have it all put away,
Sealed up in My storehouses,
To be My vengeance and recompense,
At the time that their foot falters.
Yea, their day of disaster is near,
And destiny rushes upon them.
For the LORD will vindicate His people
And take revenge for His servants,
When He sees that their might is gone,
And neither bond nor free is left.
He will say: Where are their gods,
The rock in whom they sought refuge,
Who ate the fat of their offerings
And drank their libation wine?
Let them rise up to your help,
And let them be a shield unto you!
See, then, that I, I am He;
There is no god beside Me.
I deal death and give life;
I wounded and I will heal:
None can deliver from My hand.
Lo, I raise My hand to heaven
And say: As I live forever,
When I whet My flashing blade

אִם־לֹא כִּי־צוּרָם מְכָרָם
וַיהוָה הִסְגִּירָם
כִּי לֹא כְצוּרֵנוּ צוּרָם
וְאֹיְבֵינוּ פְּלִילִים
כִּי־מִגֶּפֶן סְדֹם גַּפְנָם
וּמִשַּׁדְמֹת עֲמֹרָה
עֲנָבֵמוֹ עִנְּבֵי־רוֹשׁ
אַשְׁכְּלֹת מְרֹרֹת לָמוֹ
חֲמַת תַּנִּינִם יֵינָם
וְרֹאשׁ פְּתָנִים אַכְזָר
הֲלֹא־הוּא כָּמֻס עִמָּדִי
חָתֻם בְּאוֹצְרֹתָי
לִי נָקָם וְשִׁלֵּם
לְעֵת תָּמוּט רַגְלָם
כִּי קָרוֹב יוֹם אֵידָם
וְחָשׁ עֲתִדֹת לָמוֹ
כִּי־יָדִין יְהוָה עַמּוֹ
וְעַל־עֲבָדָיו יִתְנֶחָם
כִּי יִרְאֶה כִּי־אָזְלַת יָד
וְאֶפֶס עָצוּר וְעָזוּב
וְאָמַר אֵי אֱלֹהֵימוֹ
צוּר חָסָיוּ בוֹ
אֲשֶׁר חֵלֶב זְבָחֵימוֹ יֹאכֵלוּ
יִשְׁתּוּ יֵין נְסִיכָם
יָקוּמוּ וְיַעְזְרֻכֶם
יְהִי עֲלֵיכֶם סִתְרָה
רְאוּ עַתָּה כִּי אֲנִי אֲנִי הוּא
וְאֵין אֱלֹהִים עִמָּדִי
אֲנִי אָמִית וַאֲחַיֶּה
מָחַצְתִּי וַאֲנִי אֶרְפָּא
וְאֵין מִיָּדִי מַצִּיל
כִּי־אֶשָּׂא אֶל־שָׁמַיִם יָדִי
וְאָמַרְתִּי חַי אָנֹכִי לְעֹלָם
אִם־שַׁנּוֹתִי בְּרַק חַרְבִּי

And My hand lays hold on judgment,
Vengeance will I wreak on My foes,
Will I deal to those who reject Me.
I will make My arrows drunk with blood—
As My sword devours flesh—
Blood of the slain and the captive
From the long-haired enemy chiefs.
O nations, acclaim His people!
For He'll avenge the blood of His servants,
Wreak vengeance on His foes,
And cleanse the land of His people.

Deuteronomy 32:1–43

Deborah's Victory Song

Deborah the prophet and judge, and Barak, military commander of Israel, sing of their victory over Sisera and the army of Canaan

When locks go untrimmed in Israel,
When people dedicate themselves—
Bless the LORD!
Hear, O kings! Give ear, O potentates!
I will sing, will sing to the LORD,
Will hymn the LORD, the God of Israel.
O LORD, when You came forth from Seir,
Advanced from the country of Edom,
The earth trembled;
The heavens dripped,
Yea, the clouds dripped water,
The mountains quaked—
Before the LORD, Him of Sinai,
Before the LORD, God of Israel.
In the days of Shamgar son of Anath,
In the days of Jael, caravans ceased,

וְתֹאחֵז בְּמִשְׁפָּט יָדִי
אָשִׁיב נָקָם לְצָרָי
וְלִמְשַׂנְאַי אֲשַׁלֵּם
אַשְׁכִּיר חִצַּי מִדָּם
וְחַרְבִּי תֹּאכַל בָּשָׂר
מִדַּם חָלָל וְשִׁבְיָה
מֵרֹאשׁ פַּרְעוֹת אוֹיֵב
הַרְנִינוּ גוֹיִם עַמּוֹ
כִּי דַם־עֲבָדָיו יִקּוֹם
וְנָקָם יָשִׁיב לְצָרָיו
וְכִפֶּר אַדְמָתוֹ עַמּוֹ

בְּהִתְנַדֵּב בִּפְרֹעַ פְּרָעוֹת בְּיִשְׂרָאֵל

שִׁמְעוּ מְלָכִים הַאֲזִינוּ עָם בָּרְכוּ יְהוָה

אֲזַמֵּר אָנֹכִי לַיהוָה אָנֹכִי אָשִׁירָה רֹזְנִים

יְהוָה בְּצֵאתְךָ לַיהוָה אֱלֹהֵי יִשְׂרָאֵל

אֶרֶץ בְּצַעְדְּךָ מִשְּׂדֵה אֱדוֹם מִשֵּׂעִיר

גַּם־עָבִים נָטְפוּ רָעָשָׁה גַּם־שָׁמַיִם נָטְפוּ

זֶה הָרִים נָזְלוּ מִפְּנֵי יְהוָה מַיִם

בִּימֵי שַׁמְגַּר בֶּן־ סִינַי מִפְּנֵי יְהוָה אֱלֹהֵי יִשְׂרָאֵל

And wayfarers went
By roundabout paths.
Deliverance ceased,
Ceased in Israel,
Till you arose, O Deborah,
Arose, O mother, in Israel!
When they chose new gods,
Was there a fighter then in the gates?
No shield or spear was seen
Among forty thousand in Israel!
My heart is with Israel's leaders,
With the dedicated of the people—
Bless the LORD!
You riders on tawny she-asses,
You who sit on saddle rugs,
And you wayfarers, declare it!
Louder than the sound of archers,
There among the watering places
Let them chant the gracious acts of the
    LORD,
His gracious deliverance of Israel.
Then did the people of the LORD
March down to the gates!
Awake, awake, O Deborah!
Awake, awake, strike up the chant!
Arise, O Barak;
Take your captives, O son of Abinoam!
Then was the remnant made victor over the
    mighty,
The LORD's people won my victory over the
    warriors.
From Ephraim came they whose roots are in
    Amalek;
After you, your kin Benjamin;

וְהֹלְכֵי   בִּימֵי יָעֵל חָדְלוּ אֳרָחוֹת   עָנָת

חָדְלוּ פְרָזוֹן בְּיִשְׂרָאֵל   יֵלְכוּ אֳרָחוֹת עֲקַלְקַלּוֹת   נְתִיבוֹת

יִבְחַר   עַד שַׁקַּמְתִּי דְּבוֹרָה שַׁקַּמְתִּי אֵם בְּיִשְׂרָאֵל   חָדְלוּ

מָגֵן אִם־יֵרָאֶה   אָז לָחֶם שְׁעָרִים   אֱלֹהִים חֲדָשִׁים

לִבִּי   בְּאַרְבָּעִים אֶלֶף בְּיִשְׂרָאֵל   וָרֹמַח

הַמִּתְנַדְּבִים בָּעָם בָּרְכוּ   לְחוֹקְקֵי יִשְׂרָאֵל

יֹשְׁבֵי   רֹכְבֵי אֲתֹנוֹת צְחֹרוֹת   יְהוָה

מִקּוֹל מְחַצְצִים בֵּין   וְהֹלְכֵי עַל־דֶּרֶךְ שִׂיחוּ   עַל־מִדִּין

צִדְקֹת   שָׁם יְתַנּוּ צִדְקוֹת יְהוָה   מְשַׁאֲבִים

אָז יָרְדוּ לַשְּׁעָרִים עַם־   פְּרָזֹנוֹ בְּיִשְׂרָאֵל

עוּרִי   עוּרִי עוּרִי דְּבוֹרָה   יְהוָה

קוּם בָּרָק וּשֲׁבֵה שֶׁבְיְךָ בֶּן־   עוּרִי דַבְּרִי־שִׁיר

יְהוָה   אָז יְרַד שָׂרִיד לְאַדִּירִים עָם   אֲבִינֹעַם

מִנִּי אֶפְרַיִם שָׁרְשָׁם   יְרַד־לִי בַּגִּבּוֹרִים

From Machir came down leaders,
From Zebulun such as hold the marshal's
staff.
And Issachar's chiefs were with Deborah;
As Barak, so was Issachar—
Rushing after him into the valley.
Among the clans of Reuben
Were great decisions of heart.
Why then did you stay among the sheepfolds
And listen as they pipe for the flocks?
Among the clans of Reuben
Were great searchings of heart!
Gilead tarried beyond the Jordan;
And Dan—why did he linger by the ships?
Asher remained at the seacoast
And tarried at his landings.
Zebulun is a people that mocked at death,
Naphtali—on the open heights.
Then the kings came, they fought:
The kings of Canaan fought
At Taanach, by Megiddo's waters—
They got no spoil of silver.
The stars fought from heaven,
From their courses they fought against
Sisera.
The torrent Kishon swept them away,
The raging torrent, the torrent Kishon.
March on, my soul, with courage!
Then the horses' hoofs pounded
As headlong galloped the steeds.
"Curse Meroz!" said the angel of the LORD.
"Bitterly curse its inhabitants,
Because they came not to the aid of the
LORD,

מִנִּי   אַחֲרֶיךָ בִנְיָמִין בַּעֲמָמֶיךָ   בַּעֲמָלֵק

וּמִזְּבוּלֻן מֹשְׁכִים בְּשֵׁבֶט   מָכִיר יָרְדוּ מְחֹקְקִים

וְיִשָּׂשכָר   וְשָׂרַי בְּיִשָּׂשכָר עִם־דְּבֹרָה   סֵפֶר

בִּפְלַגּוֹת רְאוּבֵן גְּדֹלִים חִקְקֵי־   כֵּן בָּרָק בָּעֵמֶק שֻׁלַּח בְּרַגְלָיו

לִשְׁמֹעַ   לָמָּה יָשַׁבְתָּ בֵּין הַמִּשְׁפְּתַיִם   לֵב

לִפְלַגּוֹת רְאוּבֵן גְּדוֹלִים חִקְרֵי־   שְׁרִקוֹת עֲדָרִים

וְדָן   גִּלְעָד בְּעֵבֶר הַיַּרְדֵּן שָׁכֵן   לֵב

אֲשֶׁר יָשַׁב לְחוֹף   לָמָּה יָגוּר אֳנִיּוֹת

זְבֻלוּן   וְעַל מִפְרָצָיו יִשְׁכּוֹן   יַמִּים

וְנַפְתָּלִי עַל מְרוֹמֵי   עַם חֵרֵף נַפְשׁוֹ לָמוּת

אָז   בָּאוּ מְלָכִים נִלְחָמוּ   שָׂדֶה

בְּתַעְנַךְ עַל־מֵי   נִלְחֲמוּ מַלְכֵי כְנַעַן

מִן־   בֶּצַע כֶּסֶף לֹא לָקָחוּ   מְגִדּוֹ

הַכּוֹכָבִים מִמְּסִלּוֹתָם נִלְחֲמוּ עִם־   שָׁמַיִם נִלְחָמוּ

נַחַל   נַחַל קִישׁוֹן גְּרָפָם   סִיסְרָא

תִּדְרְכִי נַפְשִׁי   קְדוּמִים נַחַל קִישׁוֹן

מִדַּהֲרוֹת   אָז הָלְמוּ עִקְּבֵי־סוּס   עֹז

אוֹרוּ מֵרוֹז אָמַר מַלְאַךְ יְהֹוָה אֹרוּ אָרוֹר   דַּהֲרוֹת אַבִּירָיו

To the aid of the LORD among the warriors."
Most blessed of women be Jael,
Wife of Heber the Kenite,
Most blessed of women in tents.
He asked for water, she offered milk;
In a princely bowl she brought him curds.
Her left hand reached for the tent pin,
Her right for the workmen's hammer.
She struck Sisera, crushed his head,
Smashed and pierced his temple.
At her feet he sank, lay outstretched,
At her feet he sank, lay still;
Where he sank, there he lay—destroyed.
Through the window peered Sisera's mother,
Behind the lattice she whined:
"Why is his chariot so long in coming?
Why so late the clatter of his wheels?"
The wisest of her ladies give answer;
She, too, replies to herself:
"They must be dividing the spoil they have
    found:
A damsel or two for each man,
Spoil of dyed cloths for Sisera,
Spoil of embroidered cloths,
A couple of embroidered cloths
Round every neck as spoil."
So may all Your enemies perish, O LORD!
But may His friends be as the sun rising in
    might!
And the land was tranquil forty years.

Judges 5:2–31

לְעֶזְרַת	כִּי לֹא־בָאוּ לְעֶזְרַת יְהוָה	יִשְׁבֵּיהּ
תְּבֹרַךְ מִנָּשִׁים יָעֵל אֵשֶׁת חֶבֶר		יְהוָה בַּגִּבּוֹרִים
מַיִם	מִנָּשִׁים בָּאֹהֶל תְּבֹרָךְ	הַקֵּינִי
בְּסֵפֶל אַדִּירִים הִקְרִיבָה		שָׁאַל חָלָב נָתָנָה
וִימִינָהּ	יָדָהּ לַיָּתֵד תִּשְׁלַחְנָה	חֶמְאָה
וְהָלְמָה סִיסְרָא מָחֲקָה		לְהַלְמוּת עֲמֵלִים
בֵּין	וּמָחֲצָה וְחָלְפָה רַקָּתוֹ	רֹאשׁוֹ
בֵּין רַגְלֶיהָ כָּרַע	רַגְלֶיהָ כָּרַע נָפַל שָׁכָב	
בְּעַד	בַּאֲשֶׁר כָּרַע שָׁם נָפַל שָׁדוּד	נָפָל
מַדּוּעַ בֹּשֵׁשׁ רִכְבּוֹ	בְּעַד הַחַלּוֹן נִשְׁקְפָה וַתְּיַבֵּב אֵם סִיסְרָא בְּעַד הָאֶשְׁנָב	
חַכְמוֹת	מַדּוּעַ אֶחֱרוּ פַּעֲמֵי מַרְכְּבוֹתָיו	לָבוֹא
אַף־הִיא תָּשִׁיב אֲמָרֶיהָ		שָׂרוֹתֶיהָ תַּעֲנֶינָה
רַחַם	הֲלֹא יִמְצְאוּ יְחַלְּקוּ שָׁלָל	לָהּ
שְׁלַל צְבָעִים		רַחֲמָתַיִם לְרֹאשׁ גֶּבֶר
צֶבַע	שְׁלַל צְבָעִים רִקְמָה	לְסִיסְרָא
כֵּן יֹאבְדוּ כָל־אוֹיְבֶיךָ יְהוָה		רִקְמָתַיִם לְצַוְּארֵי שָׁלָל
וַתִּשְׁקֹט הָאָרֶץ אַרְבָּעִים שָׁנָה	וְאֹהֲבָיו כְּצֵאת הַשֶּׁמֶשׁ בִּגְבֻרָתוֹ	

43

Hannah's Prayer

And Hannah prayed:

My heart exults in the LORD;
I have triumphed through the LORD.
I gloat over my enemies;
I rejoice in Your deliverance.
There is no holy one like the LORD,
Truly, there is none beside You;
There is no rock like our God.
Talk no more with lofty pride,
Let no arrogance cross your lips!
For the LORD is an all-knowing God;
By Him actions are measured.
The bows of the mighty are broken,
And the faltering are girded with strength.
Men once sated must hire out for bread;
Men once hungry hunger no more.
While the barren woman bears seven,
The mother of many is forlorn.
The LORD deals death and gives life,
Casts down into Sheol and raises up.
The LORD makes poor and makes rich;
He casts down, He also lifts high.
He raises the poor from the dust,
Lifts up the needy from the dunghill,
Setting them with nobles,
Granting them seats of honor.
For the pillars of the earth
    are the LORD's;
He has set the world upon them.
He guards the steps of His faithful,
But the wicked perish in darkness—

וַתִּתְפַּלֵּל חַנָּה וַתֹּאמַר
עָלַץ לִבִּי בַּיהוָה
רָמָה קַרְנִי בַּיהוָה
רָחַב פִּי עַל־אוֹיְבַי
כִּי שָׂמַחְתִּי בִּישׁוּעָתֶךָ
אֵין־קָדוֹשׁ כַּיהוָה
כִּי אֵין בִּלְתֶּךָ
וְאֵין צוּר כֵּאלֹהֵינוּ
אַל־תַּרְבּוּ תְדַבְּרוּ גְּבֹהָה גְבֹהָה
יֵצֵא עָתָק מִפִּיכֶם
כִּי אֵל דֵּעוֹת יְהוָה
וְלֹא וְלוֹ נִתְכְּנוּ עֲלִלוֹת
קֶשֶׁת גִּבֹּרִים חַתִּים
וְנִכְשָׁלִים אָזְרוּ חָיִל
שְׂבֵעִים בַּלֶּחֶם נִשְׂכָּרוּ
וּרְעֵבִים חָדֵלּוּ
עַד־עֲקָרָה יָלְדָה שִׁבְעָה
וְרַבַּת בָּנִים אֻמְלָלָה
יְהוָה מֵמִית וּמְחַיֶּה
מוֹרִיד שְׁאוֹל וַיָּעַל
יְהוָה מוֹרִישׁ וּמַעֲשִׁיר
מַשְׁפִּיל אַף־מְרוֹמֵם
מֵקִים מֵעָפָר דָּל
מֵאַשְׁפֹּת יָרִים אֶבְיוֹן
לְהוֹשִׁיב עִם־נְדִיבִים
וְכִסֵּא כָבוֹד יַנְחִלֵם
כִּי לַיהוָה מְצֻקֵי אֶרֶץ
וַיָּשֶׁת עֲלֵיהֶם תֵּבֵל
רַגְלֵי חֲסִידָו יִשְׁמֹר
וּרְשָׁעִים בַּחֹשֶׁךְ יִדָּמּוּ

For not by strength shall man prevail.
The foes of the LORD shall be shattered;
He will thunder against them in the heavens.
The LORD will judge the ends of the earth.
He will give power to His king,
And triumph to His anointed one.

I Samuel 2:1–10

David's Song

David addressed the words of this song to the
  LORD, after the LORD had saved him from
  the hands of all his enemies and from the
  hands of Saul. He said:
O LORD, my crag, my fastness, my deliverer!
O God, the rock wherein I take shelter:
My shield, my mighty champion, my fortress
  and refuge!
My savior, You who rescue me from violence!
All praise! I called on the LORD,
And I was delivered from my enemies.
For the breakers of Death encompassed me,
The torrents of Belial terrified me;
The snares of Sheol encircled me,
The coils of Death engulfed me.
In my anguish I called on the LORD,
Cried out to my God;
In His Abode He heard my voice,
My cry entered His ears.
Then the earth rocked and quaked,
The foundations of heaven shook—
Rocked by His indignation.

כִּי־לֹא בְכֹחַ יִגְבַּר־אִישׁ
יְהוָה יֵחַתּוּ מְרִיבָו
עָלָו בַּשָּׁמַיִם יַרְעֵם
יְהוָה יָדִין אַפְסֵי־אָרֶץ
וְיִתֶּן־עֹז לְמַלְכּוֹ
וְיָרֵם קֶרֶן מְשִׁיחוֹ

וַיְדַבֵּר דָּוִד לַיהוָה אֶת־דִּבְרֵי
הַשִּׁירָה הַזֹּאת בְּיוֹם הִצִּיל יְהוָה אֹתוֹ
מִכַּף כָּל־אֹיְבָיו וּמִכַּף שָׁאוּל וַיֹּאמַר
יְהוָה סַלְעִי וּמְצֻדָתִי וּמְפַלְטִי־לִי
אֱלֹהֵי צוּרִי אֶחֱסֶה־בּוֹ
מָגִנִּי וְקֶרֶן יִשְׁעִי מִשְׂגַּבִּי וּמְנוּסִי
מֹשִׁעִי מֵחָמָס תֹּשִׁעֵנִי
מְהֻלָּל אֶקְרָא יְהוָה
וּמֵאֹיְבַי אִוָּשֵׁעַ
כִּי אֲפָפֻנִי מִשְׁבְּרֵי־מָוֶת
נַחֲלֵי בְלִיַּעַל יְבַעֲתֻנִי
חֶבְלֵי שְׁאוֹל סַבֻּנִי
קִדְּמֻנִי מֹקְשֵׁי־מָוֶת
בַּצַּר־לִי אֶקְרָא יְהוָה
וְאֶל־אֱלֹהַי אֶקְרָא
וַיִּשְׁמַע מֵהֵיכָלוֹ קוֹלִי
וְשַׁוְעָתִי בְּאָזְנָיו
ותגעש וַיִּתְגָּעַשׁ וַתִּרְעַשׁ הָאָרֶץ
מוֹסְדוֹת הַשָּׁמַיִם יִרְגָּזוּ
וַיִּתְגָּעֲשׁוּ כִּי־חָרָה לוֹ

47

Smoke went up from His nostrils,
From His mouth came devouring fire;
Live coals blazed forth from Him.
He bent the sky and came down,
Thick cloud beneath His feet.
He mounted a cherub and flew;
He was seen on the wings of the wind.
He made pavilions of darkness about Him,
Dripping clouds, huge thunderheads;
In the brilliance before Him
Blazed fiery coals.
The LORD thundered forth from heaven,
The Most High sent forth His voice;
He let loose bolts, and scattered them;
Lightning, and put them to rout.
The bed of the sea was exposed,
The foundations of the world were laid bare
By the mighty roaring of the LORD,
At the blast of the breath of His nostrils.
He reached down from on high, He took me,
Drew me out of the mighty waters;
He rescued me from my enemy so strong,
From foes too mighty for me.
They attacked me on my day of calamity,
But the LORD was my stay.
He brought me out to freedom,
He rescued me because He was pleased with
    me.
The LORD rewarded me according to my
    merit,
He requited the cleanness of my hands.
For I have kept the ways of the LORD
And have not been guilty before my God;
I am mindful of all His rules

עָלָה עָשָׁן בְּאַפּוֹ
וְאֵשׁ מִפִּיו תֹּאכֵל
גֶּחָלִים בָּעֲרוּ מִמֶּנּוּ
וַיֵּט שָׁמַיִם וַיֵּרַד
וַעֲרָפֶל תַּחַת רַגְלָיו
וַיִּרְכַּב עַל־כְּרוּב וַיָּעֹף
וַיֵּרָא עַל־כַּנְפֵי־רוּחַ
וַיָּשֶׁת חֹשֶׁךְ סְבִיבֹתָיו סֻכּוֹת
חַשְׁרַת־מַיִם עָבֵי שְׁחָקִים
מִנֹּגַהּ נֶגְדּוֹ
בָּעֲרוּ גַּחֲלֵי־אֵשׁ
יַרְעֵם מִן־שָׁמַיִם יְהוָה
וְעֶלְיוֹן יִתֵּן קוֹלוֹ
וַיִּשְׁלַח חִצִּים וַיְפִיצֵם
בָּרָק וַיְּהֻמֵּם וַיָּהֹם
וַיֵּרָאוּ אֲפִקֵי יָם
יִגָּלוּ מֹסְדוֹת תֵּבֵל
בְּגַעֲרַת יְהוָה
מִנִּשְׁמַת רוּחַ אַפּוֹ
יִשְׁלַח מִמָּרוֹם יִקָּחֵנִי
יַמְשֵׁנִי מִמַּיִם רַבִּים
יַצִּילֵנִי מֵאֹיְבִי עָז
מִשֹּׂנְאַי כִּי אָמְצוּ מִמֶּנִּי
יְקַדְּמֻנִי בְּיוֹם אֵידִי
וַיְהִי יְהוָה מִשְׁעָן לִי
וַיֹּצֵא לַמֶּרְחָב אֹתִי
יְחַלְּצֵנִי כִּי־חָפֵץ בִּי
יִגְמְלֵנִי יְהוָה כְּצִדְקָתִי
כְּבֹר יָדַי יָשִׁיב לִי
כִּי שָׁמַרְתִּי דַּרְכֵי יְהוָה
וְלֹא רָשַׁעְתִּי מֵאֱלֹהָי
כִּי כָל־מִשְׁפָּטָיו לְנֶגְדִּי

And have not departed from His laws.
I have been blameless before Him,
And have guarded myself against sinning—
And the LORD has requited my merit,
According to my purity in His sight.
With the loyal You deal loyally;
With the blameless hero, blamelessly.
With the pure You act in purity,
And with the perverse You are wily.
To humble folk You give victory,
And You look with scorn on the haughty.
You, O LORD, are my lamp;
The LORD lights up my darkness.
With You, I can rush a barrier,
With my God, I can scale a wall.
The way of God is perfect,
The word of the LORD is pure.
He is a shield to all who take refuge in Him.
Yea, who is a god except the LORD,
Who is a rock except God—
The God, my mighty stronghold,
Who kept my path secure;
Who made my legs like a deer's,
And set me firm on the heights;
Who trained my hands for battle,
So that my arms can bend a bow of bronze!
You have granted me the shield of Your
   protection
And Your providence has made me great.
You have let me stride on freely,
And my feet have not slipped.
I pursued my enemies and wiped them out,
I did not turn back till I destroyed them.
I destroyed them, I struck them down;

וְחֻקֹּתָיו לֹא־אָסוּר מִמֶּנָּה
וָאֶהְיֶה תָמִים לוֹ
וָאֶשְׁתַּמְּרָה מֵעֲוֹנִי
וַיָּשֶׁב יְהֹוָה לִי כְּצִדְקָתִי
כְּבֹרִי לְנֶגֶד עֵינָיו
עִם־חָסִיד תִּתְחַסָּד
עִם־גְּבוֹר תָּמִים תִּתַּמָּם
עִם־נָבָר תִּתְבָּר
וְעִם־עִקֵּשׁ תִּתַּפָּל
וְאֶת־עַם עָנִי תּוֹשִׁיעַ
וְעֵינֶיךָ עַל־רָמִים תַּשְׁפִּיל
כִּי־אַתָּה נֵירִי יְהֹוָה
וַיהֹוָה יַגִּיהַּ חָשְׁכִּי
כִּי בְכָה אָרוּץ גְּדוּד
בֵּאלֹהַי אֲדַלֶּג־שׁוּר
הָאֵל תָּמִים דַּרְכּוֹ
אִמְרַת יְהֹוָה צְרוּפָה
מָגֵן הוּא לְכֹל הַחֹסִים בּוֹ
כִּי מִי־אֵל מִבַּלְעֲדֵי יְהֹוָה
וּמִי צוּר מִבַּלְעֲדֵי אֱלֹהֵינוּ
הָאֵל מָעוּזִּי חָיִל
וַיַּתֵּר תָּמִים דַּרְכּוֹ דַּרְכִּי
מְשַׁוֶּה רַגְלַיו רַגְלַי כָּאַיָּלוֹת
וְעַל בָּמוֹתַי יַעֲמִדֵנִי
מְלַמֵּד יָדַי לַמִּלְחָמָה
וְנִחַת קֶשֶׁת־נְחוּשָׁה זְרֹעֹתָי
וַתִּתֶּן־לִי מָגֵן יִשְׁעֶךָ
וַעֲנֹתְךָ תַּרְבֵּנִי
תַּרְחִיב צַעֲדִי תַּחְתֵּנִי
וְלֹא מָעֲדוּ קַרְסֻלָּי
אֶרְדְּפָה אֹיְבַי וָאַשְׁמִידֵם
וְלֹא אָשׁוּב עַד־כַּלּוֹתָם
וָאֲכַלֵּם וָאֶמְחָצֵם

They rose no more, they lay at my feet.
You have girt me with strength for battle,
Brought low my foes before me,
Made my enemies turn tail before me,
My foes—and I wiped them out.
They looked, but there was none to deliver;
To the LORD, but He answered them not.
I pounded them like dust of the earth,
Stamped, crushed them like dirt of the
    streets.
You have rescued me from the strife of
    peoples,
Kept me to be a ruler of nations;
Peoples I knew not must serve me.
Aliens have cringed before me,
Paid me homage at the mere report of me.
Aliens have lost courage
And come trembling out of their fastnesses.
The LORD lives! Blessed is my rock!
Exalted be God, the rock
Who gives me victory;
The God who has vindicated me
And made peoples subject to me,
Rescued me from my enemies,
Raised me clear of my foes,
Saved me from lawless men!
For this I sing Your praise among the nations
And hymn Your name:
Tower of victory to His king,
Who deals graciously with His anointed,
With David and his offspring evermore.

2 Samuel 22:1–51

וְלֹא יְקוּמוּן וַיִּפְּלוּ תַּחַת רַגְלָי
וַתְּזְרֵנִי חַיִל לַמִּלְחָמָה
תַּכְרִיעַ קָמַי תַּחְתֵּנִי
וְאֹיְבַי תַּתָּה לִי עֹרֶף
מְשַׂנְאַי וָאַצְמִיתֵם
יְשַׁוְּעוּ וְאֵין מֹשִׁיעַ
אֶל־יְהוָה וְלֹא עָנָם
וְאֶשְׁחָקֵם כַּעֲפַר־אָרֶץ
כְּטִיט־חוּצוֹת אֲדִקֵּם אֶרְקָעֵם
וַתְּפַלְּטֵנִי מֵרִיבֵי עַמִּי
תְּשִׂמְרֵנִי לְרֹאשׁ גּוֹיִם
עַם לֹא־יָדַעְתִּי יַעַבְדֻנִי
בְּנֵי נֵכָר יִתְכַּחֲשׁוּ־לִי
לִשְׁמוֹעַ אֹזֶן יִשָּׁמְעוּ לִי
בְּנֵי נֵכָר יִבֹּלוּ
וְיַחְגְּרוּ מִמִּסְגְּרוֹתָם
חַי־יְהוָה וּבָרוּךְ צוּרִי
וְיָרֻם אֱלֹהֵי צוּר
יִשְׁעִי
הָאֵל הַנֹּתֵן נְקָמֹת לִי
וּמוֹרִיד עַמִּים תַּחְתֵּנִי
וּמוֹצִיאִי מֵאֹיְבָי
וּמִקָּמַי תְּרוֹמְמֵנִי
מֵאִישׁ חֲמָסִים תַּצִּילֵנִי
עַל־כֵּן אוֹדְךָ יְהוָה בַּגּוֹיִם
וּלְשִׁמְךָ אֲזַמֵּר
מַגְדִּיל מִגְדּוֹל יְשׁוּעוֹת מַלְכּוֹ
וְעֹשֶׂה־חֶסֶד לִמְשִׁיחוֹ
לְדָוִד וּלְזַרְעוֹ עַד־עוֹלָם

King Hezekiah's Poem

A poem by King Hezekiah of Judah when he
    recovered from the illness he had suffered:
I had thought:
I must depart in the middle of my days;
I have been consigned to the gates of Sheol
For the rest of my years.
I thought, I shall never see Yah,
Yah in the land of the living,
Or ever behold men again
Among those who inhabit the earth.
My dwelling is pulled up and removed from me
Like a tent of shepherds;
My life is rolled up like a web
And cut from the thrum.
Only from daybreak to nightfall
Was I kept whole,
Then it was as though a lion
Were breaking all my bones;
I cried out until morning.
(Only from daybreak to nightfall
Was I kept whole.)
I piped like a swift or a swallow,
I moaned like a dove,
As my eyes, all worn, looked to heaven:
"My LORD, I am in straits;
Be my surety!"
What can I say? He promised me,
And He it is who has wrought it.
All my sleep had fled
Because of the bitterness of my soul.
My LORD, for all that and despite it

מִכְתָּב לְחִזְקִיָּהוּ מֶלֶךְ־יְהוּדָה בַּחֲלֹתוֹ
וַיְחִי מֵחָלְיוֹ

אֲנִי אָמַרְתִּי
בִּדְמִי יָמַי אֵלֵכָה
בְּשַׁעֲרֵי שְׁאוֹל פֻּקַּדְתִּי
יֶתֶר שְׁנוֹתָי
אָמַרְתִּי לֹא־אֶרְאֶה יָהּ
יָהּ בְּאֶרֶץ הַחַיִּים
לֹא־אַבִּיט אָדָם עוֹד
עִם־יוֹשְׁבֵי חָדֶל
דּוֹרִי נִסַּע וְנִגְלָה מִנִּי
כְּאֹהֶל רֹעִי
קִפַּדְתִּי כָאֹרֵג חַיַּי
מִדַּלָּה יְבַצְּעֵנִי
מִיּוֹם עַד־לַיְלָה
תַּשְׁלִימֵנִי
שִׁוִּיתִי עַד־בֹּקֶר
כָּאֲרִי כֵּן
יְשַׁבֵּר כָּל־עַצְמוֹתָי
מִיּוֹם עַד־לַיְלָה
תַּשְׁלִימֵנִי
כְּסוּס עָגוּר כֵּן אֲצַפְצֵף
אֶהְגֶּה כַּיּוֹנָה
דַּלּוּ עֵינַי לַמָּרוֹם
אֲדֹנָי עָשְׁקָה־לִּי
עָרְבֵנִי
מָה־אֲדַבֵּר וְאָמַר־לִי
וְהוּא עָשָׂה
אֶדַּדֶּה כָל־שְׁנוֹתַי
עַל־מַר נַפְשִׁי
אֲדֹנָי עֲלֵיהֶם יִחְיוּ וּלְכָל־בָּהֶן

55

My life-breath is revived;
You have restored me to health and revived
   me.
Truly, it was for my own good
That I had such great bitterness:
You saved my life
From the pit of destruction,
For You have cast behind Your back
All my offenses.
For it is not Sheol that praises You,
Not the Land of Death that extols You;
Nor do they who descend into the Pit
Hope for Your grace.
The living, only the living
Can give thanks to You
As I do this day;
Fathers relate to children
Your acts of grace:
"It has pleased the LORD to deliver us,
That is why we offer up music
All the days of our lives
At the House of the LORD."

Isaiah 38:9–20

Refuge

In the LORD I take refuge;
how can you say to me,
"Take to the hills like a bird!
For see, the wicked bend the bow,
they set their arrow on the string

חַיֵּי רוּחִי
וְתַחֲלִימֵנִי וְהַחֲיֵנִי
הִנֵּה לְשָׁלוֹם
מַר־לִי מָר
וְאַתָּה חָשַׁקְתָּ נַפְשִׁי
מִשַּׁחַת בְּלִי
כִּי הִשְׁלַכְתָּ אַחֲרֵי גֵוְךָ
כָּל־חֲטָאָי
כִּי לֹא שְׁאוֹל תּוֹדֶךָּ
מָוֶת יְהַלְלֶךָּ
לֹא־יְשַׂבְּרוּ יוֹרְדֵי־בוֹר
אֶל־אֲמִתֶּךָ
חַי חַי
הוּא יוֹדֶךָ
כָּמוֹנִי הַיּוֹם
אָב לְבָנִים
יוֹדִיעַ אֶל־אֲמִתֶּךָ
יְהוָה לְהוֹשִׁיעֵנִי
וּנְגִנוֹתַי נְנַגֵּן
כָּל־יְמֵי חַיֵּינוּ
עַל־בֵּית יְהוָה

בַּיהוָה חָסִיתִי
אֵיךְ תֹּאמְרוּ לְנַפְשִׁי
נוּדוּ נוֹדִי הַרְכֶם צִפּוֹר:
כִּי הִנֵּה הָרְשָׁעִים יִדְרְכוּן קֶשֶׁת
כּוֹנְנוּ חִצָּם עַל־יֶתֶר

to shoot from the shadows at the upright.
When the foundations are destroyed,
what can the righteous man do?"
The LORD is in His holy palace;
the LORD—His throne is in heaven;
His eyes behold, His gaze searches mankind.
The LORD seeks out the righteous man,
but loathes the wicked one who loves injustice.
He will rain down upon the wicked blazing
    coals and sulfur;
a scorching wind shall be their lot.
For the LORD is righteous;
He loves righteous deeds;
the upright shall behold His face.

Psalms 11:1–7

The LORD Is My Shepherd

Recited for the sick, at a funeral, or at the unveiling of a tombstone

A Psalm of David.
The LORD is my shepherd; I shall not want.
He makes me lie down in green pastures;
He leads me beside the still waters.
He restores my soul;
He guides me in straight paths for His name's
    sake.
Yea, though I walk through the valley of the
    shadow of death,
I will fear no evil,
For You are with me;
Your rod and Your staff, they comfort me.

לִירוֹת בְּמוֹ־אֹפֶל לְיִשְׁרֵי־לֵב

כִּי הַשָּׁתוֹת יֵהָרֵסוּן

צַדִּיק מַה־פָּעָל

יְהוָה בְּהֵיכַל קָדְשׁוֹ

יְהוָה בַּשָּׁמַיִם כִּסְאוֹ

עֵינָיו יֶחֱזוּ עַפְעַפָּיו יִבְחֲנוּ בְּנֵי

אָדָם

יְהוָה צַדִּיק יִבְחָן

וְרָשָׁע וְאֹהֵב חָמָס שָׂנְאָה נַפְשׁוֹ

יַמְטֵר עַל־רְשָׁעִים פַּחִים אֵשׁ

וְגָפְרִית

וְרוּחַ זִלְעָפוֹת מְנָת כּוֹסָם

כִּי־צַדִּיק יְהוָה

צְדָקוֹת אָהֵב

יָשָׁר יֶחֱזוּ פָנֵימוֹ

מִזְמוֹר לְדָוִד

יְהוָה רֹעִי

לֹא אֶחְסָר

בִּנְאוֹת דֶּשֶׁא יַרְבִּיצֵנִי

עַל־מֵי מְנֻחוֹת יְנַהֲלֵנִי

נַפְשִׁי יְשׁוֹבֵב

יַנְחֵנִי בְמַעְגְּלֵי־צֶדֶק

לְמַעַן שְׁמוֹ

גַּם כִּי־אֵלֵךְ בְּגֵיא צַלְמָוֶת

לֹא־אִירָא רָע כִּי־אַתָּה עִמָּדִי

שִׁבְטְךָ וּמִשְׁעַנְתֶּךָ הֵמָּה יְנַחֲמֻנִי

You prepare a table before me in the presence
of my enemies;
You have anointed my head with oil;
My cup runs over.
Surely goodness and mercy shall follow me all
the days of my life;
And I shall dwell in the house of the LORD
forever.

Psalms 23:1–6
OJPS translation (adapted)

You Have Lifted Me Up

I extol You, O LORD,
for You have lifted me up,
and not let my enemies rejoice over me.
O LORD, my God,
I cried out to You,
and You healed me.
O LORD, You brought me up from Sheol,
preserved me from going down into the Pit.
O you faithful of the LORD, sing to Him,
and praise His holy name.
For He is angry but a moment,
and when He is pleased there is life.
One may lie down weeping at nightfall;
but at dawn there are shouts of joy.
When I was untroubled,
I thought, "I shall never be shaken,"
for You, O LORD, when You were pleased,
made me firm as a mighty mountain.

תַּעֲרֹךְ לְפָנַי שֻׁלְחָן נֶגֶד צֹרְרָי
דִּשַּׁנְתָּ בַשֶּׁמֶן רֹאשִׁי
כּוֹסִי רְוָיָה
אַךְ טוֹב וָחֶסֶד יִרְדְּפוּנִי
כָּל־יְמֵי חַיָּי
וְשַׁבְתִּי בְּבֵית־יְהוָה
לְאֹרֶךְ יָמִים

אֲרוֹמִמְךָ יְהוָה
כִּי דִלִּיתָנִי
וְלֹא־שִׂמַּחְתָּ אֹיְבַי לִי
יְהוָה אֱלֹהָי
שִׁוַּעְתִּי אֵלֶיךָ
וַתִּרְפָּאֵנִי
יְהוָה הֶעֱלִיתָ מִן־שְׁאוֹל נַפְשִׁי
חִיִּיתַנִי מִיּוֹרְדִי מִיָּרְדִי־בוֹר
זַמְּרוּ לַיהוָה חֲסִידָיו
וְהוֹדוּ לְזֵכֶר קָדְשׁוֹ
כִּי רֶגַע בְּאַפּוֹ
חַיִּים בִּרְצוֹנוֹ
בָּעֶרֶב יָלִין בֶּכִי
וְלַבֹּקֶר רִנָּה

וַאֲנִי אָמַרְתִּי בְשַׁלְוִי
בַּל־אֶמּוֹט לְעוֹלָם
יְהוָה בִּרְצוֹנְךָ
הֶעֱמַדְתָּה לְהַרְרִי עֹז

When You hid Your face,
I was terrified.
I called to You, O LORD;
to my LORD I made appeal,
"What is to be gained from my death,
from my descent into the Pit?
Can dust praise You?
Can it declare Your faithfulness?
Hear, O LORD, and have mercy on me;
O LORD, be my help!"
You turned my lament into dancing,
you undid my sackcloth and girded me with
    joy,
that my whole being might sing hymns to
    You endlessly;
O LORD my God, I will praise You forever.

Psalms 30:2–13

A Song for the Sabbath

It is good to praise the LORD,
to sing hymns to Your name, O Most High,
To proclaim Your steadfast love at daybreak,
Your faithfulness each night
With a ten-stringed harp,
with voice and lyre together.
You have gladdened me by Your deeds, O
    LORD;
I shout for joy at Your handiwork.
How great are Your works, O LORD,
how very subtle Your designs!

הִסְתַּרְתָּ פָנֶיךָ
הָיִיתִי נִבְהָל
אֵלֶיךָ יְהוָה אֶקְרָא
וְאֶל־אֲדֹנָי אֶתְחַנָּן
מַה־בֶּצַע בְּדָמִי
בְּרִדְתִּי אֶל־שָׁחַת
הֲיוֹדְךָ עָפָר
הֲיַגִּיד אֲמִתֶּךָ
שְׁמַע־יְהוָה וְחָנֵּנִי
יְהוָה הֱיֵה־עֹזֵר לִי
הָפַכְתָּ מִסְפְּדִי לְמָחוֹל לִי
פִּתַּחְתָּ שַׂקִּי וַתְּאַזְּרֵנִי שִׂמְחָה
לְמַעַן יְזַמֶּרְךָ כָבוֹד וְלֹא יִדֹּם
יְהוָה אֱלֹהַי לְעוֹלָם אוֹדֶךָּ

טוֹב לְהֹדוֹת לַיהוָה
וּלְזַמֵּר לְשִׁמְךָ עֶלְיוֹן
לְהַגִּיד בַּבֹּקֶר חַסְדֶּךָ
וֶאֱמוּנָתְךָ בַּלֵּילוֹת
עֲלֵי־עָשׂוֹר וַעֲלֵי־נָבֶל
עֲלֵי הִגָּיוֹן בְּכִנּוֹר
כִּי שִׂמַּחְתַּנִי יְהוָה בְּפָעֳלֶךָ
בְּמַעֲשֵׂי יָדֶיךָ אֲרַנֵּן
מַה־גָּדְלוּ מַעֲשֶׂיךָ יְהוָה

A brutish man cannot know,
a fool cannot understand this:
though the wicked sprout like grass,
though all evildoers blossom,
it is only that they may be destroyed forever.
But You are exalted, O LORD, for all time.
Surely, Your enemies, O LORD,
surely, Your enemies perish;
all evildoers are scattered.
You raise my horn high like that of a wild
    ox;
I am soaked in freshening oil.
I shall see the defeat of my watchful foes,
hear of the downfall of the wicked who beset
    me.
The righteous bloom like a date-palm;
they thrive like a cedar in Lebanon;
planted in the house of the LORD,
they flourish in the courts of our God.
In old age they still produce fruit;
they are full of sap and freshness,
attesting that the LORD is upright,
my rock, in whom there is no wrong.

Psalms 92:2–16

O My Soul

*Recited for the
sick, at a funeral,
at the
consecration of a
cemetery*

Bless the LORD, O my soul,
all my being, His holy name.
Bless the LORD, O my soul
and do not forget all His bounties.

מְאֹד עָמְקוּ מַחְשְׁבֹתֶיךָ
אִישׁ־בַּעַר לֹא יֵדָע
וּכְסִיל לֹא־יָבִין אֶת־זֹאת
בִּפְרֹחַ רְשָׁעִים כְּמוֹ עֵשֶׂב
וַיָּצִיצוּ כָּל־פֹּעֲלֵי אָוֶן
לְהִשָּׁמְדָם עֲדֵי־עַד
וְאַתָּה מָרוֹם לְעֹלָם יְהוָה
כִּי הִנֵּה אֹיְבֶיךָ יְהוָה
כִּי־הִנֵּה אֹיְבֶיךָ יֹאבֵדוּ
יִתְפָּרְדוּ כָּל־פֹּעֲלֵי אָוֶן
וַתָּרֶם כִּרְאֵים קַרְנִי
בַּלֹּתִי בְּשֶׁמֶן רַעֲנָן
וַתַּבֵּט עֵינִי בְּשׁוּרָי
בַּקָּמִים עָלַי מְרֵעִים תִּשְׁמַעְנָה
אָזְנָי
צַדִּיק כַּתָּמָר יִפְרָח
כְּאֶרֶז בַּלְּבָנוֹן יִשְׂגֶּה
שְׁתוּלִים בְּבֵית יְהוָה
בְּחַצְרוֹת אֱלֹהֵינוּ יַפְרִיחוּ
עוֹד יְנוּבוּן בְּשֵׂיבָה
דְּשֵׁנִים וְרַעֲנַנִּים יִהְיוּ
לְהַגִּיד כִּי־יָשָׁר יְהוָה
צוּרִי וְלֹא־עַלְתָה עַוְלָתָה בּוֹ

בָּרְכִי נַפְשִׁי אֶת־יְהוָה
וְכָל־קְרָבַי אֶת־שֵׁם קָדְשׁוֹ
בָּרְכִי נַפְשִׁי אֶת־יְהוָה
וְאַל־תִּשְׁכְּחִי כָּל־גְּמוּלָיו

He forgives all your sins,
heals all your diseases.
He redeems your life from the Pit,
surrounds you with steadfast love and
    mercy.
He satisfies you with good things in the
    prime of life,
so that your youth is renewed like the
    eagle's.
The LORD executes righteous acts
and judgments for all who are wronged.
He made known His ways to Moses,
His deeds to the children of Israel.
The LORD is compassionate and gracious,
slow to anger, abounding in steadfast love.
He will not contend forever,
or nurse His anger for all time.
He has not dealt with us according to our
    sins,
nor has He requited us according to our
    iniquities.
For as the heavens are high above the earth,
so great is His steadfast love toward those
    who fear Him.
As east is far from west,
so far has He removed our sins from us.
As a father has compassion for his children,
so the LORD has compassion for those who
    fear Him.
For He knows how we are formed;
He is mindful that we are dust.
Man, his days are like those of grass;
he blooms like a flower of the field;
a wind passes by and it is no more,

הַסֹּלֵחַ לְכָל־עֲוֺנֵכִי

הָרֹפֵא לְכָל־תַּחֲלֻאָיְכִי

הַגּוֹאֵל מִשַּׁחַת חַיָּיְכִי

הַמְעַטְּרֵכִי חֶסֶד וְרַחֲמִים

הַמַּשְׂבִּיעַ בַּטּוֹב עֶדְיֵךְ

תִּתְחַדֵּשׁ כַּנֶּשֶׁר נְעוּרָיְכִי

עֹשֵׂה צְדָקוֹת יְהוָה

וּמִשְׁפָּטִים לְכָל־עֲשׁוּקִים

יוֹדִיעַ דְּרָכָיו לְמֹשֶׁה

לִבְנֵי יִשְׂרָאֵל עֲלִילוֹתָיו

רַחוּם וְחַנּוּן יְהוָה

אֶרֶךְ אַפַּיִם וְרַב־חָסֶד

לֹא־לָנֶצַח יָרִיב

וְלֹא לְעוֹלָם יִטּוֹר

לֹא כַחֲטָאֵינוּ עָשָׂה לָנוּ

וְלֹא כַעֲוֺנֹתֵינוּ גָּמַל עָלֵינוּ

כִּי כִגְבֹהַּ שָׁמַיִם עַל־הָאָרֶץ

גָּבַר חַסְדּוֹ עַל־יְרֵאָיו

כִּרְחֹק מִזְרָח מִמַּעֲרָב

הִרְחִיק מִמֶּנּוּ אֶת־פְּשָׁעֵינוּ

כְּרַחֵם אָב עַל־בָּנִים

רִחַם יְהוָה עַל־יְרֵאָיו

כִּי־הוּא יָדַע יִצְרֵנוּ

זָכוּר כִּי־עָפָר אֲנָחְנוּ

אֱנוֹשׁ כֶּחָצִיר יָמָיו

כְּצִיץ הַשָּׂדֶה כֵּן יָצִיץ

כִּי רוּחַ עָבְרָה־בּוֹ וְאֵינֶנּוּ

its own place no longer knows it.
But the LORD's steadfast love is for all
  eternity
toward those who fear Him,
and His beneficence is for the children's
  children
of those who keep His covenant
and remember to observe His precepts.
The LORD has established His throne in
  heaven,
and His sovereign rule is over all.
Bless the LORD, O His angels,
mighty creatures who do His bidding,
ever obedient to His bidding;
bless the LORD, all His hosts,
His servants who do His will;
bless the LORD, all His works,
through the length and breadth of His
  realm;
bless the LORD, O my soul.

Psalms 103:1–22

Hallel

*Recited in Hallel
service for new
moon, festivals,
and Hanukkah*

Hallelujah.
O servants of the LORD, give praise;
praise the name of the LORD.
Let the name of the LORD be blessed
now and forever.
From east to west
the name of the LORD is praised.

וְלֹא־יַכִּירֶנּוּ עֹוד מְקֹומֹו
וְחֶסֶד יְהוָה   מֵעֹולָם וְעַד־עֹולָם
עַל־יְרֵאָיו
וְצִדְקָתֹו לִבְנֵי בָנִים
לְשֹׁמְרֵי בְרִיתֹו
וּלְזֹכְרֵי פִקֻּדָיו לַעֲשֹׂותָם
יְהוָה בַּשָּׁמַיִם הֵכִין כִּסְאֹו
וּמַלְכוּתֹו בַּכֹּל מָשָׁלָה

בָּרְכוּ יְהוָה מַלְאָכָיו
גִּבֹּרֵי כֹחַ עֹשֵׂי דְבָרֹו
לִשְׁמֹעַ בְּקֹול דְּבָרֹו
בָּרְכוּ יְהוָה כָּל־צְבָאָיו
מְשָׁרְתָיו עֹשֵׂי רְצֹונֹו
בָּרְכוּ יְהוָה כָּל־מַעֲשָׂיו
בְּכָל־מְקֹמֹות מֶמְשַׁלְתֹּו
בָּרְכִי נַפְשִׁי אֶת־יְהוָה

הַלְלוּ יָהּ
הַלְלוּ עַבְדֵי יְהוָה
הַלְלוּ אֶת־שֵׁם יְהוָה
יְהִי שֵׁם יְהוָה מְבֹרָךְ
מֵעַתָּה וְעַד־עֹולָם
מִמִּזְרַח־שֶׁמֶשׁ עַד־מְבֹואֹו
מְהֻלָּל שֵׁם יְהוָה

The LORD is exalted above all nations;
His glory is above the heavens.
Who is like the LORD our God,
who, enthroned on high,
sees what is below,
in heaven and on earth?
He raises the poor from the dust,
lifts up the needy from the refuse heap
to set them with the great,
with the great men of His people.
He sets the childless woman among her
    household
as a happy mother of children.
Hallelujah.

Psalms 113:1–9

When Israel went forth from Egypt,
the house of Judah from a people of strange
    speech,
Judah became His holy one,
Israel, His dominion.
The sea saw them and fled,
Jordan ran backward,
Mountains skipped like rams,
hills like sheep.
What alarmed you, O sea, that you fled,
Jordan, that you ran backward,
Mountains, that you skipped like rams,
hills, like sheep?
Tremble, O earth, at the presence of the
    LORD,
at the presence of Jacob,

רָם עַל־כָּל־גּוֹיִם יְהוָה
עַל הַשָּׁמַיִם כְּבוֹדוֹ
מִי כַּיהוָה אֱלֹהֵינוּ
הַמַּגְבִּיהִי לָשָׁבֶת
הַמַּשְׁפִּילִי לִרְאוֹת
בַּשָּׁמַיִם וּבָאָרֶץ
מְקִימִי מֵעָפָר דָּל
מֵאַשְׁפֹּת יָרִים אֶבְיוֹן
לְהוֹשִׁיבִי עִם־נְדִיבִים
עִם נְדִיבֵי עַמּוֹ
מוֹשִׁיבִי עֲקֶרֶת הַבַּיִת
אֵם־הַבָּנִים שְׂמֵחָה
הַלְלוּ־יָהּ

בְּצֵאת יִשְׂרָאֵל מִמִּצְרָיִם
בֵּית יַעֲקֹב מֵעַם לֹעֵז
הָיְתָה יְהוּדָה לְקָדְשׁוֹ
יִשְׂרָאֵל מַמְשְׁלוֹתָיו
הַיָּם רָאָה וַיָּנֹס
הַיַּרְדֵּן יִסֹּב לְאָחוֹר
הֶהָרִים רָקְדוּ כְאֵילִים
גְּבָעוֹת כִּבְנֵי־צֹאן
מַה־לְּךָ הַיָּם כִּי תָנוּס
הַיַּרְדֵּן תִּסֹּב לְאָחוֹר
הֶהָרִים תִּרְקְדוּ כְאֵילִים
גְּבָעוֹת כִּבְנֵי־צֹאן
מִלִּפְנֵי אָדוֹן חוּלִי אָרֶץ
מִלִּפְנֵי אֱלוֹהַּ יַעֲקֹב

who turned the rock into a pool of water,
the flinty rock into a fountain.

Psalms 114:1–8

Not to us, O LORD, not to us
but to Your name bring glory
for the sake of Your love and Your
   faithfulness.
Let the nations not say,
"Where, now, is their God?"
when our God is in heaven
and all that He wills He accomplishes.
Their idols are silver and gold,
the work of men's hands.
They have mouths, but cannot speak,
eyes, but cannot see;
they have ears, but cannot hear,
noses, but cannot smell;
they have hands, but cannot touch,
feet, but cannot walk;
they can make no sound in their throats.
Those who fashion them,
all who trust in them,
shall become like them.
O Israel, trust in the LORD!
He is their help and shield.
O house of Aaron, trust in the LORD!
He is their help and shield.
O you who fear the LORD, trust in the LORD!
He is their help and shield.
The LORD is mindful of us.
He will bless us;
He will bless the house of Israel;

הַהֹפְכִי הַצּוּר אֲגַם־מָיִם
חַלָּמִישׁ לְמַעְיְנוֹ־מָיִם

לֹא לָנוּ יְהוָה לֹא לָנוּ
כִּי־לְשִׁמְךָ תֵּן כָּבוֹד
עַל־חַסְדְּךָ עַל־אֲמִתֶּךָ
לָמָּה יֹאמְרוּ הַגּוֹיִם
אַיֵּה־נָא אֱלֹהֵיהֶם
וֵאלֹהֵינוּ בַשָּׁמָיִם
כֹּל אֲשֶׁר־חָפֵץ עָשָׂה
עֲצַבֵּיהֶם כֶּסֶף וְזָהָב
מַעֲשֵׂה יְדֵי אָדָם
פֶּה־לָהֶם וְלֹא יְדַבֵּרוּ
עֵינַיִם לָהֶם וְלֹא יִרְאוּ
אָזְנַיִם לָהֶם וְלֹא יִשְׁמָעוּ
אַף לָהֶם וְלֹא יְרִיחוּן
יְדֵיהֶם וְלֹא יְמִישׁוּן
רַגְלֵיהֶם וְלֹא יְהַלֵּכוּ
לֹא־יֶהְגּוּ בִּגְרוֹנָם
כְּמוֹהֶם יִהְיוּ
עֹשֵׂיהֶם
כֹּל אֲשֶׁר־בֹּטֵחַ בָּהֶם
יִשְׂרָאֵל בְּטַח בַּיהוָה
עֶזְרָם וּמָגִנָּם הוּא
בֵּית אַהֲרֹן בִּטְחוּ בַיהוָה
עֶזְרָם וּמָגִנָּם הוּא
יִרְאֵי יְהוָה בִּטְחוּ בַיהוָה
עֶזְרָם וּמָגִנָּם הוּא
יְהוָה זְכָרָנוּ
יְבָרֵךְ
יְבָרֵךְ אֶת־בֵּית יִשְׂרָאֵל

He will bless the house of Aaron;
He will bless those who fear the LORD,
small and great alike.
May the LORD increase your numbers,
yours and your children's also.
May you be blessed by the LORD,
Maker of heaven and earth.
The heavens belong to the LORD,
but the earth He gave over to man.
The dead cannot praise the LORD,
nor any who go down into silence.
But we will bless the LORD
now and forever.
Hallelujah.

Psalms 115:1–18

Praise the LORD, all you nations;
extol Him, all you peoples,
for great is His steadfast love toward us;
the faithfulness of the LORD endures forever.
Hallelujah.

Psalms 117:1–2

Song of Ascent

*Sung at grace
after meals on
Sabbath and
festivals*

When the LORD restores the fortunes of Zion
       —we see it as in a dream—
our mouths shall be filled with laughter,
our tongues, with songs of joy.
Then shall they say among the nations,

יְבָרֵךְ אֶת־בֵּית אַהֲרֹן
יְבָרֵךְ יִרְאֵי יְהוָה
הַקְּטַנִּים עִם־הַגְּדֹלִים
יֹסֵף יְהוָה עֲלֵיכֶם
עֲלֵיכֶם וְעַל־בְּנֵיכֶם
בְּרוּכִים אַתֶּם לַיהוָה
עֹשֵׂה שָׁמַיִם וָאָרֶץ
הַשָּׁמַיִם שָׁמַיִם לַיהוָה
וְהָאָרֶץ נָתַן לִבְנֵי־אָדָם
לֹא הַמֵּתִים יְהַלְלוּ־יָהּ
וְלֹא כָּל־יֹרְדֵי דוּמָה
וַאֲנַחְנוּ נְבָרֵךְ יָהּ
מֵעַתָּה וְעַד־עוֹלָם
הַלְלוּ־יָהּ

הַלְלוּ אֶת־יְהוָה כָּל־גּוֹיִם
שַׁבְּחוּהוּ כָּל־הָאֻמִּים
כִּי גָבַר עָלֵינוּ חַסְדּוֹ
וֶאֱמֶת־יְהוָה לְעוֹלָם
הַלְלוּ־יָהּ

בְּשׁוּב יְהוָה אֶת־שִׁיבַת צִיּוֹן
הָיִינוּ כְּחֹלְמִים
אָז יִמָּלֵא שְׂחוֹק פִּינוּ
וּלְשׁוֹנֵנוּ רִנָּה
אָז יֹאמְרוּ בַגּוֹיִם

"The LORD has done great things for them!"
The LORD will do great things for us
and we shall rejoice.
Restore our fortunes, O LORD,
like watercourses in the Negeb.
They who sow in tears
shall reap with songs of joy.
Though he goes along weeping,
carrying the seed-bag,
he shall come back with songs of joy,
carrying his sheaves.

Psalms 126:1–6

Hallelujah

Hallelujah.
Praise God in His sanctuary;
praise Him in the sky, His stronghold.
Praise Him for His mighty acts;
praise Him for His exceeding greatness.
Praise Him with blasts of the horn;
praise Him with harp and lyre.
Praise Him with timbrel and dance;
praise Him with lute and pipe.
Praise Him with resounding cymbals;
praise Him with loud-clashing cymbals.
Let all that breathes praise the LORD.
Hallelujah.

Psalms 150:1–6

הִגְדִּיל יְהֹוָה לַעֲשׂוֹת עִם־אֵלֶּה
הִגְדִּיל יְהֹוָה לַעֲשׂוֹת עִמָּנוּ
הָיִינוּ שְׂמֵחִים
שׁוּבָה יְהֹוָה אֶת־שְׁבוּתֵנוּ שְׁבִיתֵנוּ
כַּאֲפִיקִים בַּנֶּגֶב
הַזֹּרְעִים בְּדִמְעָה
בְּרִנָּה יִקְצֹרוּ
הָלוֹךְ יֵלֵךְ וּבָכֹה
נֹשֵׂא מֶשֶׁךְ־הַזָּרַע
בֹּא־יָבוֹא בְרִנָּה
נֹשֵׂא אֲלֻמֹּתָיו

הַלְלוּ יָהּ
הַלְלוּ־אֵל בְּקׇדְשׁוֹ
הַלְלוּהוּ בִּרְקִיעַ עֻזּוֹ
הַלְלוּהוּ בִגְבוּרֹתָיו
הַלְלוּהוּ כְּרֹב גֻּדְלוֹ
הַלְלוּהוּ בְּתֵקַע שׁוֹפָר
הַלְלוּהוּ בְּנֵבֶל וְכִנּוֹר
הַלְלוּהוּ בְּתֹף וּמָחוֹל
הַלְלוּהוּ בְּמִנִּים וְעֻגָב
הַלְלוּהוּ בְצִלְצְלֵי־שָׁמַע
הַלְלוּהוּ בְּצִלְצְלֵי תְרוּעָה
כֹּל הַנְּשָׁמָה תְּהַלֵּל יָהּ
הַלְלוּ־יָהּ

The Song of Asaph

Praise the LORD;
call on His name;
proclaim His deeds among the peoples.
Sing praises unto Him;
speak of all His wondrous acts.
Exult in His holy name;
let all who seek the LORD rejoice.
Turn to the LORD, to His might;
seek His presence constantly.
Remember the wonders He has done;
His portents and the judgments He has
    pronounced,
O offspring of Israel, His servant,
O descendants of Jacob, His chosen ones.
He is the LORD our God;
His judgments are throughout the earth.
Be ever mindful of His covenant,
the promise He gave for a thousand generations,
that He made with Abraham,
swore to Isaac,
and confirmed in a decree for Jacob,
for Israel, as an eternal covenant,
saying, 'To you I will give the land of Canaan
as your allotted heritage.'
You were then few in number,
a handful, merely sojourning there,
wandering from nation to nation,
from one kingdom to another.
He allowed no one to oppress them;
He reproved kings on their account,
Do not touch My anointed ones;

הוֹדוּ לַיהוָה֙
קִרְאוּ בִשְׁמ֔וֹ
הוֹדִיעוּ בָעַמִּ֖ים עֲלִילֹתָ֑יו
שִׁ֥ירוּ ל֖וֹ זַמְּרוּ־ל֑וֹ
שִׂ֕יחוּ בְּכָל־נִפְלְאֹתָֽיו
הִֽתְהַלְלוּ֙ בְּשֵׁ֣ם קָדְשׁ֔וֹ
יִשְׂמַ֕ח לֵ֖ב מְבַקְשֵׁ֥י יְהוָֽה
דִּרְשׁ֥וּ יְהוָ֖ה וְעֻזּ֑וֹ
בַּקְּשׁ֥וּ פָנָ֖יו תָּמִֽיד
זִכְר֗וּ נִפְלְאֹתָיו֙ אֲשֶׁ֣ר עָשָׂ֔ה
מֹפְתָ֖יו וּמִשְׁפְּטֵי־פִֽיהוּ
זֶ֖רַע יִשְׂרָאֵ֣ל עַבְדּ֑וֹ
בְּנֵ֥י יַעֲקֹ֖ב בְּחִירָֽיו
ה֖וּא יְהוָ֣ה אֱלֹהֵ֑ינוּ
בְּכָל־הָאָ֖רֶץ מִשְׁפָּטָֽיו
זִכְר֤וּ לְעוֹלָם֙ בְּרִית֔וֹ
דָּבָ֥ר צִוָּ֖ה לְאֶ֥לֶף דּֽוֹר
אֲשֶׁ֤ר כָּרַת֙ אֶת־אַבְרָהָ֔ם
וּשְׁבוּעָת֖וֹ לְיִצְחָֽק
וַיַּעֲמִידֶ֤הָ לְיַעֲקֹב֙ לְחֹ֔ק
לְיִשְׂרָאֵ֖ל בְּרִ֥ית עוֹלָֽם
לֵאמֹ֗ר לְךָ֙ אֶתֵּ֣ן אֶֽרֶץ־כְּנָ֑עַן
חֶ֖בֶל נַחֲלַתְכֶֽם

בִּֽהְיוֹתְכֶם֙ מְתֵ֣י מִסְפָּ֔ר
כִּמְעַ֖ט וְגָרִ֥ים בָּֽהּ
וַיִּֽתְהַלְּכוּ֙ מִגּ֣וֹי אֶל־גּ֔וֹי
וּמִמַּמְלָכָ֖ה אֶל־עַ֥ם אַחֵֽר
לֹֽא־הִנִּ֥יחַ לְאִ֖ישׁ לְעָשְׁקָ֑ם
וַיּ֖וֹכַח עֲלֵיהֶ֥ם מְלָכִֽים
אַֽל־תִּגְּעוּ֙ בִּמְשִׁיחָ֔י

do not harm My prophets.'
"Sing to the LORD, all the earth.
proclaim His victory day after day.
Tell of His glory among the nations,
His wondrous deeds among all peoples.
For the LORD is great and much acclaimed,
He is held in awe by all divine beings.
All the gods of the peoples are mere idols,
but the LORD made the heavens.
Glory and majesty are before Him;
strength and joy are in His place.
"Ascribe to the LORD, O families of the
    peoples,
ascribe to the LORD glory and strength.
Ascribe to the LORD the glory of His name,
bring tribute and enter before Him,
bow down to the LORD majestic in holiness.
Tremble in His presence, all the earth!
The world stands firm; it cannot be shaken.
Let the heavens rejoice and the earth exult;
let them declare among the nations, "The
    LORD is King!"
Let the sea and all within it thunder,
the fields and everything in them exult;
then shall all the trees of the forest shout for
    joy
at the presence of the LORD,
for He is coming to rule the earth.
Praise the LORD for He is good;
His steadfast love is eternal.

וּבִנְבִיאַי אַל־תָּרֵעוּ

שִׁירוּ לַיהוָה כָּל־הָאָרֶץ

בַּשְּׂרוּ מִיּוֹם־אֶל־יוֹם יְשׁוּעָתוֹ

סַפְּרוּ בַגּוֹיִם אֶת־כְּבוֹדוֹ

בְּכָל־הָעַמִּים נִפְלְאֹתָיו

כִּי גָדוֹל יְהוָה וּמְהֻלָּל מְאֹד

וְנוֹרָא הוּא עַל־כָּל־אֱלֹהִים

כִּי כָּל־אֱלֹהֵי הָעַמִּים אֱלִילִים

וַיהוָה שָׁמַיִם עָשָׂה

הוֹד וְהָדָר לְפָנָיו

עֹז וְחֶדְוָה בִּמְקֹמוֹ

הָבוּ לַיהוָה מִשְׁפְּחוֹת עַמִּים

הָבוּ לַיהוָה כָּבוֹד וָעֹז

הָבוּ לַיהוָה כְּבוֹד שְׁמוֹ

שְׂאוּ מִנְחָה וּבֹאוּ לְפָנָיו

הִשְׁתַּחֲווּ לַיהוָה בְּהַדְרַת־קֹדֶשׁ

חִילוּ מִלְּפָנָיו כָּל־הָאָרֶץ

אַף־תִּכּוֹן תֵּבֵל בַּל־תִּמּוֹט

יִשְׂמְחוּ הַשָּׁמַיִם וְתָגֵל הָאָרֶץ

וְיֹאמְרוּ בַגּוֹיִם יְהוָה מָלָךְ

יִרְעַם הַיָּם וּמְלוֹאוֹ

יַעֲלֹץ הַשָּׂדֶה וְכָל־אֲשֶׁר־בּוֹ

אָז יְרַנְּנוּ עֲצֵי הַיָּעַר

מִלִּפְנֵי יְהוָה

כִּי־בָא לִשְׁפּוֹט אֶת־הָאָרֶץ

הוֹדוּ לַיהוָה כִּי טוֹב

כִּי לְעוֹלָם חַסְדּוֹ

Declare:
Deliver us, O God, our deliverer,
and gather us and save us from the nations,
to acclaim Your holy name,
to glory in Your praise.

1 Chronicles 16:8–35

וְאִמְרוּ
הוֹשִׁיעֵנוּ אֱלֹהֵי יִשְׁעֵנוּ
וְקַבְּצֵנוּ וְהַצִּילֵנוּ מִן־הַגּוֹיִם
לְהֹדוֹת לְשֵׁם קָדְשֶׁךָ
לְהִשְׁתַּבֵּחַ בִּתְהִלָּתֶךָ

POETIC MOMENTS

So the Lord God cast a deep sleep upon the
man; and, while he slept, He took one of
his ribs and closed up the flesh at that spot.
And the Lord God fashioned the rib that
He had taken from the man into a woman;
and He brought her to the man. Then the
man said,
> "This one at last
> Is bone of my bones
> And flesh of my flesh.
> This one shall be called Woman,
> For from man was she taken."

Genesis 2:21–23

In the course of time, Cain brought an
offering to the LORD from the fruit of the
soil; and Abel, for his part, brought the
choicest of the firstlings of his flock. The
LORD paid heed to Abel and his offering,
but to Cain and his offering He paid no
heed. Cain was much distressed and his
face fell. And the LORD said to Cain,
> "Why are you distressed,
> And why is your face fallen?
> Surely, if you do right,
> There is uplift.

וַיַּפֵּל יְהוָה אֱלֹהִים תַּרְדֵּמָה עַל־הָאָדָם
וַיִּישָׁן וַיִּקַּח אַחַת מִצַּלְעֹתָיו וַיִּסְגֹּר בָּשָׂר
תַּחְתֶּנָּה וַיִּבֶן יְהוָה אֱלֹהִים אֶת־
הַצֵּלָע אֲשֶׁר־לָקַח מִן־הָאָדָם לְאִשָּׁה
וַיְבִאֶהָ אֶל־הָאָדָם
וַיֹּאמֶר הָאָדָם
זֹאת הַפַּעַם
עֶצֶם מֵעֲצָמַי
וּבָשָׂר מִבְּשָׂרִי
לְזֹאת יִקָּרֵא אִשָּׁה
כִּי מֵאִישׁ לֻקֳחָה־זֹּאת

וַיְהִי מִקֵּץ יָמִים וַיָּבֵא קַיִן מִפְּרִי
הָאֲדָמָה מִנְחָה לַיהוָה וְהֶבֶל הֵבִיא
גַם־הוּא מִבְּכֹרוֹת צֹאנוֹ וּמֵחֶלְבֵהֶן וַיִּשַׁע
יְהוָה אֶל־הֶבֶל וְאֶל־מִנְחָתוֹ וְאֶל־קַיִן
וְאֶל־מִנְחָתוֹ לֹא שָׁעָה וַיִּחַר לְקַיִן מְאֹד
וַיִּפְּלוּ פָּנָיו וַיֹּאמֶר יְהוָה אֶל־קַיִן
לָמָּה חָרָה לָךְ
וְלָמָּה נָפְלוּ פָנֶיךָ
הֲלוֹא אִם־תֵּיטִיב
שְׂאֵת

But if you do not do right
Sin couches at the door;
Its urge is toward you,
Yet you can be its master."

Genesis 4:3–7

*From "The New
Order" as
presented by God
to Noah after the
flood*

Whoever sheds the blood of man,
By man shall his blood be shed;
For in His image
Did God make man.

Genesis 9:6

*Rebekah's family
blesses her when
she leaves to
marry Isaac*

O sister!
May you grow
Into thousands of myriads;
May your offspring seize
The gates of their foes.

Genesis 24:60

וְאִם לֹא תֵיטִיב
לַפֶּתַח חַטָּאת רֹבֵץ
וְאֵלֶיךָ תְּשׁוּקָתוֹ
וְאַתָּה תִּמְשָׁל־בּוֹ

שֹׁפֵךְ דַּם הָאָדָם
בָּאָדָם דָּמוֹ יִשָּׁפֵךְ
כִּי בְּצֶלֶם אֱלֹהִים
עָשָׂה אֶת־הָאָדָם

אֲחֹתֵנוּ
אַתְּ הֲיִי
לְאַלְפֵי רְבָבָה
וְיִירַשׁ זַרְעֵךְ
אֵת שַׁעַר שֹׂנְאָיו

*The Israelites'
song when God
provides water in
the desert at Be'er*

Spring up, O well—sing to it—
The well which the chieftains dug,
Which the nobles of the people started
With maces, with their own staffs.

Numbers 21:17–18

*A vision of the
prophet Isaiah*

In the year that King Uzziah died, I beheld
    my LORD seated on a high and lofty throne;
    and the skirts of His robe filled the Temple.
    Seraphs stood in attendance on Him. Each
    of them had six wings: with two he covered
    his face, with two he covered his legs, and
    with two he would fly.
And one would call to the other,
"Holy, holy, holy!
The LORD of Hosts!
His presence fills all the earth!"
The doorposts would shake at the sound of
    the one who called, and the House kept
    filling with smoke. I cried,
"Woe is me; I am lost!
For I am a man of unclean lips
And I live among a people
Of unclean lips;
Yet my own eyes have beheld
The King LORD of Hosts."

עֲלִי בְאֵר עֱנוּ-לָהּ
בְּאֵר חֲפָרוּהָ שָׂרִים
כָּרוּהָ נְדִיבֵי הָעָם
בִּמְחֹקֵק בְּמִשְׁעֲנֹתָם

בִּשְׁנַת-מוֹת הַמֶּלֶךְ עֻזִּיָּהוּ וָאֶרְאֶה
אֶת-אֲדֹנָי יֹשֵׁב עַל-כִּסֵּא רָם וְנִשָּׂא וְשׁוּלָיו
מְלֵאִים אֶת-הַהֵיכָל שְׂרָפִים עֹמְדִים
מִמַּעַל לוֹ שֵׁשׁ כְּנָפַיִם שֵׁשׁ כְּנָפַיִם לְאֶחָד
בִּשְׁתַּיִם יְכַסֶּה פָנָיו וּבִשְׁתַּיִם יְכַסֶּה רַגְלָיו
וּבִשְׁתַּיִם יְעוֹפֵף
וְקָרָא זֶה אֶל-זֶה וְאָמַר
קָדוֹשׁ קָדוֹשׁ קָדוֹשׁ
יְהוָה צְבָאוֹת
מְלֹא כָל-הָאָרֶץ כְּבוֹדוֹ
וַיָּנֻעוּ אַמּוֹת הַסִּפִּים מִקּוֹל הַקּוֹרֵא
וְהַבַּיִת יִמָּלֵא עָשָׁן וָאֹמַר
אוֹי-לִי כִּי-נִדְמֵיתִי
כִּי אִישׁ טְמֵא-שְׂפָתַיִם אָנֹכִי
וּבְתוֹךְ עַם-טְמֵא שְׂפָתַיִם
אָנֹכִי יוֹשֵׁב
כִּי אֶת-הַמֶּלֶךְ יְהוָה צְבָאוֹת
רָאוּ עֵינָי

Then one of the seraphs flew over to me with
    a live coal, which he had taken from the
    altar with a pair of tongs. He touched it to
    my lips and declared,
"Now that this has touched your lips,
Your guilt shall depart
And your sin be purged away."

Isaiah 6:1–7

Ask the LORD for rain
In the season of late rain.
It is the LORD who causes storms;
And He will provide rainstorms for them,
Grass in the fields for everyone.

Zechariah 10:1

Oh, the worthless shepherd
Who abandons the flock!
Let a sword descend upon his arm
And upon his right eye!
His arm shall shrivel up;
His right eye shall go blind.

Zechariah 11:17

וַיָּעָף אֵלַי אֶחָד מִן־הַשְּׂרָפִים וּבְיָדוֹ
רִצְפָּה בְּמֶלְקָחַיִם לָקַח מֵעַל הַמִּזְבֵּחַ
וַיַּגַּע עַל־פִּי וַיֹּאמֶר
הִנֵּה נָגַע זֶה עַל־שְׂפָתֶיךָ
וְסָר עֲוֹנֶךָ
וְחַטָּאתְךָ תְּכֻפָּר

שַׁאֲלוּ מֵיְהוָה מָטָר
בְּעֵת מַלְקוֹשׁ
יְהוָה עֹשֶׂה חֲזִיזִים
וּמְטַר־גֶּשֶׁם יִתֵּן לָהֶם
לְאִישׁ עֵשֶׂב בַּשָּׂדֶה

הוֹי רֹעִי הָאֱלִיל
עֹזְבִי הַצֹּאן
חֶרֶב עַל־זְרוֹעוֹ
וְעַל־עֵין יְמִינוֹ
זְרֹעוֹ יָבוֹשׁ תִּיבָשׁ
וְעֵין יְמִינוֹ כָּהֹה תִכְהֶה

How good and how pleasant it is
that brothers dwell together.
It is like fine oil on the head
running down onto the beard,
the beard of Aaron,
that comes down over the collar of his robe;
like the dew of Hermon
that falls upon the mountains of Zion.
There the LORD ordained blessing,
everlasting life.

Psalms 133:1–3

*The vision of
Nebuchadnezzar,
king of Babylon*

In the visions of my mind in bed
I saw a tree of great height in the midst of the
      earth;
The tree grew and became mighty;
Its top reached heaven,
And it was visible to the ends of the earth.
Its foliage was beautiful
And its fruit abundant;
There was food for all in it.
Beneath it the beasts of the field found shade,
And the birds of the sky dwelt on its
      branches;
All creatures fed on it.

הִנֵּה מַה־טּוֹב וּמַה־נָּעִים
שֶׁבֶת אַחִים גַּם־יָחַד
כַּשֶּׁמֶן הַטּוֹב עַל־הָרֹאשׁ
יֹרֵד עַל־הַזָּקָן
זְקַן־אַהֲרֹן
שֶׁיֹּרֵד עַל־פִּי מִדּוֹתָיו
כְּטַל־חֶרְמוֹן
שֶׁיֹּרֵד עַל־הַרְרֵי צִיּוֹן
כִּי שָׁם צִוָּה יְהוָה אֶת־הַבְּרָכָה
חַיִּים עַד־הָעוֹלָם

וְחֶזְוֵי רֵאשִׁי עַל־מִשְׁכְּבִי
חָזֵה הֲוֵית וַאֲלוּ אִילָן בְּגוֹא אַרְעָא
וְרוּמֵהּ שַׂגִּיא
רְבָה אִילָנָא וּתְקִף
וְרוּמֵהּ יִמְטֵא לִשְׁמַיָּא
וַחֲזוֹתֵהּ לְסוֹף כָּל־אַרְעָא
עָפְיֵהּ שַׁפִּיר
וְאִנְבֵּהּ שַׂגִּיא
וּמָזוֹן לְכֹלָּא־בֵהּ
תְּחֹתוֹהִי תַּטְלֵל חֵיוַת בָּרָא
וּבְעַנְפוֹהִי יְדֻרָן צִפֲּרֵי שְׁמַיָּא
וּמִנֵּהּ יִתְּזִין כָּל־בִּשְׂרָא

In the vision of my mind in bed, I looked and
   saw a holy Watcher coming down from
   heaven. He called loudly and said:
"Hew down the tree, lop off its branches,
Strip off its foliage, scatter its fruit.
Let the beasts of the field flee from beneath it
And the birds from its branches,
But leave the stump with its roots in the
   ground.
In fetters of iron and bronze
In the grass of the field,
Let him be drenched with the dew of heaven,
And share earth's verdure with the beasts.
Let his mind be altered from that of a man,
And let him be given the mind of a beast,
And let seven seasons pass over him.
This sentence is decreed by the Watchers;
This verdict is commanded by the Holy Ones
So that all creatures may know
That the Most High is sovereign over the
   realm of man,
And He gives it to whom He wishes
And He may set over it even the lowest of
   men."

Daniel 4:7–14

חָזֵה הֲוֵית בְּחֶזְוֵי רֵאשִׁי עַל־מִשְׁכְּבִי
וַאֲלוּ עִיר וְקַדִּישׁ מִן־שְׁמַיָּא נָחִת
קָרֵא בְחַיִל וְכֵן אָמַר
גֹּדּוּ אִילָנָא וְקַצִּצוּ עַנְפּוֹהִי
אַתַּרוּ עָפְיֵהּ וּבַדַּרוּ אִנְבֵּהּ
תְּנֻד חֵיוְתָא מִן־תַּחְתּוֹהִי
וְצִפְּרַיָּא מִן־עַנְפוֹהִי
בְּרַם עִקַּר שָׁרְשׁוֹהִי בְּאַרְעָא שְׁבֻקוּ
וּבֶאֱסוּר דִּי־פַרְזֶל וּנְחָשׁ
בְּדִתְאָא דִּי בָרָא
וּבְטַל שְׁמַיָּא יִצְטַבַּע
וְעִם־חֵיוְתָא חֲלָקֵהּ בַּעֲשַׂב אַרְעָא
לִבְבֵהּ מִן־אֲנָשָׁא אֲנָשָׁא יְשַׁנּוֹן
וּלְבַב חֵיוָה יִתְיְהִב לֵהּ
וְשִׁבְעָה עִדָּנִין יַחְלְפוּן עֲלוֹהִי
בִּגְזֵרַת עִירִין פִּתְגָמָא
וּמֵאמַר קַדִּישִׁין שְׁאֵלְתָא
עַד־דִּבְרַת דִּי יִנְדְּעוּן חַיַּיָּא
דִּי־שַׁלִּיט עליא עִלָּאָה בְּמַלְכוּת אנושא
אֲנָשָׁא
וּלְמַן־דִּי יִצְבֵּא יִתְּנִנַּהּ
וּשְׁפַל אֲנָשִׁים יְקִים עליה עֲלַהּ

TESTAMENTS & PRONOUNCEMENTS

The Testament of Jacob

*Jacob foretells the
future of his sons
and their
offspring*

Assemble and hearken, O sons of Jacob;
Hearken to Israel your father:
Reuben, you are my first-born,
My might and first fruit of my vigor,
Exceeding in rank
And exceeding in honor.
Unstable as water, you shall excel no longer;
For when you mounted your father's bed,
You brought disgrace—my couch he
    mounted!
Simeon and Levi are a pair;
Their weapons are tools of lawlessness.
Let not my person be included in their
    council,
Let not my being be counted in their assembly.
For when angry they slay men,
And when pleased they maim oxen.
Cursed be their anger so fierce,
And their wrath so relentless.
I will divide them in Jacob,
Scatter them in Israel.
You, O Judah, your brothers shall praise;
Your hand shall be on the nape of your foes;
Your father's sons shall bow low to you.
Judah is a lion's whelp;
On prey, my son, have you grown.
He crouches, lies down like a lion,

הֵקָּבְצוּ וְשִׁמְעוּ בְּנֵי יַעֲקֹב

וְשִׁמְעוּ אֶל־יִשְׂרָאֵל אֲבִיכֶם

רְאוּבֵן בְּכֹרִי אַתָּה

כֹּחִי וְרֵאשִׁית אוֹנִי

יֶתֶר שְׂאֵת

וְיֶתֶר עָז

פַּחַז כַּמַּיִם אַל־תּוֹתַר

כִּי עָלִיתָ מִשְׁכְּבֵי אָבִיךָ

אָז חִלַּלְתָּ יְצוּעִי עָלָה

שִׁמְעוֹן וְלֵוִי אַחִים

כְּלֵי חָמָס מְכֵרֹתֵיהֶם

בְּסֹדָם אַל־תָּבֹא נַפְשִׁי

בִּקְהָלָם אַל־תֵּחַד כְּבֹדִי

כִּי בְאַפָּם הָרְגוּ אִישׁ

וּבִרְצֹנָם עִקְּרוּ־שׁוֹר

אָרוּר אַפָּם כִּי עָז

וְעֶבְרָתָם כִּי קָשָׁתָה

אֲחַלְּקֵם בְּיַעֲקֹב

וַאֲפִיצֵם בְּיִשְׂרָאֵל

יְהוּדָה אַתָּה יוֹדוּךָ אַחֶיךָ

יָדְךָ בְּעֹרֶף אֹיְבֶיךָ

יִשְׁתַּחֲווּ לְךָ בְּנֵי אָבִיךָ

גּוּר אַרְיֵה יְהוּדָה

מִטֶּרֶף בְּנִי עָלִיתָ

כָּרַע רָבַץ כְּאַרְיֵה

Like the king of beasts—who dare rouse
    him?
The scepter shall not depart from Judah,
Nor the ruler's staff from between his feet;
So that tribute shall come to him
And the homage of peoples be his.
He tethers his ass to a vine,
His ass's foal to a choice vine;
He washes his garment in wine,
His robe in blood of grapes.
His eyes are darker than wine;
His teeth are whiter than milk.
Zebulun shall dwell by the seashore;
He shall be a haven for ships,
And his flank shall rest on Sidon.
Issachar is a strong-boned ass,
Crouching among the sheepfolds.
When he saw how good was security,
And how pleasant was the country,
He bent his shoulder to the burden,
And became a toiling serf.
Dan shall govern his people,
As one of the tribes of Israel.
Dan shall be a serpent by the road,
A viper by the path,
That bites the horse's heels
So that his rider is thrown backward.
I wait for Your deliverance, O LORD!
Gad shall be raided by raiders,
But he shall raid at their heels.
Asher's bread shall be rich,
And he shall yield royal dainties.
Naphtali is a hind let loose,
Which yields lovely fawns.

וּכְלָבִיא מִי יְקִימֶנּוּ
לֹא-יָסוּר שֵׁבֶט מִיהוּדָה
וּמְחֹקֵק מִבֵּין רַגְלָיו
עַד כִּי-יָבֹא שִׁילֹה שִׁילוֹ
וְלוֹ יְקְּהַת עַמִּים
אֹסְרִי לַגֶּפֶן עירה עִירוֹ
וְלַשֹּׂרֵקָה בְּנִי אֲתֹנוֹ
כִּבֶּס בַּיַּיִן לְבֻשׁוֹ
וּבְדַם-עֲנָבִים סותה סוּתוֹ
חַכְלִילִי עֵינַיִם מִיָּיִן
וּלְבֶן-שִׁנַּיִם מֵחָלָב
זְבוּלֻן לְחוֹף יַמִּים יִשְׁכֹּן
וְהוּא לְחוֹף אֳנִיֹּת
וְיַרְכָתוֹ עַל-צִידֹן
יִשָּׂשכָר חֲמֹר גָּרֶם
רֹבֵץ בֵּין הַמִּשְׁפְּתָיִם
וַיַּרְא מְנֻחָה כִּי טוֹב
וְאֶת-הָאָרֶץ כִּי נָעֵמָה
וַיֵּט שִׁכְמוֹ לִסְבֹּל
וַיְהִי לְמַס-עֹבֵד
דָּן יָדִין עַמּוֹ
כְּאַחַד שִׁבְטֵי יִשְׂרָאֵל
יְהִי-דָן נָחָשׁ עֲלֵי-דֶרֶךְ
שְׁפִיפֹן עֲלֵי-אֹרַח
הַנֹּשֵׁךְ עִקְּבֵי-סוּס
וַיִּפֹּל רֹכְבוֹ אָחוֹר
לִישׁוּעָתְךָ קִוִּיתִי יְהוָה
גָּד גְּדוּד יְגוּדֶנּוּ
וְהוּא יָגֻד עָקֵב
מֵאָשֵׁר שְׁמֵנָה לַחְמוֹ
וְהוּא יִתֵּן מַעֲדַנֵּי-מֶלֶךְ
נַפְתָּלִי אַיָּלָה שְׁלֻחָה
הַנֹּתֵן אִמְרֵי-שָׁפֶר

Joseph is a wild ass,
A wild ass by a spring
—Wild colts on a hillside.
Archers bitterly assailed him;
They shot at him and harried him.
Yet his bow stayed taut,
And his arms were made firm
By the hands of the Mighty One of Jacob—
There, the Shepherd, the Rock of Israel—
The God of your father who helps you,
And Shaddai who blesses you
With blessings of heaven above,
Blessings of the deep that couches below,
Blessings of the breast and womb.
The blessings of your father
Surpass the blessings of my ancestors,
To the utmost bounds of the eternal hills.
May they rest on the head of Joseph,
On the brow of the elect of his brothers.
Benjamin is a ravenous wolf;
In the morning he consumes the foe,
And in the evening he divides the spoil.

Genesis 49:2–27

The Last Words of David

These are the last words of David:
The utterance of David son of Jesse,
The utterance of the man set on high,
The anointed of the God of Jacob,
The favorite of the songs of Israel:

בֵּן פֹּרָת יוֹסֵף
בֵּן פֹּרָת עֲלֵי־עָיִן
בָּנוֹת צָעֲדָה עֲלֵי־שׁוּר
וַיְמָרֲרֻהוּ וָרֹבּוּ
וַיִּשְׂטְמֻהוּ בַּעֲלֵי חִצִּים
וַתֵּשֶׁב בְּאֵיתָן קַשְׁתּוֹ
וַיָּפֹזּוּ זְרֹעֵי יָדָיו
מִידֵי אֲבִיר יַעֲקֹב
מִשָּׁם רֹעֶה אֶבֶן יִשְׂרָאֵל
מֵאֵל אָבִיךָ וְיַעְזְרֶךָּ
וְאֵת שַׁדַּי וִיבָרְכֶךָּ
בִּרְכֹת שָׁמַיִם מֵעָל
בִּרְכֹת תְּהוֹם רֹבֶצֶת תָּחַת
בִּרְכֹת שָׁדַיִם וָרָחַם
בִּרְכֹת אָבִיךָ
גָּבְרוּ עַל־בִּרְכֹת הוֹרַי
עַד־תַּאֲוַת גִּבְעֹת עוֹלָם
תִּהְיֶיןָ לְרֹאשׁ יוֹסֵף
וּלְקָדְקֹד נְזִיר אֶחָיו
בִּנְיָמִין זְאֵב יִטְרָף
בַּבֹּקֶר יֹאכַל עַד
וְלָעֶרֶב יְחַלֵּק שָׁלָל

וְאֵלֶּה דִּבְרֵי דָוִד הָאַחֲרֹנִים
נְאֻם דָּוִד בֶּן־יִשַׁי
וּנְאֻם הַגֶּבֶר הֻקַם עָל
מְשִׁיחַ אֱלֹהֵי יַעֲקֹב
וּנְעִים זְמִרוֹת יִשְׂרָאֵל

The spirit of the LORD has spoken through
   me,
His message is on my tongue;
The God of Israel has spoken,
The Rock of Israel said concerning me:
"He who rules men justly,
He who rules in awe of God
Is like the light of morning at sunrise,
A morning without clouds—
Through sunshine and rain
Bringing vegetation out of the earth."
Is not my House established before God?
For He has granted me an eternal pact,
Drawn up in full and secured.
Will He not cause all my success
And my every desire to blossom?
But the wicked shall all
Be raked aside like thorns;
For no one will take them in his hand.
Whoever touches them
Must arm himself with iron
And the shaft of a spear;
And they must be burned up on the spot.

2 Samuel 23:1–7

Desert of the Sea

Like the gales
That race through the Negeb,
It comes from the desert,
The terrible land.

רוּחַ יְהוָה דִּבֶּר־בִּי
וּמִלָּתוֹ עַל־לְשׁוֹנִי
אָמַר אֱלֹהֵי יִשְׂרָאֵל
לִי דִבֶּר צוּר יִשְׂרָאֵל
מוֹשֵׁל בָּאָדָם צַדִּיק
מוֹשֵׁל יִרְאַת אֱלֹהִים
וּכְאוֹר בֹּקֶר יִזְרַח־שָׁמֶשׁ
בֹּקֶר לֹא עָבוֹת
מִנֹּגַהּ מִמָּטָר
דֶּשֶׁא מֵאָרֶץ
כִּי־לֹא־כֵן בֵּיתִי עִם־אֵל
כִּי בְרִית עוֹלָם שָׂם לִי
עֲרוּכָה בַכֹּל וּשְׁמֻרָה
כִּי־כָל־יִשְׁעִי וְכָל־חֵפֶץ
כִּי־לֹא יַצְמִיחַ
וּבְלִיַּעַל כְּקוֹץ
מֻנָד כֻּלָּהַם
כִּי־לֹא בְיָד יִקָּחוּ
וְאִישׁ יִגַּע בָּהֶם
יִמָּלֵא בַרְזֶל
וְעֵץ חֲנִית
וּבָאֵשׁ שָׂרוֹף יִשָּׂרְפוּ בַּשָּׁבֶת

כְּסוּפוֹת
בַּנֶּגֶב לַחֲלֹף
מִמִּדְבָּר בָּא
מֵאֶרֶץ נוֹרָאָה

A harsh prophecy
Has been announced to me:
"The betrayer is betraying,
The ravager ravaging.
Advance, Elam!
Lay siege, Media!
I have put an end
To all her sighing."
Therefore my loins
Are seized with trembling;
I am gripped by pangs
Like a woman in travail,
Too anguished to hear,
Too frightened to see.
My mind is confused,
I shudder in panic.
My night of pleasure
He has turned to terror:
"Set the table!"
To "Let the watchman watch!"
"Eat and drink!"
To "Up, officers! Grease the shields!"
For thus my LORD said to me:
"Go, set up a sentry;
Let him announce what he sees.
He will see mounted men,
Horsemen in pairs—
Riders on asses,
Riders on camels—
And he will listen closely,
Most attentively."
And like a lion he called out:
 "On my LORD's lookout I stand
Ever by day,

חָזוּת קָשָׁה

הֻגַּד־לִי

הַבּוֹגֵד בּוֹגֵד

וְהַשּׁוֹדֵד שׁוֹדֵד

עֲלִי עֵילָם

צוּרִי מָדַי

כָּל־אַנְחָתָה

הִשְׁבַּתִּי

עַל־כֵּן

מָלְאוּ מָתְנַי חַלְחָלָה

צִירִים אֲחָזוּנִי

כְּצִירֵי יוֹלֵדָה

נַעֲוֵיתִי מִשְּׁמֹעַ

נִבְהַלְתִּי מֵרְאוֹת

תָּעָה לְבָבִי

פַּלָּצוּת בִּעֲתָתְנִי

אֵת נֶשֶׁף חִשְׁקִי

שָׂם לִי לַחֲרָדָה

עָרֹךְ הַשֻּׁלְחָן

צָפֹה הַצָּפִית

אָכוֹל שָׁתֹה

קוּמוּ הַשָּׂרִים מִשְׁחוּ מָגֵן

כִּי כֹה אָמַר אֵלַי אֲדֹנָי

לֵךְ הַעֲמֵד הַמְצַפֶּה

אֲשֶׁר יִרְאֶה יַגִּיד

וְרָאָה רֶכֶב

צֶמֶד פָּרָשִׁים

רֶכֶב חֲמוֹר

רֶכֶב גָּמָל

וְהִקְשִׁיב קֶשֶׁב

רַב־קָשֶׁב

וַיִּקְרָא אַרְיֵה

עַל־מִצְפֶּה אֲדֹנָי אָנֹכִי עֹמֵד

תָּמִיד יוֹמָם

And at my post I watch
Every night.
And there they come, mounted men—
Horsemen in pairs!"
Then he spoke up and said,
"Fallen, fallen is Babylon,
And all the images of her gods
Have crashed to the ground!"
My threshing, the product of my threshing
    floor:
What I have heard from the LORD of Hosts,
The God of Israel—
That I have told to you.

Isaiah 21:1–10

Dumah

A call comes to me from Seir:
"Watchman, what of the night?
Watchman, what of the night?"
The watchman replied,
"Morning came, and so did night.
If you would inquire, inquire.
Come back again."

Isaiah 21:11–12

וְעַל־מִשְׁמַרְתִּי אָנֹכִי נִצָּב

כָּל־הַלֵּילוֹת

וְהִנֵּה־זֶה בָא רֶכֶב אִישׁ

צֶמֶד פָּרָשִׁים

וַיַּעַן וַיֹּאמֶר

נָפְלָה נָפְלָה בָּבֶל

וְכָל־פְּסִילֵי אֱלֹהֶיהָ

שִׁבַּר לָאָרֶץ

מְדֻשָׁתִי וּבֶן־גָּרְנִי

אֲשֶׁר שָׁמַעְתִּי מֵאֵת יְהוָה צְבָאוֹת

אֱלֹהֵי יִשְׂרָאֵל

הִגַּדְתִּי לָכֶם

אֵלַי קֹרֵא מִשֵּׂעִיר

שֹׁמֵר מַה־מִּלַּיְלָה

שֹׁמֵר מַה־מִּלֵּיל

אָמַר שֹׁמֵר

אָתָה בֹקֶר וְגַם־לָיְלָה

אִם־תִּבְעָיוּן בְּעָיוּ

שֻׁבוּ אֵתָיוּ

In the Steppe

In the scrub, in the steppe, you will lodge,
O caravans of the Dedanites!
Meet the thirsty with water,
You who dwell in the land of Tema;
Greet the fugitive with bread.
For they have fled before swords:
Before the whetted sword,
Before the bow that was drawn,
Before the stress of war.

Isaiah 21:13–15

בַּיַּעַר בַּעֲרָב תָּלִינוּ
אֹרְחוֹת דְּדָנִים
לִקְרַאת צָמֵא הֵתָיוּ מָיִם
יֹשְׁבֵי אֶרֶץ תֵּימָא
בְּלַחְמוֹ קִדְּמוּ נֹדֵד
כִּי־מִפְּנֵי חֲרָבוֹת נָדָדוּ
מִפְּנֵי חֶרֶב נְטוּשָׁה
וּמִפְּנֵי קֶשֶׁת דְּרוּכָה
וּמִפְּנֵי כֹּבֶד מִלְחָמָה

LAMENTS

Song of the Bow: David's Lament

David weeps over the deaths of Saul and Jonathan

Your glory, O Israel
Lies slain on your heights;
How have the mighty fallen!
Tell it not in Gath,
Do not proclaim it in the streets of
    Ashkelon,
Lest the daughters of the Philistine rejoice,
Lest the daughters of the uncircumcised
    exult.
O hills of Gilboa—
Let there be no dew or rain on you,
Or bountiful fields,
For there the shield of warriors lay rejected,
The shield of Saul,
Polished with oil no more.
From the blood of slain,
From the fat of warriors—
The bow of Jonathan
Never turned back;
The sword of Saul
Never withdrew empty.
Saul and Jonathan,
Beloved and cherished,
Never parted
In life or in death!
They were swifter than eagles,
They were stronger than lions!

הַצְּבִי יִשְׂרָאֵל
עַל־בָּמוֹתֶיךָ חָלָל
אֵיךְ נָפְלוּ גִבּוֹרִים
אַל־תַּגִּידוּ בְגַת
אַל־תְּבַשְּׂרוּ בְּחוּצֹת אַשְׁקְלוֹן
פֶּן־תִּשְׂמַחְנָה בְּנוֹת פְּלִשְׁתִּים
פֶּן־תַּעֲלֹזְנָה בְּנוֹת הָעֲרֵלִים
הָרֵי בַגִּלְבֹּעַ
אַל־טַל וְאַל־מָטָר עֲלֵיכֶם
וּשְׂדֵי תְרוּמֹת
כִּי שָׁם נִגְעַל מָגֵן גִּבּוֹרִים
מָגֵן שָׁאוּל
בְּלִי מָשִׁיחַ בַּשָּׁמֶן
מִדַּם חֲלָלִים
מֵחֵלֶב גִּבּוֹרִים
קֶשֶׁת יְהוֹנָתָן
לֹא נָשׂוֹג אָחוֹר
וְחֶרֶב שָׁאוּל
לֹא תָשׁוּב רֵיקָם
שָׁאוּל וִיהוֹנָתָן
הַנֶּאֱהָבִים וְהַנְּעִימִם
בְּחַיֵּיהֶם וּבְמוֹתָם
לֹא נִפְרָדוּ
מִנְּשָׁרִים קַלּוּ
מֵאֲרָיוֹת גָּבֵרוּ

Daughters of Israel,
Weep over Saul,
Who clothed you in crimson and finery,
Who decked your robes with jewels of gold.
How have the mighty fallen
In the thick of battle—
Jonathan, slain on your heights!
I grieve for you,
My brother Jonathan,
You were most dear to me.
Your love was wonderful to me
More than the love of women.
How have the mighty fallen,
The weapons of war perished!

2 Samuel 1:19–27

A Cry in Ramah

A cry is heard in Ramah—
Wailing, bitter weeping—
Rachel weeping for her children.
She refuses to be comforted
For her children, who are gone.
Thus said the LORD:
Restrain your voice from weeping,
Your eyes from shedding tears;
For there is a reward for your labor
               —declares the LORD:
They shall return from the enemy's land.
And there is hope for your future

בְּנוֹת יִשְׂרָאֵל
אֶל־שָׁאוּל בְּכֶינָה
הַמַּלְבִּשְׁכֶם שָׁנִי עִם־עֲדָנִים
הַמַּעֲלֶה עֲדִי זָהָב עַל לְבוּשְׁכֶן
אֵיךְ נָפְלוּ גִבֹּרִים
בְּתוֹךְ הַמִּלְחָמָה
יְהוֹנָתָן עַל־בָּמוֹתֶיךָ חָלָל
צַר־לִי עָלֶיךָ
אָחִי יְהוֹנָתָן
נָעַמְתָּ לִּי מְאֹד
נִפְלְאַתָה אַהֲבָתְךָ לִי
מֵאַהֲבַת נָשִׁים
אֵיךְ נָפְלוּ גִבּוֹרִים
וַיֹּאבְדוּ כְּלֵי מִלְחָמָה

כֹּה אָמַר יְהוָה
קוֹל בְּרָמָה נִשְׁמָע
נְהִי בְּכִי תַמְרוּרִים
רָחֵל מְבַכָּה עַל־בָּנֶיהָ
מֵאֲנָה לְהִנָּחֵם
עַל־בָּנֶיהָ כִּי אֵינֶנּוּ
כֹּה אָמַר יְהוָה
מִנְעִי קוֹלֵךְ מִבֶּכִי
וְעֵינַיִךְ מִדִּמְעָה
כִּי יֵשׁ שָׂכָר לִפְעֻלָּתֵךְ
נְאֻם־יְהוָה
וְשָׁבוּ מֵאֶרֶץ אוֹיֵב
וְיֵשׁ־תִּקְוָה לְאַחֲרִיתֵךְ

—declares the LORD:
Your children shall return to their country.

Jeremiah 31:15–17

Lamentations over Tyre I

O you who dwell at the gateway of the sea,
Who trade with the peoples on many
  coastlands:
Thus said the Lord God:
O Tyre, you boasted,
I am perfect in beauty.
Your frontiers were on the high seas,
Your builders perfected your beauty.
From cypress trees of Senir
They fashioned your planks;
They took a cedar from Lebanon
To make a mast for you.
From oak trees of Bashan
They made your oars;
Of boxwood from the isles of Kittim,
Inlaid with ivory,
They made your decks.
Embroidered linen from Egypt
Was the cloth
That served you for sails;
Of blue and purple from the coasts of Elishah
Were your awnings.
The inhabitants of Sidon and Arvad

נְאֻם־יְהוָה
וְשָׁבוּ בָנִים לִגְבוּלָם

הֲיֹשַׁבְתִּי הַיֹּשֶׁבֶת עַל־מְבוֹאֹת יָם
רֹכֶלֶת הָעַמִּים אֶל־אִיִּים רַבִּים
כֹּה אָמַר אֲדֹנָי יְהוִה
צוֹר אַתְּ אָמַרְתְּ
אֲנִי כְּלִילַת יֹפִי
בְּלֵב יַמִּים גְּבוּלָיִךְ
בֹּנַיִךְ כָּלְלוּ יָפְיֵךְ
בְּרוֹשִׁים מִשְּׂנִיר
בָּנוּ לָךְ אֵת כָּל־לֻחֹתָיִם
אֶרֶז מִלְּבָנוֹן לָקָחוּ
לַעֲשׂוֹת תֹּרֶן עָלָיִךְ
אַלּוֹנִים מִבָּשָׁן
עָשׂוּ מִשּׁוֹטָיִךְ
קַרְשֵׁךְ עָשׂוּ־שֵׁן בַּת־אֲשֻׁרִים
מֵאִיֵּי כִתִּים כִּתִּיִּים
שֵׁשׁ־בְּרִקְמָה מִמִּצְרַיִם
הָיָה מִפְרָשֵׂךְ
לִהְיוֹת לָךְ לְנֵס
תְּכֵלֶת וְאַרְגָּמָן מֵאִיֵּי אֱלִישָׁה
הָיָה מְכַסֵּךְ
יֹשְׁבֵי צִידוֹן וְאַרְוַד

Were your rowers;
Your skilled men, O Tyre, were within you,
They were your pilots.
Gebal's elders and craftsmen were within
  you,
Making your repairs.
All the ships of the sea, with their crews,
Were in your harbor
To traffic in your wares.
Men of Paras, Lud, and Put
Were in your army,
Your fighting men;
They hung shields and helmets in your
  midst,
They lent splendor to you.
Men of Arvad and Helech
Manned your walls all around,
And men of Gammad were stationed in your
  towers;
They hung their quivers all about your walls;
They perfected your beauty.

Ezekiel 27:3–11

Lamentations over Tyre II

So you were full and richly laden
On the high seas.
Your oarsmen brought you out
Into the mighty waters;

הָיוּ שָׁטִים לָךְ
חֲכָמַיִךְ צוֹר הָיוּ בָךְ
הֵמָּה חֹבְלָיִךְ
זִקְנֵי גְבַל וַחֲכָמֶיהָ הָיוּ בָךְ
מַחֲזִיקֵי בִּדְקֵךְ
כָּל־אֳנִיּוֹת הַיָּם
וּמַלָּחֵיהֶם הָיוּ בָךְ
לַעֲרֹב מַעֲרָבֵךְ
פָּרַס וְלוּד וּפוּט
הָיוּ בְחֵילֵךְ
אַנְשֵׁי מִלְחַמְתֵּךְ
מָגֵן וְכוֹבַע תִּלּוּ־בָךְ
הֵמָּה נָתְנוּ הֲדָרֵךְ
בְּנֵי אַרְוַד וְחֵילֵךְ
עַל־חוֹמוֹתַיִךְ סָבִיב
וְגַמָּדִים בְּמִגְדְּלוֹתַיִךְ הָיוּ
שִׁלְטֵיהֶם תִּלּוּ עַל־חוֹמוֹתַיִךְ סָבִיב
הֵמָּה כָּלְלוּ יָפְיֵךְ

וַתִּמָּלְאִי וַתִּכְבְּדִי מְאֹד
בְּלֵב יַמִּים
בְּמַיִם רַבִּים הֱבִיאוּךְ
הַשָּׁטִים אֹתָךְ

The tempest wrecked you
On the high seas.
Your wealth, your wares, your merchandise,
Your sailors and your pilots,
The men who made your repairs,
Those who carried on your traffic,
And all the fighting men within you—
All the multitude within you—
Shall go down into the depths of the sea
On the day of your downfall.
At the outcry of your pilots
The billows shall heave;
And all the oarsmen and mariners,
All the pilots of the sea,
Shall come down from their ships
And stand on the ground.
They shall raise their voices over you
And cry out bitterly;
They shall cast dust on their heads
And strew ashes on themselves.
On your account, they shall make
Bald patches on their heads,
And shall gird themselves
    with sackcloth.
They shall weep over you,
    brokenhearted,
With bitter lamenting;
They shall intone a dirge over you as they
    wail,
And lament for you thus:
Who was like Tyre when she was silenced
In the midst of the sea?
When your wares were unloaded from the
    seas,

רוּחַ הַקָּדִים שְׁבָרֵךְ
בְּלֵב יַמִּים
הוֹנֵךְ וְעִזְבוֹנַיִךְ
מַעֲרָבֵךְ מַלָּחַיִךְ וְחֹבְלָיִךְ
מַחֲזִיקֵי בִּדְקֵךְ
וְעֹרְבֵי מַעֲרָבֵךְ
וְכָל־אַנְשֵׁי מִלְחַמְתֵּךְ אֲשֶׁר־בָּךְ
וּבְכָל־קְהָלֵךְ אֲשֶׁר בְּתוֹכֵךְ
יִפְּלוּ בְּלֵב יַמִּים
בְּיוֹם מַפַּלְתֵּךְ
לְקוֹל זַעֲקַת חֹבְלָיִךְ
יִרְעֲשׁוּ מִגְרֹשׁוֹת
וְיָרְדוּ מֵאָנִיּוֹתֵיהֶם
כֹּל תֹּפְשֵׂי מָשׁוֹט
מַלָּחִים כֹּל חֹבְלֵי הַיָּם
אֶל־הָאָרֶץ יַעֲמֹדוּ
וְהִשְׁמִיעוּ עָלַיִךְ בְּקוֹלָם
וְיִזְעֲקוּ מָרָה
וְיַעֲלוּ עָפָר עַל־רָאשֵׁיהֶם
בָּאֵפֶר יִתְפַּלָּשׁוּ
וְהִקְרִיחוּ אֵלַיִךְ קָרְחָה
וְחָגְרוּ שַׂקִּים
וּבָכוּ אֵלַיִךְ בְּמַר־נֶפֶשׁ
מִסְפֵּד מָר
וְנָשְׂאוּ אֵלַיִךְ בְּנִיהֶם קִינָה
וְקוֹנְנוּ עָלַיִךְ
מִי כְצוֹר כְּדֻמָּה
בְּתוֹךְ הַיָּם
בְּצֵאת עִזְבוֹנַיִךְ מִיַּמִּים

You satisfied many peoples;
With your great wealth and merchandise
You enriched the kings of the earth.
But when you were wrecked on the seas,
In the deep waters sank your merchandise
And all the crew aboard you.
All the inhabitants of the coastlands
Are appalled over you;
Their kings are aghast,
Their faces contorted.
The merchants among the peoples hissed at
    you;
You have become a horror,
And have ceased to be forever.

Ezekiel 27:25–36

Lament for the King of Tyre

You were the seal of perfection,
Full of wisdom and flawless in beauty.
You were in Eden, the garden of God;
Every precious stone was your adornment:
Carnelian, chrysolite, and amethyst;
Beryl, lapis lazuli, and jasper;
Sapphire, turquoise, and emerald;
And gold beautifully wrought for you,
Mined for you, prepared the day you were
    created.
I created you as a cherub

הִשְׁבַּעַתָּ עַמִּים רַבִּים
בְּרֹב הוֹנַיִךְ וּמַעֲרָבַיִךְ
הֶעֱשַׁרְתָּ מַלְכֵי־אָרֶץ
עֵת נִשְׁבֶּרֶת מִיַּמִּים
בְּמַעֲמַקֵּי־מָיִם
מַעֲרָבֵךְ וְכָל־קְהָלֵךְ בְּתוֹכֵךְ נָפָלוּ
כֹּל יֹשְׁבֵי הָאִיִּים
שָׁמְמוּ עָלַיִךְ
וּמַלְכֵיהֶם שָׂעֲרוּ שַׂעַר
רָעֲמוּ פָנִים
סֹחֲרִים בָּעַמִּים שָׁרְקוּ עָלַיִךְ
בַּלָּהוֹת הָיִית
וְאֵינֵךְ עַד־עוֹלָם

אַתָּה חוֹתֵם תָּכְנִית
מָלֵא חָכְמָה וּכְלִיל יֹפִי
בְּעֵדֶן גַּן־אֱלֹהִים הָיִיתָ
כָּל־אֶבֶן יְקָרָה מְסֻכָתֶךָ
אֹדֶם פִּטְדָה וְיָהֲלֹם
תַּרְשִׁישׁ שֹׁהַם וְיָשְׁפֵה
סַפִּיר נֹפֶךְ וּבָרְקַת
וְזָהָב מְלֶאכֶת תֻּפֶּיךָ
וּנְקָבֶיךָ בָּךְ בְּיוֹם הִבָּרַאֲךָ כּוֹנָנוּ
אַתְּ־כְּרוּב

121

With outstretched shielding wings;
And you resided on God's holy mountain;
You walked among stones of fire.
You were blameless in your ways,
From the day you were created
Until wrongdoing was found in you.
By your far-flung commerce
You were filled with lawlessness
And you sinned.
So I have struck you down
From the mountain of God,
And I have destroyed you, O shielding
  cherub,
From among the stones of fire.
You grew haughty because of your beauty,
You debased your wisdom for the sake of
  your splendor;
I have cast you to the ground,
I have made you an object for kings to stare
  at.
By the greatness of your guilt,
Through the dishonesty of your trading,
You desecrated your sanctuaries.
So I made a fire issue from you,
And it has devoured you;
I have reduced you to ashes on the ground,
In the sight of all who behold you.
All who knew you among the peoples
Are appalled at your doom.
You have become a horror
And have ceased to be, forever.

Ezekiel 28:12–19

מִמְשַׁח הַסּוֹכֵךְ
וּנְתַתִּיךָ בְּהַר קֹדֶשׁ אֱלֹהִים הָיִיתָ
בְּתוֹךְ אַבְנֵי־אֵשׁ הִתְהַלָּכְתָּ
תָּמִים אַתָּה בִּדְרָכֶיךָ
מִיּוֹם הִבָּרְאָךְ
עַד־נִמְצָא עַוְלָתָה בָּךְ
בְּרֹב רְכֻלָּתְךָ
מָלוּ תוֹכְךָ חָמָס
וַתֶּחֱטָא
וָאֲחַלֶּלְךָ
מֵהַר אֱלֹהִים
וָאַבֶּדְךָ כְּרוּב הַסֹּכֵךְ
מִתּוֹךְ אַבְנֵי־אֵשׁ
גָּבַהּ לִבְּךָ בְּיָפְיֶךָ
שִׁחַתָּ חָכְמָתְךָ עַל־יִפְעָתֶךָ
עַל־אֶרֶץ הִשְׁלַכְתִּיךָ
לִפְנֵי מְלָכִים נְתַתִּיךָ לְרַאֲוָה בָךְ
מֵרֹב עֲוֹנֶיךָ
בְּעֶוֶל רְכֻלָּתְךָ
חִלַּלְתָּ מִקְדָּשֶׁיךָ
וָאוֹצִא־אֵשׁ מִתּוֹכְךָ
הִיא אֲכָלָתְךָ
וָאֶתֶּנְךָ לְאֵפֶר עַל־הָאָרֶץ
לְעֵינֵי כָּל־רֹאֶיךָ
כָּל־יוֹדְעֶיךָ בָּעַמִּים
שָׁמְמוּ עָלֶיךָ
בַּלָּהוֹת הָיִיתָ
וְאֵינְךָ עַד־עוֹלָם

Pharaoh King of Egypt

O great beast among the nations, you are
    doomed!
You are like the dragon in the seas,
Thrusting through their streams,
Stirring up the water with your feet
And muddying their streams!
Thus said the LORD GOD:
I will cast My net over you
In an assembly of many peoples,
And you shall be hauled up in My toils.
And I will fling you to the ground,
Hurl you upon the open field.
I will cause all the birds of the sky
To settle upon you.
I will cause the beasts of all the earth
To batten on you.
I will cast your carcass upon the hills
And fill the valleys with your rotting flesh.
I will drench the earth
With your oozing blood upon the hills,
And the watercourses shall be filled with
    your gore.
When you are snuffed out,
I will cover the sky
And darken its stars;
I will cover the sun with clouds
And the moon shall not give its light.
All the lights that shine in the sky
I will darken above you;
And I will bring darkness upon your land
               —declares the LORD GOD.

כְּפִיר גּוֹיִם נִדְמֵיתָ
וְאַתָּה כַּתַּנִּים בַּיַּמִּים
וַתָּגַח בְּנַהֲרוֹתֶיךָ
וַתִּדְלַח־מַיִם בְּרַגְלֶיךָ
וַתִּרְפֹּס נַהֲרוֹתָם
כֹּה אָמַר אֲדֹנָי יְהוִה
וּפָרַשְׂתִּי עָלֶיךָ אֶת־רִשְׁתִּי
בִּקְהַל עַמִּים רַבִּים
וְהֶעֱלוּךָ בְּחֶרְמִי
וּנְטַשְׁתִּיךָ בָאָרֶץ
עַל־פְּנֵי הַשָּׂדֶה אֲטִילֶךָ
וְהִשְׁכַּנְתִּי עָלֶיךָ
כָּל־עוֹף הַשָּׁמַיִם
וְהִשְׂבַּעְתִּי מִמְּךָ
חַיַּת כָּל־הָאָרֶץ
וְנָתַתִּי אֶת־בְּשָׂרְךָ עַל־הֶהָרִים
וּמִלֵּאתִי הַגֵּאָיוֹת רָמוּתֶךָ
וְהִשְׁקֵיתִי אֶרֶץ צָפָתְךָ
מִדָּמְךָ אֶל־הֶהָרִים
וַאֲפִקִים יִמָּלְאוּן מִמֶּךָּ
וְכִסֵּיתִי בְכַבּוֹתְךָ שָׁמַיִם
וְהִקְדַּרְתִּי אֶת־כֹּכְבֵיהֶם
שֶׁמֶשׁ בֶּעָנָן אֲכַסֶּנּוּ
וְיָרֵחַ לֹא־יָאִיר אוֹרוֹ
כָּל־מְאוֹרֵי אוֹר בַּשָּׁמַיִם
אַקְדִּירֵם עָלֶיךָ
וְנָתַתִּי חֹשֶׁךְ עַל־אַרְצֶךָ
נְאֻם אֲדֹנָי יְהוִה

I will vex the hearts of many peoples
When I bring your shattered remnants
among the nations,
To countries which you never knew.
I will strike many peoples with horror over
    your fate;
And their kings shall be aghast over you,
When I brandish My sword before them.
They shall tremble continually,
Each man for his own life,
On the day of your downfall.
For thus said the LORD GOD:
The sword of the king of Babylon shall come
    upon you.
I will cause your multitude to fall
By the swords of warriors,
All the most ruthless among the nations.
They shall ravage the splendor of Egypt,
And all her masses shall be wiped out.
I will make all her cattle vanish from beside
    abundant waters;
The feet of man shall not muddy them any
    more,
Nor shall the hoofs of cattle muddy them.
Then I will let their waters settle,
And make their rivers flow like oil
                    —declares the LORD GOD:
When I lay the land of Egypt waste,
When the land is emptied of the life that
    filled it,
When I strike down all its inhabitants.
And they shall know that I am the LORD.
This is a dirge, and it shall be intoned;
The women of the nations shall intone it,

וְהִכְעַסְתִּי לֵב עַמִּים רַבִּים
בַּהֲבִיאִי שִׁבְרְךָ בַּגּוֹיִם
עַל־אֲרָצוֹת אֲשֶׁר לֹא־יְדַעְתָּם
וַהֲשִׁמּוֹתִי עָלֶיךָ עַמִּים רַבִּים
וּמַלְכֵיהֶם יִשְׂעֲרוּ עָלֶיךָ שַׂעַר
בְּעוֹפְפִי חַרְבִּי עַל־פְּנֵיהֶם
וְחָרְדוּ לִרְגָעִים
אִישׁ לְנַפְשׁוֹ
בְּיוֹם מַפַּלְתֶּךָ
כִּי כֹּה אָמַר אֲדֹנָי יְהוִה
חֶרֶב מֶלֶךְ־בָּבֶל תְּבוֹאֶךָ
בְּחַרְבוֹת גִּבּוֹרִים
אַפִּיל הֲמוֹנֶךָ
עָרִיצֵי גוֹיִם כֻּלָּם
וְשָׁדְדוּ אֶת־גְּאוֹן מִצְרַיִם
וְנִשְׁמַד כָּל־הֲמוֹנָהּ
וְהַאֲבַדְתִּי אֶת־כָּל־בְּהֶמְתָּהּ מֵעַל מַיִם
רַבִּים
וְלֹא תִדְלָחֶם רֶגֶל־אָדָם עוֹד
וּפַרְסוֹת בְּהֵמָה לֹא תִדְלָחֶם
אָז אַשְׁקִיעַ מֵימֵיהֶם
וְנַהֲרוֹתָם כַּשֶּׁמֶן אוֹלִיךְ
נְאֻם אֲדֹנָי יְהוִה
בְּתִתִּי אֶת־אֶרֶץ מִצְרַיִם שְׁמָמָה
וּנְשַׁמָּה אֶרֶץ מִמְּלֹאָהּ
בְּהַכּוֹתִי אֶת־כָּל־יוֹשְׁבֵי בָהּ
וְיָדְעוּ כִּי־אֲנִי יְהוָה
קִינָה הִיא וְקוֹנְנוּהָ
בְּנוֹת הַגּוֹיִם תְּקוֹנֵנָּה אוֹתָהּ

They shall intone it over Egypt and all her
  multitude
             — declares the LORD GOD.

Ezekiel 32:2–16

Deliver Me

A psalm of David when he fled from his son
  Absalom.
O LORD, my foes are so many!
Many are those who attack me;
many say of me,
"There is no deliverance for him through
  God." *Selah.*
But You, O LORD, are a shield about me,
my glory, He who holds my head high.
I cry aloud to the LORD,
and He answers me from His holy mountain.
  Selah.
I lie down and sleep and wake again,
for the LORD sustains me.
I have no fear of the myriad forces
arrayed against me on every side.
Rise, O LORD!
Deliver me, O my God!
For You slap all my enemies in the face;
You break the teeth of the wicked.
Deliverance is the LORD's;
Your blessing be upon Your people! *Selah.*

Psalms 3:1–9

עַל־מִצְרַיִם וְעַל־כָּל־הֶהָמוֹנָה תְּקוֹנֵנָה
אוֹתָהּ
נְאֻם אֲדֹנָי יְהוִה

מִזְמוֹר לְדָוִד בְּבָרְחוֹ מִפְּנֵי
אַבְשָׁלוֹם בְּנוֹ
יְהוָה מָה־רַבּוּ צָרָי
רַבִּים קָמִים עָלָי
רַבִּים אֹמְרִים לְנַפְשִׁי
אֵין יְשׁוּעָתָה לּוֹ בֵאלֹהִים סֶלָה
וְאַתָּה יְהוָה מָגֵן בַּעֲדִי
כְּבוֹדִי וּמֵרִים רֹאשִׁי
קוֹלִי אֶל־יְהוָה אֶקְרָא
וַיַּעֲנֵנִי מֵהַר קָדְשׁוֹ סֶלָה
אֲנִי שָׁכַבְתִּי וָאִישָׁנָה הֱקִיצוֹתִי
כִּי יְהוָה יִסְמְכֵנִי
לֹא־אִירָא מֵרִבְבוֹת עָם
אֲשֶׁר סָבִיב שָׁתוּ עָלָי
קוּמָה יְהוָה
הוֹשִׁיעֵנִי אֱלֹהַי
כִּי־הִכִּיתָ אֶת־כָּל־אֹיְבַי לֶחִי
שִׁנֵּי רְשָׁעִים שִׁבַּרְתָּ
לַיהוָה הַיְשׁוּעָה
עַל־עַמְּךָ בִרְכָתֶךָ סֶלָה

I Am Weary

O LORD, do not punish me in anger,
do not chastise me in fury.
Have mercy on me, O LORD, for I languish;
heal me, O LORD, for my bones shake with
     terror.
My whole being is stricken with terror,
while You, LORD—O, how long!
O LORD, turn! Rescue me!
Deliver me as befits Your faithfulness.
For there is no praise of You among the dead;
in Sheol, who can acclaim You?
I am weary with groaning;
every night I drench my bed,
I melt my couch in tears.
My eyes are wasted by vexation,
worn out because of all my foes.
Away from me, all you evildoers,
for the LORD heeds the sound of my
     weeping.
The LORD heeds my plea,
the LORD accepts my prayer.
All my enemies will be frustrated and
     stricken with terror;
they will turn back in an instant, frustrated.

Psalms 6:2–11

יְהוָה אַל־בְּאַפְּךָ תוֹכִיחֵנִי
וְאַל־בַּחֲמָתְךָ תְיַסְּרֵנִי
חָנֵּנִי יְהוָה כִּי אֻמְלַל אָנִי
רְפָאֵנִי יְהוָה כִּי נִבְהֲלוּ עֲצָמָי
וְנַפְשִׁי נִבְהֲלָה מְאֹד
וְאַתְּ וְאַתָּה יְהוָה עַד־מָתָי
שׁוּבָה יְהוָה חַלְּצָה נַפְשִׁי
הוֹשִׁיעֵנִי לְמַעַן חַסְדֶּךָ
כִּי אֵין בַּמָּוֶת זִכְרֶךָ
בִּשְׁאוֹל מִי יוֹדֶה־לָּךְ
יָגַעְתִּי בְּאַנְחָתִי
אַשְׂחֶה בְכָל־לַיְלָה מִטָּתִי
בְּדִמְעָתִי עַרְשִׂי אַמְסֶה
עָשְׁשָׁה מִכַּעַס עֵינִי
עָתְקָה בְּכָל־צוֹרְרָי
סוּרוּ מִמֶּנִּי כָּל־פֹּעֲלֵי אָוֶן
כִּי־שָׁמַע יְהוָה קוֹל בִּכְיִי
שָׁמַע יְהוָה תְּחִנָּתִי
יְהוָה תְּפִלָּתִי יִקָּח
יֵבֹשׁוּ וְיִבָּהֲלוּ מְאֹד כָּל־אֹיְבָי
יָשֻׁבוּ יֵבֹשׁוּ רָגַע

How Long?

How long, O LORD; will You ignore me
    forever?
How long will You hide Your face from me?
How long will I have cares on my mind,
grief in my heart all day?
How long will my enemy have the upper
    hand?
Look at me, answer me, O LORD, my God!
Restore the luster to my eyes,
lest I sleep the sleep of death;
lest my enemy say, "I have overcome him,"
my foes exult when I totter.
But I trust in Your faithfulness,
my heart will exult in Your deliverance.
I will sing to the LORD,
for He has been good to me.

Psalms 13:2–6

Protect Me, O God

*Recited at a
funeral,
unveiling of a
tombstone, in a
house of
mourning*

Protect me, O God, for I seek refuge in You.
I say to the LORD,
"You are my LORD, my benefactor;
there is none above You."
As to the holy and mighty ones that are in
    the land,
my whole desire concerning them is that
those who espouse another god

עַד־אָנָה יְהוָה תִּשְׁכָּחֵנִי נֶצַח
עַד־אָנָה תַּסְתִּיר אֶת־פָּנֶיךָ מִמֶּנִּי
עַד־אָנָה אָשִׁית עֵצוֹת בְּנַפְשִׁי
יָגוֹן בִּלְבָבִי יוֹמָם
עַד־אָנָה יָרוּם אֹיְבִי עָלָי
הַבִּיטָה עֲנֵנִי יְהוָה אֱלֹהָי
הָאִירָה עֵינַי
פֶּן־אִישַׁן הַמָּוֶת
פֶּן־יֹאמַר אֹיְבִי יְכָלְתִּיו
צָרַי יָגִילוּ כִּי אֶמּוֹט
וַאֲנִי בְּחַסְדְּךָ בָטַחְתִּי
יָגֵל לִבִּי בִּישׁוּעָתֶךָ
אָשִׁירָה לַיהוָה
כִּי גָמַל עָלָי

שָׁמְרֵנִי אֵל כִּי־חָסִיתִי בָךְ
אָמַרְתְּ לַיהוָה
אֲדֹנָי אַתָּה טוֹבָתִי
בַּל־עָלֶיךָ
לִקְדוֹשִׁים אֲשֶׁר־בָּאָרֶץ הֵמָּה
וְאַדִּירֵי כָּל־חֶפְצִי־בָם
יִרְבּוּ עַצְּבוֹתָם
אַחֵר מָהָרוּ

133

may have many sorrows!
I will have no part of their bloody libations;
their names will not pass my lips.
The LORD is my allotted share and portion;
You control my fate.
Delightful country has fallen to my lot;
lovely indeed is my estate.
I bless the LORD who has guided me;
my conscience admonishes me at night.
I am ever mindful of the LORD's presence;
He is at my right hand; I shall never be
    shaken.
So my heart rejoices,
my whole being exults,
and my body rests secure.
For You will not abandon me to Sheol,
or let Your faithful one see the Pit.
You will teach me the path of life.
In Your presence is perfect joy;
delights are ever in Your right hand.

Psalms 16:1–11

My Soul Cries for You

Like a hind crying for water
my soul cries for You, O God;
my soul thirsts for God, the living God;
O when will I come to appear before God!
My tears have been my food day and night;
I am ever taunted with, "Where is your
    God?"

בַּל־אַסִּיךְ נִסְכֵּיהֶם מִדָּם
וּבַל־אֶשָּׂא אֶת־שְׁמוֹתָם עַל־שְׂפָתָי
יְהֹוָה מְנָת־חֶלְקִי וְכוֹסִי
אַתָּה תּוֹמִיךְ גּוֹרָלִי
חֲבָלִים נָפְלוּ־לִי בַּנְּעִמִים
אַף־נַחֲלָת שָׁפְרָה עָלָי
אֲבָרֵךְ אֶת־יְהֹוָה אֲשֶׁר יְעָצָנִי
אַף־לֵילוֹת יִסְּרוּנִי כִלְיוֹתָי
שִׁוִּיתִי יְהֹוָה לְנֶגְדִּי תָמִיד
כִּי מִימִינִי בַּל־אֶמּוֹט
לָכֵן שָׂמַח לִבִּי
וַיָּגֶל כְּבוֹדִי
אַף־בְּשָׂרִי יִשְׁכֹּן לָבֶטַח
כִּי לֹא־תַעֲזֹב נַפְשִׁי לִשְׁאוֹל
לֹא־תִתֵּן חֲסִידְךָ לִרְאוֹת שָׁחַת
תּוֹדִיעֵנִי אֹרַח חַיִּים
שֹׂבַע שְׂמָחוֹת אֶת־פָּנֶיךָ
נְעִמוֹת בִּימִינְךָ נֶצַח

כְּאַיָּל תַּעֲרֹג עַל־אֲפִיקֵי־מָיִם
כֵּן נַפְשִׁי תַעֲרֹג אֵלֶיךָ אֱלֹהִים
צָמְאָה נַפְשִׁי לֵאלֹהִים לְאֵל חָי
מָתַי אָבוֹא
וְאֵרָאֶה פְּנֵי אֱלֹהִים
הָיְתָה־לִּי דִמְעָתִי לֶחֶם יוֹמָם
וָלָיְלָה
בֶּאֱמֹר אֵלַי כָּל־הַיּוֹם אַיֵּה אֱלֹהֶיךָ

When I think of this, I pour out my soul:
how I walked with the crowd, moved with
    them,
the festive throng, to the House of God
with joyous shouts of praise.
Why so downcast, my soul,
why disquieted within me?
Have hope in God;
I will yet praise Him
for His saving presence.
O my God, my soul is downcast;
therefore I think of You
in this land of Jordan and Hermon,
in Mount Mizar,
where deep calls to deep
in the roar of Your cataracts;
all Your breakers and billows have swept over
    me.
By day may the LORD vouchsafe His faithful
    care,
so that at night a song to Him may be with
    me,
a prayer to the God of my life.
I say to God, my rock,
"Why have You forgotten me,
why must I walk in gloom,
oppressed by my enemy?"
Crushing my bones,
my foes revile me,
taunting me always with, "Where is your
    God?"
Why so downcast, my soul,
why disquieted within me?
Have hope in God;

אֵלֶּה אֶזְכְּרָה וְאֶשְׁפְּכָה עָלַי
נַפְשִׁי
כִּי אֶעֱבֹר בַּסָּךְ
אֶדַּדֵּם עַד־בֵּית אֱלֹהִים
בְּקוֹל־רִנָּה וְתוֹדָה הָמוֹן חוֹגֵג
מַה־תִּשְׁתּוֹחֲחִי נַפְשִׁי
וַתֶּהֱמִי עָלָי
הוֹחִילִי לֵאלֹהִים
כִּי־עוֹד אוֹדֶנּוּ
יְשׁוּעוֹת פָּנָיו
אֱלֹהַי עָלַי נַפְשִׁי תִשְׁתּוֹחָח
עַל־כֵּן אֶזְכָּרְךָ
מֵאֶרֶץ יַרְדֵּן וְחֶרְמוֹנִים
מֵהַר מִצְעָר
תְּהוֹם־אֶל־תְּהוֹם קוֹרֵא
לְקוֹל צִנּוֹרֶיךָ
כָּל־מִשְׁבָּרֶיךָ וְגַלֶּיךָ עָלַי עָבָרוּ
יוֹמָם יְצַוֶּה יְהוָה חַסְדּוֹ
וּבַלַּיְלָה שִׁירֹה עִמִּי
תְּפִלָּה לְאֵל חַיָּי
אוֹמְרָה לְאֵל סַלְעִי
לָמָה שְׁכַחְתָּנִי
לָמָּה־קֹדֵר אֵלֵךְ
בְּלַחַץ אוֹיֵב
בְּרֶצַח בְּעַצְמוֹתַי
חֵרְפוּנִי צוֹרְרָי
בְּאָמְרָם אֵלַי כָּל־הַיּוֹם אַיֵּה
אֱלֹהֶיךָ
מַה־תִּשְׁתּוֹחֲחִי נַפְשִׁי
וּמַה־תֶּהֱמִי עָלָי
הוֹחִילִי לֵאלֹהִים

I will yet praise Him,
my ever-present help, my God.

Psalms 42:2–12

Purge Me with Hyssop

For the leader. A psalm of David, when
    Nathan the prophet came to him after he
    had come to Bathsheba.
Have mercy upon me, O God,
as befits Your faithfulness;
in keeping with Your abundant compassion,
blot out my transgressions.
Wash me thoroughly of my iniquity,
and purify me of my sin;
for I recognize my transgressions,
and am ever conscious of my sin.
Against You alone have I sinned,
and done what is evil in Your sight;
so You are just in Your sentence,
and right in Your judgment.
Indeed I was born with iniquity;
with sin my mother conceived me.
Indeed You desire truth about that which is
    hidden;
teach me wisdom about secret things.
Purge me with hyssop till I am pure;
wash me till I am whiter than snow.
Let me hear tidings of joy and gladness;
let the bones You have crushed exult.
Hide Your face from my sins;

כִּי־עֹוד אֹודֶנּוּ
יְשׁוּעֹת פָּנַי וֵאלֹהָי

לַמְנַצֵּחַ מִזְמֹור לְדָוִד בְּבֹוא־
אֵלָיו נָתָן הַנָּבִיא כַּאֲשֶׁר־בָּא אֶל־בַּת־
שָׁבַע
חָנֵּנִי אֱלֹהִים
כְּחַסְדֶּךָ
כְּרֹב רַחֲמֶיךָ
מְחֵה פְשָׁעָי
הרבה הֶרֶב כַּבְּסֵנִי מֵעֲוֺנִי
וּמֵחַטָּאתִי טַהֲרֵנִי
כִּי־פְשָׁעַי אֲנִי אֵדָע
וְחַטָּאתִי נֶגְדִּי תָמִיד
לְךָ לְבַדְּךָ חָטָאתִי
וְהָרַע בְּעֵינֶיךָ עָשִׂיתִי
לְמַעַן תִּצְדַּק בְּדָבְרֶךָ
תִּזְכֶּה בְשָׁפְטֶךָ
הֵן־בְּעָוֺון חֹולָלְתִּי
וּבְחֵטְא יֶחֱמַתְנִי אִמִּי
הֵן־אֱמֶת חָפַצְתָּ בַטֻּחֹות
וּבְסָתֻם חָכְמָה תֹודִיעֵנִי
תְּחַטְּאֵנִי בְאֵזֹוב וְאֶטְהָר
תְּכַבְּסֵנִי וּמִשֶּׁלֶג אַלְבִּין
תַּשְׁמִיעֵנִי שָׂשֹׂון וְשִׂמְחָה
תָּגֵלְנָה עֲצָמֹות דִּכִּיתָ
הַסְתֵּר פָּנֶיךָ מֵחֲטָאָי

139

blot out all my iniquities.
Fashion a pure heart for me, O God;
create in me a steadfast spirit.
Do not cast me out of Your presence,
or take Your holy spirit away from me.
Let me again rejoice in Your help;
let a vigorous spirit sustain me.
I will teach transgressors Your ways,
that sinners may return to You.
Save me from bloodguilt,
O God, God, my deliverer,
that I may sing forth Your beneficence.
O LORD, open my lips,
and let my mouth declare Your praise.
You do not want me to bring sacrifices;
You do not desire burnt offerings;
True sacrifice to God is a contrite spirit;
God, You will not despise
a contrite and crushed heart.
May it please You to make Zion prosper;
rebuild the walls of Jerusalem.
Then You will want sacrifices offered in
    righteousness,
burnt and whole offerings;
then bulls will be offered on Your altar.

Psalms 51:1–21

וְכָל־עֲוֺנֹתַי מְחֵה
לֵב טָהוֹר בְּרָא־לִי אֱלֹהִים
וְרוּחַ נָכוֹן חַדֵּשׁ בְּקִרְבִּי
אַל־תַּשְׁלִיכֵנִי מִלְּפָנֶיךָ
וְרוּחַ קָדְשְׁךָ אַל־תִּקַּח מִמֶּנִּי
הָשִׁיבָה לִּי שְׂשׂוֹן יִשְׁעֶךָ
וְרוּחַ נְדִיבָה תִסְמְכֵנִי
אֲלַמְּדָה פֹשְׁעִים דְּרָכֶיךָ
וְחַטָּאִים אֵלֶיךָ יָשׁוּבוּ
הַצִּילֵנִי מִדָּמִים
אֱלֹהִים אֱלֹהֵי תְּשׁוּעָתִי
תְּרַנֵּן לְשׁוֹנִי צִדְקָתֶךָ
אֲדֹנָי שְׂפָתַי תִּפְתָּח
וּפִי יַגִּיד תְּהִלָּתֶךָ
כִּי לֹא־תַחְפֹּץ זֶבַח וְאֶתֵּנָה
עוֹלָה לֹא תִרְצֶה
זִבְחֵי אֱלֹהִים רוּחַ נִשְׁבָּרָה
לֵב־נִשְׁבָּר וְנִדְכֶּה
אֱלֹהִים לֹא תִבְזֶה
הֵיטִיבָה בִרְצוֹנְךָ אֶת־צִיּוֹן
תִּבְנֶה חוֹמוֹת יְרוּשָׁלָ͏ִם
אָז תַּחְפֹּץ זִבְחֵי־צֶדֶק
עוֹלָה וְכָלִיל
אָז יַעֲלוּ עַל־מִזְבַּחֲךָ פָרִים

By the Rivers of Babylon

By the rivers of Babylon,
there we sat,
sat and wept,
as we thought of Zion.
There on the poplars
we hung up our lyres,
for our captors asked us there for songs,
our tormentors, for amusement,
"Sing us one of the songs of Zion."
How can we sing a song of the LORD
on alien soil?
If I forget you, O Jerusalem,
let my right hand wither;
let my tongue stick to my palate
if I cease to think of you,
if I do not keep Jerusalem in memory
even at my happiest hour.
Remember, O LORD, against the Edomites
the day of Jerusalem's fall;
how they cried, "Strip her, strip her
to her very foundations!"
Fair Babylon, you predator,
a blessing on him who repays you in kind
what you have inflicted on us;
a blessing on him who seizes your babies
and dashes them against the rocks!

Psalms 137:1–9

עַל נַהֲרוֹת בָּבֶל
שָׁם יָשַׁבְנוּ
גַּם־בָּכִינוּ
בְּזָכְרֵנוּ אֶת־צִיּוֹן
עַל־עֲרָבִים בְּתוֹכָהּ
תָּלִינוּ כִּנֹּרוֹתֵינוּ
כִּי שָׁם שְׁאֵלוּנוּ שׁוֹבֵינוּ דִּבְרֵי־שִׁיר
וְתוֹלָלֵינוּ שִׂמְחָה
שִׁירוּ לָנוּ מִשִּׁיר צִיּוֹן
אֵיךְ נָשִׁיר אֶת־שִׁיר־יְהוָה
עַל אַדְמַת נֵכָר
אִם־אֶשְׁכָּחֵךְ יְרוּשָׁלָ͏ִם
תִּשְׁכַּח יְמִינִי
תִּדְבַּק־לְשׁוֹנִי לְחִכִּי
אִם־לֹא אֶזְכְּרֵכִי
אִם־לֹא אַעֲלֶה אֶת־יְרוּשָׁלַ͏ִם
עַל רֹאשׁ שִׂמְחָתִי
זְכֹר יְהוָה לִבְנֵי אֱדוֹם
אֵת יוֹם יְרוּשָׁלָ͏ִם
הָאֹמְרִים עָרוּ עָרוּ
עַד הַיְסוֹד בָּהּ
בַּת־בָּבֶל הַשְּׁדוּדָה
אַשְׁרֵי שֶׁיְשַׁלֶּם־לָךְ
אֶת־גְּמוּלֵךְ שֶׁגָּמַלְתְּ לָנוּ
אַשְׁרֵי שֶׁיֹּאחֵז וְנִפֵּץ אֶת־עֹלָלַיִךְ
אֶל־הַסָּלַע

Lamentations

Alas!
Lonely sits the city
Once great with people!
She that was great among nations
Is become like a widow;
The princess among states
Is become a thrall.
Bitterly she weeps in the night,
Her cheek wet with tears.
There is none to comfort her
Of all her friends.
All her allies have betrayed her;
They have become her foes.
Judah has gone into exile
Because of misery and harsh oppression;
When she settled among the nations,
She found no rest;
All her pursuers overtook her
In the narrow places.
Zion's roads are in mourning,
Empty of festival pilgrims;
All her gates are deserted.
Her priests sigh,
Her maidens are unhappy—
She is utterly disconsolate!
Her enemies are now the masters,
Her foes are at ease,
Because the LORD has afflicted her
For her many transgressions;
Her infants have gone into captivity
Before the enemy.
Gone from Fair Zion are all

אֵיכָה
יָשְׁבָה בָדָד הָעִיר
רַבָּתִי עָם
הָיְתָה כְּאַלְמָנָה
רַבָּתִי בַגּוֹיִם
שָׂרָתִי בַּמְּדִינוֹת
הָיְתָה לָמַס
בָּכוֹ תִבְכֶּה בַּלַּיְלָה
וְדִמְעָתָהּ עַל לֶחֱיָהּ
אֵין־לָהּ מְנַחֵם
מִכָּל־אֹהֲבֶיהָ
כָּל־רֵעֶיהָ בָּגְדוּ בָהּ
הָיוּ לָהּ לְאֹיְבִים
גָּלְתָה יְהוּדָה
מֵעֹנִי וּמֵרֹב עֲבֹדָה
הִיא יָשְׁבָה בַגּוֹיִם
לֹא מָצְאָה מָנוֹחַ
כָּל־רֹדְפֶיהָ הִשִּׂיגוּהָ
בֵּין הַמְּצָרִים
דַּרְכֵי צִיּוֹן אֲבֵלוֹת
מִבְּלִי בָּאֵי מוֹעֵד
כָּל־שְׁעָרֶיהָ שׁוֹמֵמִין
כֹּהֲנֶיהָ נֶאֱנָחִים
בְּתוּלֹתֶיהָ נּוּגוֹת
וְהִיא מַר־לָהּ
הָיוּ צָרֶיהָ לְרֹאשׁ
אֹיְבֶיהָ שָׁלוּ
כִּי־יְהֹוָה הוֹגָהּ
עַל רֹב־פְּשָׁעֶיהָ
עוֹלָלֶיהָ הָלְכוּ שְׁבִי
לִפְנֵי־צָר
וַיֵּצֵא מן בת מִבַּת־צִיּוֹן

That were her glory;
Her leaders were like stags
That found no pasture;
They could only walk feebly
Before the pursuer.
All the precious things she had
In the days of old
Jerusalem recalled
In her days of woe and sorrow,
When her people fell by enemy hands
With none to help her;
When enemies looked on and gloated
Over her downfall.
Jerusalem has greatly sinned,
Therefore she is become a mockery.
All who admired her despise her,
For they have seen her disgraced;
And she can only sigh
And shrink back.
Her uncleanness clings to her skirts.
She gave no thought to her future;
She has sunk appallingly,
With none to comfort her.—
See, O LORD, my misery;
How the enemy jeers!
The foe has laid hands
On everything dear to her.
She has seen her Sanctuary
Invaded by nations
Which you have denied admission
Into Your community.
All her inhabitants sigh
As they search for bread;
They have bartered their treasures for food,

כָּל־הֲדָרָהּ
הָיוּ שָׂרֶיהָ כְּאַיָּלִים
לֹא־מָצְאוּ מִרְעֶה
וַיֵּלְכוּ בְלֹא־כֹחַ
לִפְנֵי רוֹדֵף
זָכְרָה יְרוּשָׁלַ͏ִם
יְמֵי עָנְיָהּ וּמְרוּדֶיהָ
כֹּל מַחֲמֻדֶיהָ אֲשֶׁר הָיוּ
מִימֵי קֶדֶם
בִּנְפֹּל עַמָּהּ בְּיַד־צָר
וְאֵין עוֹזֵר לָהּ
רָאוּהָ צָרִים שָׂחֲקוּ
עַל מִשְׁבַּתֶּהָ
חֵטְא חָטְאָה יְרוּשָׁלַ͏ִם
עַל־כֵּן לְנִידָה הָיָתָה
כָּל־מְכַבְּדֶיהָ הִזִּילוּהָ
כִּי־רָאוּ עֶרְוָתָהּ
גַּם־הִיא נֶאֶנְחָה
וַתָּשָׁב אָחוֹר
טֻמְאָתָהּ בְּשׁוּלֶיהָ
לֹא זָכְרָה אַחֲרִיתָהּ
וַתֵּרֶד פְּלָאִים
אֵין מְנַחֵם לָהּ
רְאֵה יְהוָה אֶת־עָנְיִי
כִּי הִגְדִּיל אוֹיֵב
יָדוֹ פָּרַשׂ צָר
עַל כָּל־מַחֲמַדֶּיהָ
כִּי־רָאֲתָה
גוֹיִם בָּאוּ מִקְדָּשָׁהּ
אֲשֶׁר צִוִּיתָה לֹא־יָבֹאוּ
בַקָּהָל לָךְ
כָּל־עַמָּהּ נֶאֱנָחִים
מְבַקְשִׁים לֶחֶם
נָתְנוּ מַחֲמוֹדֵּיהֶם מַחֲמַדֵּיהֶם בְּאֹכֶל

To keep themselves alive.—
See, O LORD, and behold,
How abject I have become!

Lamentations 1:1–11

The LORD has done what He purposed,
Has carried out the decree
That He ordained long ago;
He has torn down without pity.
He has let the foe rejoice over you,
Has exalted the might of your enemies.
Their heart cried out to the LORD.
O wall of Fair Zion,
Shed tears like a torrent
Day and night!
Give yourself no respite,
Your eyes no rest.
Arise, cry out in the night
At the beginning of the watches,
Pour out your heart like water
In the presence of the LORD!
Lift up your hands to Him
For the life of your infants,
Who faint for hunger
At every street corner.
See, O LORD, and behold,
To whom You have done this!
Alas, women eat their own fruit,
Their new-born babes!
Alas, priest and prophet are slain
In the Sanctuary of the LORD!
Prostrate in the streets lie
Both young and old.

לְהָשִׁיב נָפֶשׁ
רְאֵה יְהֹוָה֙ וְהַבִּ֔יטָה
כִּ֥י הָיִ֖יתִי זוֹלֵלָֽה

עָשָׂ֨ה יְהֹוָ֜ה אֲשֶׁ֣ר זָמָ֗ם
בִּצַּ֣ע אֶמְרָת֗וֹ
אֲשֶׁ֤ר צִוָּה֙ מִֽימֵי־קֶ֔דֶם
הָרַ֖ס וְלֹ֣א חָמָ֑ל
וַיְשַׂמַּ֤ח עָלַ֙יִךְ֙ אוֹיֵ֔ב
הֵרִ֖ים קֶ֥רֶן צָרָֽיִךְ
צָעַ֥ק לִבָּ֖ם אֶל־אֲדֹנָ֑י
חוֹמַ֣ת בַּת־צִיּ֗וֹן
הוֹרִ֤ידִי כַנַּ֙חַל֙ דִּמְעָ֔ה
יוֹמָ֣ם וָלַ֔יְלָה
אַֽל־תִּתְּנִ֤י פוּגַת֙ לָ֔ךְ
אַל־תִּדֹּ֖ם בַּת־עֵינֵֽךְ
ק֣וּמִי רֹ֗נִּי בליל בַלַּ֙יְלָה֙
לְרֹאשׁ֙ אַשְׁמֻר֔וֹת
שִׁפְכִ֤י כַמַּ֙יִם֙ לִבֵּ֔ךְ
נֹ֖כַח פְּנֵ֣י אֲדֹנָ֑י
שְׂאִ֧י אֵלָ֣יו כַּפַּ֗יִךְ
עַל־נֶ֙פֶשׁ֙ עֽוֹלָלַ֔יִךְ
הָעֲטוּפִ֥ים בְּרָעָ֖ב
בְּרֹ֥אשׁ כָּל־חוּצֽוֹת
רְאֵ֤ה יְהֹוָה֙ וְהַבִּ֔יטָה
לְמִ֖י עוֹלַ֣לְתָּ כֹּ֑ה
אִם־תֹּאכַ֨לְנָה נָשִׁ֤ים פִּרְיָם֙
עֹלְלֵ֣י טִפֻּחִ֔ים
אִם־יֵהָרֵ֛ג בְּמִקְדַּ֥שׁ אֲדֹנָ֖י
כֹּהֵ֣ן וְנָבִ֑יא
שָׁכְב֨וּ לָאָ֤רֶץ חוּצוֹת֙
נַ֣עַר וְזָקֵ֔ן

My maidens and youths
Are fallen by the sword;
You slew them on Your day of wrath,
You slaughtered without pity.
You summoned, as on a festival,
My neighbors from roundabout.
On the day of the wrath of the LORD,
None survived or escaped;
Those whom I bore and reared
My foe has consumed.

Lamentations 2:17–22

My eyes shall flow without cease,
Without respite,
Until the LORD looks down
And beholds from heaven.
My eyes have brought me grief
Over all the maidens of my city.
My foes have snared me like a bird,
Without any cause.
They have ended my life in a pit
And cast stones at me.
Waters flowed over my head;
I said: I am lost!
I have called your name, O LORD,
From the depths of the Pit.
Hear my plea;
Do not shut Your ear
To my groan, to my cry!
You have ever drawn nigh when I called You;
You have said, "Do not fear!"
You have championed my cause, O LORD,
You have redeemed my life.

בְּתוּלֹתַי וּבַחוּרַי
נָפְלוּ בֶחָרֶב
הָרַגְתָּ בְּיוֹם אַפֶּךָ
טָבַחְתָּ לֹא חָמָלְתָּ
תִּקְרָא כְיוֹם מוֹעֵד
מְגוּרַי מִסָּבִיב
וְלֹא הָיָה בְּיוֹם אַף־יְהוָה
פָּלִיט וְשָׂרִיד
אֲשֶׁר־טִפַּחְתִּי וְרִבִּיתִי
אֹיְבִי כִלָּם

עֵינַי נִגְּרָה וְלֹא תִדְמֶה
מֵאֵין הֲפֻגוֹת
עַד־יַשְׁקִיף
וְיֵרֶא יְהוָה מִשָּׁמָיִם
עֵינִי עוֹלְלָה לְנַפְשִׁי
מִכֹּל בְּנוֹת עִירִי
צוֹד צָדוּנִי כַּצִּפּוֹר אֹיְבַי
חִנָּם
צָמְתוּ בַבּוֹר חַיָּי
וַיַּדּוּ־אֶבֶן בִּי
צָפוּ־מַיִם עַל־רֹאשִׁי
אָמַרְתִּי נִגְזָרְתִּי
קָרָאתִי שִׁמְךָ יְהוָה
מִבּוֹר תַּחְתִּיּוֹת
קוֹלִי שָׁמָעְתָּ
אַל־תַּעְלֵם אָזְנְךָ
לְרַוְחָתִי לְשַׁוְעָתִי
קָרַבְתָּ בְּיוֹם אֶקְרָאֶךָ
אָמַרְתָּ אַל־תִּירָא
רַבְתָּ אֲדֹנָי רִיבֵי נַפְשִׁי
גָּאַלְתָּ חַיָּי

You have seen, O LORD, the wrong done me;
Oh, vindicate my right!
You have seen all their malice,
All their designs against me;
You have heard, O LORD, their taunts,
All their designs against me,
The mouthings and pratings of my
    adversaries
Against me all day long.
See how, at their ease or at work,
I am the butt of their gibes.
Give them, O LORD, their deserts
According to their deeds.
Give them anguish of heart;
Your curse be upon them!
Oh, pursue them in wrath and destroy them
From under the heavens of the LORD!

Lamentations 3:49–66

Alas!
The gold is dulled,
Debased the finest gold!
The sacred gems are spilled
At every street corner.
The precious children of Zion;
Once valued as gold—
Alas, they are accounted as earthen pots,
Work of a potter's hands!
Even jackals offer the breast
And suckle their young;
But my poor people has turned cruel,
Like ostriches of the desert.
The tongue of the suckling cleaves

רָאִיתָה יְהֹוָה עַוָּתָתִי
שָׁפְטָה מִשְׁפָּטִי
רָאִיתָה כָּל־נִקְמָתָם
כָּל־מַחְשְׁבֹתָם לִי
שָׁמַעְתָּ חֶרְפָּתָם יְהֹוָה
כָּל־מַחְשְׁבֹתָם עָלָי
שִׂפְתֵי קָמַי וְהֶגְיוֹנָם
עָלַי כָּל־הַיּוֹם
שִׁבְתָּם וְקִימָתָם הַבִּיטָה
אֲנִי מַנְגִּינָתָם
תָּשִׁיב לָהֶם גְּמוּל יְהֹוָה
כְּמַעֲשֵׂה יְדֵיהֶם
תִּתֵּן לָהֶם מְגִנַּת־לֵב
תַּאֲלָתְךָ לָהֶם
תִּרְדֹּף בְּאַף וְתַשְׁמִידֵם
מִתַּחַת שְׁמֵי יְהֹוָה

אֵיכָה
יוּעַם זָהָב
יִשְׁנֶא הַכֶּתֶם הַטּוֹב
תִּשְׁתַּפֵּכְנָה אַבְנֵי־קֹדֶשׁ
בְּרֹאשׁ כָּל־חוּצוֹת
בְּנֵי צִיּוֹן הַיְקָרִים
הַמְסֻלָּאִים בַּפָּז
אֵיכָה נֶחְשְׁבוּ לְנִבְלֵי־חֶרֶשׂ
מַעֲשֵׂה יְדֵי יוֹצֵר
גַּם־תַּנִּין תַּנִּים חָלְצוּ שַׁד
הֵינִיקוּ גּוּרֵיהֶן
בַּת־עַמִּי לְאַכְזָר
כִּי עֵנִים כַּיְעֵנִים בַּמִּדְבָּר
דָּבַק לְשׁוֹן יוֹנֵק

To its palate for thirst.
Little children beg for bread;
None gives them a morsel.
Those who feasted on dainties
Lie famished in the streets;
Those who were reared in purple
Have embraced refuse heaps.
The guilt of my poor people
Exceeded the iniquity of Sodom,
Which was overthrown in a moment,
Without a hand striking it.
Her elect were purer than snow,
Whiter than milk;
Their limbs were ruddier than coral,
Their bodies were like sapphire.
Now their faces are blacker than soot,
They are not recognized in the streets;
Their skin has shriveled on their bones,
It has become dry as wood.
Better off were the slain of the sword
Than those slain by famine,
Who pined away, as though wounded,
For lack of the fruits of the field.
With their own hands, tenderhearted women
Have cooked their children;
Such became their fare,
In the disaster of my poor people.

Lamentations 4:1–10

Remember, O LORD, what has befallen us;
Behold, and see our disgrace!
Our heritage has passed to aliens,
Our homes to strangers.

אֵל־חִכּוֹ בַּצָּמָא
עוֹלָלִים שָׁאֲלוּ לֶחֶם
פֹּרֵשׂ אֵין לָהֶם
הָאֹכְלִים לְמַעֲדַנִּים
נָשַׁמּוּ בַּחוּצוֹת
הָאֱמֻנִים עֲלֵי תוֹלָע
חִבְּקוּ אַשְׁפַּתּוֹת
וַיִּגְדַּל עֲוֹן בַּת־עַמִּי
מֵחַטַּאת סְדֹם
הַהֲפוּכָה כְמוֹ־רָגַע
וְלֹא־חָלוּ בָהּ יָדָיִם
זַכּוּ נְזִירֶיהָ מִשֶּׁלֶג
צַחוּ מֵחָלָב
אָדְמוּ עֶצֶם מִפְּנִינִים
סַפִּיר גִּזְרָתָם
חָשַׁךְ מִשְּׁחוֹר תָּאֳרָם
לֹא נִכְּרוּ בַּחוּצוֹת
צָפַד עוֹרָם עַל־עַצְמָם
יָבֵשׁ הָיָה כָעֵץ
טוֹבִים הָיוּ חַלְלֵי־חֶרֶב
מֵחַלְלֵי רָעָב
שֶׁהֵם יָזוּבוּ מְדֻקָּרִים
מִתְּנוּבֹת שָׂדָי
יְדֵי נָשִׁים רַחֲמָנִיּוֹת
בִּשְּׁלוּ יַלְדֵיהֶן
הָיוּ לְבָרוֹת לָמוֹ
בְּשֶׁבֶר בַּת־עַמִּי

זְכֹר יְהוָה מֶה־הָיָה לָנוּ
הַבִּיטָה וּרְאֵה אֶת־חֶרְפָּתֵנוּ
נַחֲלָתֵנוּ נֶהֶפְכָה לְזָרִים
בָּתֵּינוּ לְנָכְרִים

We have become orphans, fatherless;
Our mothers are like widows.
We must pay to drink our own water,
Obtain our own kindling at a price.
We are hotly pursued;
Exhausted, we are given no rest.
We hold out a hand to Egypt;
To Assyria, for our fill of bread.
Our fathers sinned and are no more;
And we must bear their guilt.
Slaves are ruling over us,
With none to rescue us from them.
We get our bread at the peril of our lives,
Because of the sword of the wilderness.
Our skin glows like an oven,
With the fever of famine.
They have ravished women in Zion,
Maidens in the towns of Judah.
Princes have been hanged by them;
No respect has been shown to elders.
Young men must carry millstones,
And youths stagger under loads of wood.
The old men are gone from the gate,
The young men from their music.
Gone is the joy of our hearts;
Our dancing is turned into mourning.
The crown has fallen from our head;
Woe to us that we have sinned!
Because of this our hearts are sick,
Because of these our eyes are dimmed:
Because of Mount Zion, which lies desolate;
Jackals prowl over it.
But You, O LORD, are enthroned forever,
Your throne endures through the ages.

יְתוֹמִים הָיִ֙ינוּ֙ אֵ֣ין וְאֵ֣ין אָ֔ב
אִמֹּתֵ֖ינוּ כְּאַלְמָנֽוֹת
מֵימֵ֙ינוּ֙ בְּכֶ֣סֶף שָׁתִ֔ינוּ
עֵצֵ֖ינוּ בִּמְחִ֥יר יָבֹֽאוּ
עַ֤ל צַוָּארֵ֙נוּ֙ נִרְדָּ֔פְנוּ
יָגַ֖עְנוּ לֹ֥א וְלֹ֖א הֽוּנַֽח־לָֽנוּ
מִצְרַ֙יִם֙ נָתַ֣נּוּ יָ֔ד
אַשּׁ֖וּר לִשְׂבֹּ֥עַ לָֽחֶם
אֲבֹתֵ֤ינוּ חָֽטְאוּ֙ אֵינָ֔ם וְאֵינָ֑ם
אֲנַ֕חְנוּ וַֽאֲנַ֥חְנוּ עֲוֹנֹֽתֵיהֶ֖ם סָבָֽלְנוּ
עֲבָדִים֙ מָ֣שְׁלוּ בָ֔נוּ
פֹּרֵ֖ק אֵ֥ין מִיָּדָֽם
בְּנַפְשֵׁ֙נוּ֙ נָבִ֣יא לַחְמֵ֔נוּ
מִפְּנֵ֖י חֶ֥רֶב הַמִּדְבָּֽר
עוֹרֵ֙נוּ֙ כְּתַנּ֣וּר נִכְמָ֔רוּ
מִפְּנֵ֖י זַלְעֲפ֥וֹת רָעָֽב
נָשִׁים֙ בְּצִיּ֣וֹן עִנּ֔וּ
בְּתֻלֹ֖ת בְּעָרֵ֥י יְהוּדָֽה
שָׂרִים֙ בְּיָדָ֣ם נִתְל֔וּ
פְּנֵ֥י זְקֵנִ֖ים לֹ֥א נֶהְדָּֽרוּ
בַּחוּרִים֙ טְח֣וֹן נָשָׂ֔אוּ
וּנְעָרִ֖ים בָּעֵ֥ץ כָּשָֽׁלוּ
זְקֵנִים֙ מִשַּׁ֣עַר שָׁבָ֔תוּ
בַּחוּרִ֖ים מִנְּגִֽינָתָֽם
שָׁבַת֙ מְשׂ֣וֹשׂ לִבֵּ֔נוּ
נֶהְפַּ֥ךְ לְאֵ֖בֶל מְחֹלֵֽנוּ
נָֽפְלָה֙ עֲטֶ֣רֶת רֹאשֵׁ֔נוּ
אֽוֹי־נָ֥א לָ֖נוּ כִּ֥י חָטָֽאנוּ
עַל־זֶ֗ה הָיָ֤ה דָוֶה֙ לִבֵּ֔נוּ
עַל־אֵ֖לֶּה חָֽשְׁכ֥וּ עֵינֵֽינוּ
עַ֤ל הַר־צִיּוֹן֙ שֶׁשָּׁמֵ֔ם
שֽׁוּעָלִ֖ים הִלְּכוּ־בֽוֹ
אַתָּ֤ה יְהוָה֙ לְעוֹלָ֣ם תֵּשֵׁ֔ב
כִּסְאֲךָ֖ לְדֹ֥ר וָדֽוֹר

Why have You forgotten us utterly,
Forsaken us for all time?
Take us back, O LORD, to Yourself,
And let us come back;
Renew our days as of old!
For truly, You have rejected us,
Bitterly raged against us.
Take us back, O LORD, to Yourself,
And let us come back;
Renew our days as of old!

Lamentations 5:1–22

Alas for the Day

Listen to this, O elders,
Give ear, all inhabitants of the land.
Has the like of this happened in your days
Or in the days of your fathers?
Tell your children about it,
And let your children tell theirs,
And their children the next generation!
What the cutter has left, the locust has
    devoured;
What the locust has left, the grub has
    devoured;
And what the grub has left, the hopper has
    devoured.
Wake up, you drunkards, and weep,
Wail, all you swillers of wine—
For the new wine that is denied you!
For a nation has invaded my land,

לָמָּה לָנֶ֫צַח תִּשְׁכָּחֵ֫נוּ
תַּעַזְבֵ֫נוּ לְאֹ֫רֶךְ יָמִֽים
הֲשִׁיבֵ֫נוּ יְהוָ֤ה אֵלֶ֫יךָ
וְנָשׁוּבָה
חַדֵּשׁ יָמֵ֫ינוּ כְּקֶֽדֶם
כִּי אִם־מָאֹס מְאַסְתָּ֫נוּ
קָצַ֫פְתָּ עָלֵ֫ינוּ עַד־מְאֹֽד
[הֲשִׁיבֵ֫נוּ יְהוָ֤ה אֵלֶ֫יךָ
וְנָשׁוּבָה
חַדֵּשׁ יָמֵ֫ינוּ כְּקֶֽדֶם]

שִׁמְעוּ־זֹאת הַזְּקֵנִ֫ים
וְהַאֲזִ֫ינוּ כֹּל יוֹשְׁבֵי הָאָ֫רֶץ
הֶהָ֫יְתָה זֹּאת בִּֽימֵיכֶ֫ם
וְאִם בִּֽימֵי אֲבֹֽתֵיכֶ֫ם
עָלֶ֫יהָ לִבְנֵיכֶ֫ם סַפֵּ֫רוּ
וּבְנֵיכֶ֫ם לִבְנֵיהֶ֫ם
וּבְנֵיהֶ֫ם לְדוֹר אַחֵֽר
יֶ֫תֶר הַגָּזָ֫ם אָכַל הָֽאַרְבֶּ֫ה
וְיֶ֫תֶר הָֽאַרְבֶּ֫ה אָכַל הַיָּ֫לֶק
וְיֶ֫תֶר הַיֶּ֫לֶק אָכַל הֶחָסִֽיל
הָקִ֫יצוּ שִׁכּוֹרִ֫ים וּבְכ֫וּ
וְהֵילִ֫לוּ כָּל־שֹׁ֫תֵי יָ֫יִן
עַל־עָסִ֫יס כִּי נִכְרַ֫ת מִפִּיכֶֽם
כִּֽי־גוֹי עָלָ֫ה עַל־אַרְצִ֫י

Vast beyond counting,
With teeth like the teeth of a lion,
With the fangs of a lion's breed.
They have laid my vines waste
And splintered my fig trees:
They have stripped off their bark and thrown
    it away;
Their runners have turned white.
Lament—like a maiden girt with sackcloth
For the husband of her youth!
Offering and libation have ceased
From the House of the LORD;
The priests must mourn
Who minister to the LORD.
The country is ravaged,
The ground must mourn;
For the new grain is ravaged,
The new wine is dried up,
The new oil has failed.
Farmers are dismayed
And vine dressers wail
Over wheat and barley;
For the crops of the field are lost.
The vine has dried up,
The fig tree withers,
Pomegranate, palm, and apple—
All the trees of the field are sear.
And joy has dried up
Among men.
Gird yourselves and lament, O priests,
Wail, O ministers of the altar;
Come, spend the night in sackcloth,
O ministers of my God.
For offering and libation are withheld

עָצוּם וְאֵין מִסְפָּר
שִׁנָּיו שִׁנֵּי אַרְיֵה
וּמְתַלְּעוֹת לָבִיא לוֹ
שָׂם גַּפְנִי לְשַׁמָּה
וּתְאֵנָתִי לִקְצָפָה
חָשֹׂף חֲשָׂפָהּ וְהִשְׁלִיךְ
הִלְבִּינוּ שָׂרִיגֶיהָ
אֱלִי כִּבְתוּלָה חֲגֻרַת־שַׂק
עַל־בַּעַל נְעוּרֶיהָ
הָכְרַת מִנְחָה וָנֶסֶךְ
מִבֵּית יְהוָה
אָבְלוּ הַכֹּהֲנִים
מְשָׁרְתֵי יְהוָה
שֻׁדַּד שָׂדֶה
אָבְלָה אֲדָמָה
כִּי שֻׁדַּד דָּגָן
הוֹבִישׁ תִּירוֹשׁ
אֻמְלַל יִצְהָר
הֹבִישׁוּ אִכָּרִים
הֵילִילוּ כֹּרְמִים
עַל־חִטָּה וְעַל־שְׂעֹרָה
כִּי אָבַד קְצִיר שָׂדֶה
הַגֶּפֶן הוֹבִישָׁה
וְהַתְּאֵנָה אֻמְלָלָה
רִמּוֹן גַּם־תָּמָר וְתַפּוּחַ
כָּל־עֲצֵי הַשָּׂדֶה יָבֵשׁוּ
כִּי־הֹבִישׁ שָׂשׂוֹן
מִן־בְּנֵי אָדָם
חִגְרוּ וְסִפְדוּ הַכֹּהֲנִים
הֵילִילוּ מְשָׁרְתֵי מִזְבֵּחַ
בֹּאוּ לִינוּ בַשַּׂקִּים
מְשָׁרְתֵי אֱלֹהָי
כִּי נִמְנַע מִבֵּית אֱלֹהֵיכֶם

From the House of your God.
Solemnize a fast,
Proclaim an assembly;
Gather the elders—all the inhabitants of the land—
In the House of the LORD your God,
And cry out to the LORD.
Alas for the day!
For the day of the LORD is near;
It shall come like havoc from Shaddai.
For food is cut off
Before our very eyes,
And joy and gladness
From the House of our God.
The seeds have shriveled
Under their clods.
The granaries are desolate,
Barns are in ruins,
For the new grain has failed.
How the beasts groan!
The herds of cattle are bewildered
Because they have no pasture,
And the flocks of sheep are dazed.
To You, O LORD, I call.
For fire has consumed
The pastures in the wilderness,
And flame has devoured
All the trees of the countryside.
The very beasts of the field
Cry out to You;
For the watercourses are dried up,
And fire has consumed
The pastures in the wilderness.

Joel 1 2–20

מִנְחָה וָנֶסֶךְ
קַדְּשׁוּ־צוֹם
קִרְאוּ עֲצָרָה
אִסְפוּ זְקֵנִים כֹּל יֹשְׁבֵי הָאָרֶץ
בֵּית יְהוָה אֱלֹהֵיכֶם
וְזַעֲקוּ אֶל־יְהוָה
אֲהָהּ לַיּוֹם
כִּי קָרוֹב יוֹם יְהוָה
וּכְשֹׁד מִשַּׁדַּי יָבוֹא
הֲלוֹא נֶגֶד עֵינֵינוּ
אֹכֶל נִכְרָת
מִבֵּית אֱלֹהֵינוּ
שִׂמְחָה וָגִיל
עָבְשׁוּ פְרֻדוֹת
תַּחַת מֶגְרְפֹתֵיהֶם
נָשַׁמּוּ אֹצָרוֹת
נֶהֶרְסוּ מַמְּגֻרוֹת
כִּי הֹבִישׁ דָּגָן
מַה־נֶּאֶנְחָה בְהֵמָה
נָבֹכוּ עֶדְרֵי בָקָר
כִּי אֵין מִרְעֶה לָהֶם
גַּם־עֶדְרֵי הַצֹּאן נֶאְשָׁמוּ
אֵלֶיךָ יְהוָה אֶקְרָא
כִּי אֵשׁ אָכְלָה
נְאוֹת מִדְבָּר
וְלֶהָבָה לִהֲטָה
כָּל־עֲצֵי הַשָּׂדֶה
גַּם־בַּהֲמוֹת שָׂדֶה
תַּעֲרוֹג אֵלֶיךָ
כִּי יָבְשׁוּ אֲפִיקֵי מָיִם
וְאֵשׁ אָכְלָה
נְאוֹת הַמִּדְבָּר

JUDGMENT ORACLES

The Moon
Will Be Ashamed

Terror, and pit, and trap
Upon you who dwell on earth!
He who flees at the report of the terror
Shall fall into the pit;
And he who climbs out of the pit
Shall be caught in the trap.
For sluices are opened on high,
And earth's foundations tremble.
The earth is breaking, breaking;
The earth is crumbling, crumbling.
The earth is tottering, tottering;
The earth is swaying like a drunkard;
It is rocking to and fro like a hut.
Its iniquity shall weigh it down,
And it shall fall, to rise no more.
In that day, the LORD will punish
The host of heaven in heaven
And the kings of the earth on earth.
They shall be gathered in a dungeon
As captives are gathered;
And shall be locked up in a prison.
But after many days they shall be
   remembered.
Then the moon shall be ashamed,
And the sun shall be abashed.
For the LORD of Hosts will reign

פַּחַד וָפַחַת וָפָח
עָלֶיךָ יוֹשֵׁב הָאָרֶץ
וְהָיָה הַנָּס מִקּוֹל הַפַּחַד
יִפֹּל אֶל־הַפַּחַת
וְהָעוֹלֶה מִתּוֹךְ הַפַּחַת
יִלָּכֵד בַּפָּח
כִּי־אֲרֻבּוֹת מִמָּרוֹם נִפְתָּחוּ
וַיִּרְעֲשׁוּ מוֹסְדֵי אָרֶץ

רֹעָה הִתְרֹעֲעָה הָאָרֶץ
פּוֹר הִתְפּוֹרְרָה אָרֶץ
מוֹט הִתְמוֹטְטָה אָרֶץ
נוֹעַ תָּנוּעַ אֶרֶץ כַּשִּׁכּוֹר
וְהִתְנוֹדְדָה כַּמְּלוּנָה
וְכָבַד עָלֶיהָ פִּשְׁעָהּ
וְנָפְלָה וְלֹא־תֹסִיף קוּם

וְהָיָה בַּיּוֹם הַהוּא יִפְקֹד יְהוָה
עַל־צְבָא הַמָּרוֹם בַּמָּרוֹם
וְעַל־מַלְכֵי הָאֲדָמָה עַל־הָאֲדָמָה
וְאֻסְּפוּ אֲסֵפָה
אַסִּיר עַל־בּוֹר
וְסֻגְּרוּ עַל־מַסְגֵּר
וּמֵרֹב יָמִים יִפָּקֵדוּ

וְחָפְרָה הַלְּבָנָה
וּבוֹשָׁה הַחַמָּה
כִּי־מָלַךְ יְהוָה צְבָאוֹת

On Mount Zion and in Jerusalem,
And the Presence will be revealed to His
elders.

Isaiah 24:17–23

The Streets of Jerusalem

Roam the streets of Jerusalem,
Search its squares,
Look about and take note:
You will not find a man,
There is none who acts justly,
Who seeks integrity—
That I should pardon her.
Even when they say, "As the LORD lives,"
They are sure to be swearing falsely.
O LORD, Your eyes look for integrity.
You have struck them, but they sensed no
   pain;
You have consumed them, but they would
   accept no discipline.
They made their faces harder than rock,
They refused to turn back.
Then I thought: These are just poor folk;
They act foolishly;
For they do not know the way of the LORD,
The rules of their God.
So I will go to the wealthy
And speak with them:
Surely they know the way of the LORD,
The rules of their God.

בְּהַר צִיּוֹן וּבִירוּשָׁלַ‍ִם
וְנֶגֶד זְקֵנָיו כָּבוֹד

שׁוֹטְטוּ בְּחוּצוֹת יְרוּשָׁלַ‍ִם
וּרְאוּ־נָא וּדְעוּ
וּבַקְשׁוּ בִרְחוֹבוֹתֶיהָ
אִם־תִּמְצְאוּ אִישׁ
אִם־יֵשׁ עֹשֶׂה מִשְׁפָּט
מְבַקֵּשׁ אֱמוּנָה
וְאֶסְלַח לָהּ
וְאִם חַי־יְהוָֹה יֹאמֵרוּ
לָכֵן לַשֶּׁקֶר יִשָּׁבֵעוּ
יְהוָֹה עֵינֶיךָ הֲלוֹא לֶאֱמוּנָה
הִכִּיתָה אֹתָם וְלֹא־חָלוּ
כִּלִּיתָם מֵאֲנוּ קַחַת מוּסָר
חִזְּקוּ פְנֵיהֶם מִסֶּלַע
מֵאֲנוּ לָשׁוּב
וַאֲנִי אָמַרְתִּי אַךְ־דַּלִּים הֵם
נוֹאָלוּ
כִּי לֹא יָדְעוּ דֶּרֶךְ יְהוָֹה
מִשְׁפַּט אֱלֹהֵיהֶם
אֵלֲכָה־לִּי אֶל־הַגְּדֹלִים
וַאֲדַבְּרָה אוֹתָם
כִּי הֵמָּה יָדְעוּ דֶּרֶךְ יְהוָֹה
מִשְׁפַּט אֱלֹהֵיהֶם

But they as well had broken the yoke,
Had snapped the bonds.
Therefore,
The lion of the forest strikes them down,
The wolf of the desert ravages them.
A leopard lies in wait by their towns;
Whoever leaves them will be torn in pieces.
For their transgressions are many,
Their rebellious acts unnumbered.
Why should I forgive you?
Your children have forsaken Me
And sworn by no-gods.
When I fed them their fill,
They committed adultery
And went trooping to the harlot's house.
They were well-fed, lusty stallions,
Each neighing at another's wife.
Shall I not punish such deeds?
                              —says the LORD—

Jeremiah 5:1–9

Howl, Shepherds

Howl, you shepherds, and yell,
Strew dust on yourselves, you lords of the
      flock!
For the day of your slaughter draws near.
I will break you in pieces,
And you shall fall like a precious vessel.
Flight shall fail the shepherds,
And escape, the lords of the flock.

אַךְ הֵמָּה יַחְדָּו שָׁבְרוּ עֹל
נִתְּקוּ מוֹסֵרוֹת
עַל־כֵּן
הִכָּם אַרְיֵה מִיַּעַר
זְאֵב עֲרָבוֹת יְשָׁדְדֵם
נָמֵר שֹׁקֵד עַל־עָרֵיהֶם
כָּל־הַיּוֹצֵא מֵהֵנָּה יִטָּרֵף
כִּי רַבּוּ פִּשְׁעֵיהֶם
עָצְמוּ מְשֻׁבוֹתֵיהֶם
אֵי לָזֹאת אסלוח אֶסְלַח־לָךְ
בָּנַיִךְ עֲזָבוּנִי
וַיִּשָּׁבְעוּ בְּלֹא אֱלֹהִים
וָאַשְׂבִּעַ אוֹתָם
וַיִּנְאָפוּ
וּבֵית זוֹנָה יִתְגֹּדָדוּ
סוּסִים מְיֻזָּנִים מַשְׁכִּים הָיוּ
אִישׁ אֶל־אֵשֶׁת רֵעֵהוּ יִצְהָלוּ
הַעַל־אֵלֶּה לוֹא־אֶפְקֹד
נְאֻם־יְהוָה

הֵילִילוּ הָרֹעִים וְזַעֲקוּ
וְהִתְפַּלְּשׁוּ אַדִּירֵי הַצֹּאן
כִּי־מָלְאוּ יְמֵיכֶם לִטְבוֹחַ
וּתְפוֹצוֹתִיכֶם
וּנְפַלְתֶּם כִּכְלִי חֶמְדָּה
וְאָבַד מָנוֹס מִן־הָרֹעִים
וּפְלֵיטָה מֵאַדִּירֵי הַצֹּאן

Hark, the outcry of the shepherds,
And the howls of the lords of the flock!
For the LORD is ravaging their pasture.
The peaceful meadows shall be wiped out
By the fierce wrath of the LORD.
Like a lion, He has gone forth from His lair;
The land has become a desolation,
Because of the oppressive wrath,
Because of His fierce anger.

Jeremiah 25:34–38

Wail

Wail, alas for the day!
For a day is near;
A day of the LORD is near.
It will be a day of cloud,
An hour of invading nations.
A sword shall pierce Egypt,
And Nubia shall be seized with trembling,
When men fall slain in Egypt
And her wealth is seized
And her foundations are overthrown.
Nubia, Put, and Lud, and all the mixed
    populations, and Cub, and the inhabitants
    of the allied countries shall fall by the
    sword with them.
Thus said the LORD:
Those who support Egypt shall fall,
And her proud strength shall sink;
There they shall fall by the sword,

קוֹל צַעֲקַת הָרֹעִים
וִילְלַת אַדִּירֵי הַצֹּאן
כִּי־שֹׁדֵד יְהוָה אֶת־מַרְעִיתָם
וְנָדַמּוּ נְאוֹת הַשָּׁלוֹם
מִפְּנֵי חֲרוֹן אַף־יְהוָה
עָזַב כַּכְּפִיר סֻכּוֹ
כִּי־הָיְתָה אַרְצָם לְשַׁמָּה
מִפְּנֵי חֲרוֹן הַיּוֹנָה
וּמִפְּנֵי חֲרוֹן אַפּוֹ

הֵילִילוּ הָהּ לַיּוֹם
כִּי־קָרוֹב יוֹם
וְקָרוֹב יוֹם לַיהוָה
יוֹם עָנָן
עֵת גּוֹיִם יִהְיֶה
וּבָאָה חֶרֶב בְּמִצְרַיִם
וְהָיְתָה חַלְחָלָה בְּכוּשׁ
בִּנְפֹל חָלָל בְּמִצְרָיִם
וְלָקְחוּ הֲמוֹנָהּ
וְנֶהֶרְסוּ יְסוֹדֹתֶיהָ
כּוּשׁ וּפוּט וְלוּד וְכָל־הָעֶרֶב וְכוּב וּבְנֵי
אֶרֶץ הַבְּרִית אִתָּם בַּחֶרֶב יִפֹּלוּ
כֹּה אָמַר יְהוָה
וְנָפְלוּ סֹמְכֵי מִצְרַיִם
וְיָרַד גְּאוֹן עֻזָּהּ
מִמִּגְדֹּל סְוֵנֵה

From Migdol to Syene
—declares the LORD GOD.

Ezekiel 30:2–6

Lofty Egypt

O mortal, say to Pharaoh king of Egypt and
   his hordes:
Who was comparable to you in greatness?
Assyria was a cedar in Lebanon
With beautiful branches and shady thickets,
Of lofty stature,
With its top among leafy trees.
Waters nourished it,
The deep made it grow tall,
Washing with its streams
The place where it was planted,
Making its channels well up
To all the trees of the field.
Therefore it exceeded in stature
All the trees of the field;
Its branches multiplied and its boughs grew
   long
Because of the abundant water
That welled up for it.
In its branches nested
All the birds of the sky;
All the beasts of the field
Bore their young under its boughs,
And in its shadow lived
All the great nations.

בַּחֶרֶב יִפְּלוּ־בָהּ
נְאֻם אֲדֹנָי יְהוִה

בֶּן־אָדָם אֱמֹר אֶל־פַּרְעֹה
מֶלֶךְ־מִצְרַיִם וְאֶל־הֲמוֹנוֹ
אֶל־מִי דָּמִיתָ בְגָדְלֶךָ
הִנֵּה אַשּׁוּר אֶרֶז בַּלְּבָנוֹן
יְפֵה עָנָף וְחֹרֶשׁ מֵצַל
וּגְבַהּ קוֹמָה
וּבֵין עֲבֹתִים הָיְתָה צַמַּרְתּוֹ
מַיִם גִּדְּלוּהוּ
תְּהוֹם רֹמְמָתְהוּ
אֶת־נַהֲרֹתֶיהָ
הֹלֵךְ סְבִיבוֹת מַטָּעָהּ
וְאֶת־תְּעָלֹתֶיהָ שִׁלְּחָה
אֶל כָּל־עֲצֵי הַשָּׂדֶה
עַל־כֵּן גָּבְהָא קֹמָתוֹ
מִכֹּל עֲצֵי הַשָּׂדֶה
וַתִּרְבֶּינָה סַרְעַפֹּתָיו וַתֶּאֱרַכְנָה פארתו
פֹארֹתָיו
מִמַּיִם רַבִּים
בְּשַׁלְּחוֹ
בִּסְעַפֹּתָיו קִנְנוּ
כָּל־עוֹף הַשָּׁמַיִם
וְתַחַת פֹּארֹתָיו יָלְדוּ
כֹּל חַיַּת הַשָּׂדֶה
וּבְצִלּוֹ יֵשְׁבוּ
כֹּל גּוֹיִם רַבִּים

173

It was beautiful in its height,
In the length of its branches,
Because its stock stood
By abundant waters.
Cedars in the garden of God
Could not compare with it;
Cypresses could not match its boughs,
And plane trees could not vie with its
    branches;
No tree in the garden of God
Was its peer in beauty.
I made it beautiful
In the profusion of its branches;
And all the trees of Eden envied it
In the garden of God.

Ezekiel 31:2–9

The LORD Roars from Zion

The LORD roars from Zion,
Shouts aloud from Jerusalem;
And the pastures of the shepherds shall
    languish,
And the summit of Carmel shall wither.
Thus said the LORD:
For three transgressions of Damascus,
For four, I will not revoke it:
Because they threshed Gilead
With threshing boards of iron.

וַיְּיְף בְּגָדְלוֹ
בְּאֹרֶךְ דָּלִיּוֹתָיו
כִּי־הָיָה שָׁרְשׁוֹ
אֶל־מַיִם רַבִּים
אֲרָזִים לֹא־עֲמָמֻהוּ בְּגַן־אֱלֹהִים
בְּרוֹשִׁים לֹא דָמוּ אֶל־סְעַפֹּתָיו
וְעַרְמֹנִים לֹא־הָיוּ כְּפֹארֹתָיו
כָּל־עֵץ בְּגַן־אֱלֹהִים
לֹא־דָמָה אֵלָיו בְּיָפְיוֹ
יָפֶה עֲשִׂיתִיו
בְּרֹב דָּלִיּוֹתָיו
וַיְקַנְאֻהוּ כָּל־עֲצֵי־עֵדֶן
אֲשֶׁר בְּגַן הָאֱלֹהִים

יְהוָה מִצִּיּוֹן יִשְׁאָג
וּמִירוּשָׁלִַם יִתֵּן קוֹלוֹ
וְאָבְלוּ נְאוֹת הָרֹעִים
וְיָבֵשׁ רֹאשׁ הַכַּרְמֶל
כֹּה אָמַר יְהוָה
עַל־שְׁלֹשָׁה פִּשְׁעֵי דַמֶּשֶׂק
וְעַל־אַרְבָּעָה לֹא אֲשִׁיבֶנּוּ
עַל־דּוּשָׁם
בַּחֲרֻצוֹת הַבַּרְזֶל אֶת־הַגִּלְעָד

175

I will send down fire upon the palace of
   Hazael,
And it shall devour the fortresses of Ben-hadad.
I will break the gate bars of Damascus,
And wipe out the inhabitants from the Vale of
   Aven
And the sceptered ruler of Beth-eden;
And the people of Aram shall be exiled to
   Kir
                      —said the LORD.

Amos 1:2–5

Who Can Prophesy

Hear this word, O people of Israel,
That the LORD has spoken concerning you,
Concerning the whole family that I brought up
   from the land of Egypt:
You alone have I singled out
Of all the families of the earth—
That is why I will call you to account
For all your iniquities.
Can two walk together
Without having met?
Does a lion roar in the forest
When he has no prey?
Does a great beast let out a cry from its den
Without having made a capture?
Does a bird drop on the ground—in a trap—
With no snare there?
Does a trap spring up from the ground

וְשִׁלַּחְתִּי אֵשׁ בְּבֵית חֲזָאֵל
וְאָכְלָה אַרְמְנוֹת בֶּן־הֲדָד
וְשָׁבַרְתִּי בְּרִיחַ דַּמֶּשֶׂק
וְהִכְרַתִּי יוֹשֵׁב מִבִּקְעַת־אָוֶן
וְתוֹמֵךְ שֵׁבֶט מִבֵּית עֶדֶן
וְגָלוּ עַם־אֲרָם קִירָה
אָמַר יְהוָה

שִׁמְעוּ אֶת־הַדָּבָר הַזֶּה
אֲשֶׁר דִּבֶּר יְהוָה עֲלֵיכֶם בְּנֵי יִשְׂרָאֵל
עַל כָּל־הַמִּשְׁפָּחָה אֲשֶׁר הֶעֱלֵיתִי מֵאֶרֶץ
מִצְרַיִם לֵאמֹר
רַק אֶתְכֶם יָדַעְתִּי
מִכֹּל מִשְׁפְּחוֹת הָאֲדָמָה
עַל־כֵּן אֶפְקֹד עֲלֵיכֶם
אֵת כָּל־עֲוֹנֹתֵיכֶם
הֲיֵלְכוּ שְׁנַיִם יַחְדָּו
בִּלְתִּי אִם־נוֹעָדוּ
הֲיִשְׁאַג אַרְיֵה בַּיַּעַר
וְטֶרֶף אֵין לוֹ
הֲיִתֵּן כְּפִיר קוֹלוֹ מִמְּעֹנָתוֹ
בִּלְתִּי אִם־לָכָד
הֲתִפֹּל צִפּוֹר עַל־פַּח הָאָרֶץ
וּמוֹקֵשׁ אֵין לָהּ
הֲיַעֲלֶה־פַּח מִן־הָאֲדָמָה

Unless it has caught something?
When a ram's horn is sounded in a town,
Do the people not take alarm?
Can misfortune come to a town
If the LORD has not caused it?
Indeed, my LORD GOD does nothing
Without having revealed His purpose
To His servants the prophets.
A lion has roared,
Who can but fear?
My LORD GOD has spoken,
Who can but prophesy?
Proclaim in the fortresses of Ashdod
And in the fortresses of the land of Egypt!
Say:
Gather on the hill of Samaria
And witness the great outrages within her
And the oppression in her midst.
They are incapable of doing right
                    —declares the LORD.

Amos 3:1–10

Nineveh's Pride

Ah, city of crime,
Utterly treacherous,
Full of violence,
Where killing never stops!
Crack of whip
And rattle of wheel,
Galloping steed

וְלָכוֹד לֹא יִלְכּוֹד
אִם־יִתָּקַע שׁוֹפָר בְּעִיר
וְעָם לֹא יֶחֱרָדוּ
אִם־תִּהְיֶה רָעָה בְּעִיר
וַיהוָה לֹא עָשָׂה
כִּי לֹא יַעֲשֶׂה אֲדֹנָי יְהוִה דָּבָר
כִּי אִם־גָּלָה סוֹדוֹ
אֶל־עֲבָדָיו הַנְּבִיאִים
אַרְיֵה שָׁאָג
מִי לֹא יִירָא
אֲדֹנָי יְהוִה דִּבֶּר
מִי לֹא יִנָּבֵא
הַשְׁמִיעוּ עַל־אַרְמְנוֹת בְּאַשְׁדּוֹד
וְעַל־אַרְמְנוֹת בְּאֶרֶץ מִצְרָיִם
וְאִמְרוּ
הֵאָסְפוּ עַל־הָרֵי שֹׁמְרוֹן
וּרְאוּ מְהוּמֹת רַבּוֹת בְּתוֹכָהּ
וַעֲשׁוּקִים בְּקִרְבָּהּ
וְלֹא־יָדְעוּ עֲשׂוֹת־נְכֹחָה
נְאֻם־יְהוָה

הוֹי עִיר דָּמִים
כֻּלָּהּ כַּחַשׁ
פֶּרֶק מְלֵאָה
לֹא יָמִישׁ טָרֶף
קוֹל שׁוֹט
וְקוֹל רַעַשׁ אוֹפָן
וְסוּס דֹּהֵר

And bounding chariot!
Charging horsemen,
Flashing swords,
And glittering spears!
Hosts of slain
And heaps of corpses,
Dead bodies without number—
They stumble over bodies.
Because of the countless harlotries of the
   harlot,
The winsome mistress of sorcery,
Who ensnared nations with her harlotries
And peoples with her sorcery,
I am going to deal with you
          —declares the LORD of Hosts.
I will lift up your skirts over your face
And display your nakedness to the nations
And your shame to kingdoms.
I will throw loathsome things over you
And disfigure you
And make a spectacle of you.
All who see you will recoil from you
And will say,
"Nineveh has been ravaged!"
Who will console her?
Where shall I look for
Anyone to comfort you?
Were you any better than No-amon,
Which sat by the Nile,
Surrounded by water—
Its rampart a river,
Its wall consisting of sea?
Populous Nubia
And teeming Egypt,

וּמֶרְכָּבָה מְרַקֵּדָה
פָּרָשׁ מַעֲלֶה
וְלַהַב חֶרֶב
וּבְרַק חֲנִית
וְרֹב חָלָל
וְכֹבֶד פָּגֶר
וְאֵין קֵצֶה לַגְּוִיָּה
יכשלו וְכָשְׁלוּ בִּגְוִיָּתָם
מֵרֹב זְנוּנֵי זוֹנָה
טוֹבַת חֵן בַּעֲלַת כְּשָׁפִים
הַמֹּכֶרֶת גּוֹיִם בִּזְנוּנֶיהָ
וּמִשְׁפָּחוֹת בִּכְשָׁפֶיהָ
הִנְנִי אֵלַיִךְ
נְאֻם יְהוָה צְבָאוֹת
וְגִלֵּיתִי שׁוּלַיִךְ עַל־פָּנָיִךְ
וְהַרְאֵיתִי גוֹיִם מַעְרֵךְ
וּמַמְלָכוֹת קְלוֹנֵךְ
וְהִשְׁלַכְתִּי עָלַיִךְ שִׁקֻּצִים
וְנִבַּלְתִּיךְ
וְשַׂמְתִּיךְ כְּרֹאִי
וְהָיָה כָל־רֹאַיִךְ יִדּוֹד מִמֵּךְ
וְאָמַר
שָׁדְדָה נִינְוֵה
מִי יָנוּד לָהּ
מֵאַיִן אֲבַקֵּשׁ
מְנַחֲמִים לָךְ
הֲתֵיטְבִי מִנֹּא אָמוֹן
הַיֹּשְׁבָה בַּיְאֹרִים
מַיִם סָבִיב לָהּ
אֲשֶׁר־חֵיל יָם
מִיָּם חוֹמָתָהּ
כּוּשׁ עָצְמָה
וּמִצְרַיִם וְאֵין קֵצֶה

181

Put and the Libyans—
They were her helpers.
Yet even she was exiled,
She went into captivity.
Her babes, too, were dashed in pieces
At every street corner.
Lots were cast for her honored men,
And all her nobles were bound in chains.
You too shall be drunk
And utterly overcome;
You too shall seek
A refuge from the enemy.
All your forts are fig trees
With ripe fruit;
If shaken they will fall
Into the mouths of devourers.
Truly, the troops within you are women;
The gates of your land have opened themselves
To your enemies;
Fire has consumed your gate bars.
Draw water for the siege,
Strengthen your forts;
Tread the clay,
Trample the mud,
Grasp the brick mold!
There fire will devour you,
The sword will put an end to you;
It will devour you like the grub.
Multiply like grubs,
Multiply like locusts!
You had more traders
Than the sky has stars—
The grubs cast their skins and fly away.
Your guards were like locusts,

פּוּט וְלוּבִים
הָיוּ בְּעֶזְרָתֵךְ
גַּם־הִיא לַגֹּלָה
הָלְכָה בַשֶּׁבִי
גַּם עֹלָלֶיהָ יְרֻטְּשׁוּ
בְּרֹאשׁ כָּל־חוּצוֹת
וְעַל־נִכְבַּדֶּיהָ יַדּוּ גוֹרָל
וְכָל־גְּדוֹלֶיהָ רֻתְּקוּ בַזִּקִּים
גַּם־אַתְּ תִּשְׁכְּרִי
תְּהִי נַעֲלָמָה
גַּם־אַתְּ תְּבַקְשִׁי
מָעוֹז מֵאוֹיֵב
כָּל־מִבְצָרַיִךְ תְּאֵנִים
עִם־בִּכּוּרִים
אִם־יִנּוֹעוּ וְנָפְלוּ
עַל־פִּי אוֹכֵל
הִנֵּה עַמֵּךְ נָשִׁים בְּקִרְבֵּךְ
לְאֹיְבַיִךְ
פָּתוֹחַ נִפְתְּחוּ שַׁעֲרֵי אַרְצֵךְ
אָכְלָה אֵשׁ בְּרִיחָיִךְ
מֵי מָצוֹר שַׁאֲבִי־לָךְ
חַזְּקִי מִבְצָרָיִךְ
בֹּאִי בַטִּיט
וְרִמְסִי בַחֹמֶר
הַחֲזִיקִי מַלְבֵּן
שָׁם תֹּאכְלֵךְ אֵשׁ
תַּכְרִיתֵךְ חֶרֶב
תֹּאכְלֵךְ כַּיָּלֶק
הִתְכַּבֵּד כַּיֶּלֶק
הִתְכַּבְּדִי כָאַרְבֶּה
הִרְבֵּית רֹכְלַיִךְ
מִכּוֹכְבֵי הַשָּׁמָיִם
יֶלֶק פָּשַׁט וַיָּעֹף
מִנְּזָרַיִךְ כָּאַרְבֶּה

183

Your marshals like piles of hoppers
Which settle on the stone fences
On a chilly day;
When the sun comes out, they fly away,
And where they are nobody knows.
Your shepherds are slumbering,
O king of Assyria;
Your sheepmasters are lying inert;
Your people are scattered over the hills,
And there is none to gather them.
There is no healing for your injury;
Your wound is grievous.
All who hear the news about you
Clap their hands over you.
For who has not suffered
From your constant malice?

Nahum 3:1–19

Howl, Cypresses

Throw open your gates, O Lebanon,
And let fire consume your cedars!
Howl, cypresses, for cedars have fallen!
How the mighty are ravaged!
Howl, you oaks of Bashan,
For the stately forest is laid low!
Hark, the wailing of the shepherds,
For their rich pastures are ravaged;
Hark, the roaring of the great beasts,
For the jungle of the Jordan is ravaged.

Zechariah 11:1–3

וְטַפְסְרַיִךְ כְּגוֹב גֹּבָי
הַחוֹנִים בַּגְּדֵרוֹת
בְּיוֹם קָרָה
שֶׁמֶשׁ זָרְחָה וְנוֹדַד
וְלֹא־נוֹדַע מְקוֹמוֹ אַיָּם
נָמוּ רֹעֶיךָ
מֶלֶךְ אַשּׁוּר
יִשְׁכְּנוּ אַדִּירֶיךָ
נָפֹשׁוּ עַמְּךָ עַל־הֶהָרִים
וְאֵין מְקַבֵּץ
אֵין־כֵּהָה לְשִׁבְרֶךָ
נַחְלָה מַכָּתֶךָ
כֹּל שֹׁמְעֵי שִׁמְעֲךָ
תָּקְעוּ כַף עָלֶיךָ
כִּי עַל־מִי לֹא־עָבְרָה
רָעָתְךָ תָּמִיד

פְּתַח לְבָנוֹן דְּלָתֶיךָ
וְתֹאכַל אֵשׁ בַּאֲרָזֶיךָ
הֵילֵל בְּרוֹשׁ כִּי־נָפַל אֶרֶז
אֲשֶׁר אַדִּרִים שֻׁדָּדוּ
הֵילִילוּ אַלּוֹנֵי בָשָׁן
כִּי יָרַד יַעַר הבצור הַבָּצִיר
קוֹל יִלְלַת הָרֹעִים
כִּי שֻׁדְּדָה אַדַּרְתָּם
קוֹל שַׁאֲגַת כְּפִירִים
כִּי שֻׁדַּד גְּאוֹן הַיַּרְדֵּן

PROPHECIES OF SALVATION AND CONSOLATION

Swords into Plowshares

In the days to come,
The Mount of the LORD's House
Shall stand firm above the mountains
And tower above the hills;
And all the nations
Shall gaze on it with joy.
And the many peoples shall go and say:
"Come,
Let us go up to the Mount of the LORD,
To the House of the God of Jacob;
That He may instruct us in His ways,
And that we may walk in His paths."
For instruction shall come forth from Zion,
The word of the LORD from Jerusalem.
Thus He will judge among the nations
And arbitrate for the many peoples,
And they shall beat their swords into
    plowshares
And their spears into pruning hooks:
Nation shall not take up
Sword against nation;
They shall never again know war.

Isaiah 2:2–4

וְהָיָה בְּאַחֲרִית הַיָּמִים
נָכוֹן יִהְיֶה הַר בֵּית־יְהוָה
בְּרֹאשׁ הֶהָרִים
וְנִשָּׂא מִגְּבָעוֹת
וְנָהֲרוּ אֵלָיו
כָּל־הַגּוֹיִם
וְהָלְכוּ עַמִּים רַבִּים וְאָמְרוּ
לְכוּ
וְנַעֲלֶה אֶל־הַר־יְהוָה
אֶל־בֵּית אֱלֹהֵי יַעֲקֹב
וְיֹרֵנוּ מִדְּרָכָיו
וְנֵלְכָה בְּאֹרְחֹתָיו
כִּי מִצִּיּוֹן תֵּצֵא תוֹרָה
וּדְבַר־יְהוָה מִירוּשָׁלָיִם
וְשָׁפַט בֵּין הַגּוֹיִם
וְהוֹכִיחַ לְעַמִּים רַבִּים
וְכִתְּתוּ חַרְבוֹתָם לְאִתִּים
וַחֲנִיתוֹתֵיהֶם לְמַזְמֵרוֹת
לֹא־יִשָּׂא גוֹי
אֶל־גּוֹי חֶרֶב
וְלֹא־יִלְמְדוּ עוֹד מִלְחָמָה

I Will Betroth You

Assuredly,
I will speak coaxingly to her
And lead her through the wilderness
And speak to her tenderly.
I will give her her vineyards from there,
And the Valley of Achor as a plowland of
    hope.
There she shall respond as in the days of her
    youth,
When she came up from the land of Egypt.
And in that day
                —declares the LORD—
You will call [Me] Ishi,
And no more will you call Me Baali.
For I will remove the names of the Baalim
    from her mouth,
And they shall nevermore be mentioned by
    name
In that day, I will make a covenant for them
    with the beasts of the field, the birds of the
    air, and the creeping things of the ground;
    I will also banish bow, sword, and war
    from the land. Thus I will let them lie
    down in safety.
And I will espouse you forever:
I will espouse you with righteousness and
    justice,
And with goodness and mercy,
And I will espouse you with faithfulness;
Then you shall be devoted to the LORD.
In that day,

לָכֵן
הִנֵּה אָנֹכִי מְפַתֶּיהָ
וְהֹלַכְתִּיהָ הַמִּדְבָּר
וְדִבַּרְתִּי עַל־לִבָּהּ
וְנָתַתִּי לָהּ אֶת־כְּרָמֶיהָ מִשָּׁם
וְאֶת־עֵמֶק עָכוֹר לְפֶתַח תִּקְוָה
וְעָנְתָה שָּׁמָּה כִּימֵי נְעוּרֶיהָ
וּכְיוֹם עֲלֹתָהּ מֵאֶרֶץ־מִצְרָיִם
וְהָיָה בַיּוֹם־הַהוּא
נְאֻם־יְהוָה
תִּקְרְאִי אִישִׁי
וְלֹא־תִקְרְאִי־לִי עוֹד בַּעְלִי
וַהֲסִרֹתִי אֶת־שְׁמוֹת הַבְּעָלִים מִפִּיהָ
וְלֹא־יִזָּכְרוּ עוֹד בִּשְׁמָם
וְכָרַתִּי לָהֶם בְּרִית בַּיּוֹם הַהוּא עִם־חַיַּת
הַשָּׂדֶה וְעִם־עוֹף הַשָּׁמַיִם וְרֶמֶשׂ הָאֲדָמָה
וְקֶשֶׁת וְחֶרֶב וּמִלְחָמָה אֶשְׁבּוֹר מִן־הָאָרֶץ
וְהִשְׁכַּבְתִּים לָבֶטַח
וְאֵרַשְׂתִּיךְ לִי לְעוֹלָם
וְאֵרַשְׂתִּיךְ לִי בְּצֶדֶק וּבְמִשְׁפָּט
וּבְחֶסֶד וּבְרַחֲמִים
וְאֵרַשְׂתִּיךְ לִי בֶּאֱמוּנָה
וְיָדַעַתְּ אֶת־יְהוָה
וְהָיָה בַּיּוֹם הַהוּא

I will respond

—declares the LORD.

I will respond to the sky,
And it shall respond to the earth;
And the earth shall respond
With new grain and wine and oil,
And they shall respond to Jezreel.
I will sow her in the land as My own;
And take Lo-ruhamah back in favor;
And I will say to Lo-ammi, "[You are] My
   people,"
And he will respond, "[You are] my God."

Hosea 2:16–25

Paternal Love

God's love of Israel described as a parent-child relationship

I fell in love with Israel
When he was still a child;
And I have called him My son
Ever since Egypt.
Thus were they called,
But they went their own way;
They sacrifice to Baalim
And offer to carved images.
I have pampered Ephraim,
Taking them in My arms;
But they have ignored
My healing care.
I drew them with human ties,
With cords of love;
But I seemed to them as one

אֶעֱנֶה
נְאֻם־יְהֹוָה
אֶעֱנֶה אֶת־הַשָּׁמָיִם
וְהֵם יַעֲנוּ אֶת־הָאָרֶץ
וְהָאָרֶץ תַּעֲנֶה
אֶת־הַדָּגָן וְאֶת־הַתִּירוֹשׁ וְאֶת־הַיִּצְהָר
וְהֵם יַעֲנוּ אֶת־יִזְרְעֶאל
וּזְרַעְתִּיהָ לִי בָּאָרֶץ
וְרִחַמְתִּי אֶת־לֹא רֻחָמָה
וְאָמַרְתִּי לְלֹא־עַמִּי עַמִּי־אַתָּה
וְהוּא יֹאמַר אֱלֹהָי

כִּי נַעַר יִשְׂרָאֵל
וָאֹהֲבֵהוּ
וּמִמִּצְרַיִם
קָרָאתִי לִבְנִי
קָרְאוּ לָהֶם
כֵּן הָלְכוּ מִפְּנֵיהֶם
לַבְּעָלִים יְזַבֵּחוּ
וְלַפְּסִלִים יְקַטֵּרוּן
וְאָנֹכִי תִרְגַּלְתִּי לְאֶפְרַיִם
קָחָם עַל־זְרוֹעֹתָיו
וְלֹא יָדְעוּ
כִּי רְפָאתִים
בְּחַבְלֵי אָדָם אֶמְשְׁכֵם
בַּעֲבֹתוֹת אַהֲבָה
וָאֶהְיֶה לָהֶם

Who imposed a yoke on their jaws,
Though I was offering them food.
No!
They return to the land of Egypt,
And Assyria is their king.
Because they refuse to repent,
A sword shall descend upon their towns
And consume their limbs
And devour them because of their designs.
For My people persists
In its defection from Me;
When it is summoned upward,
It does not rise at all.
How can I give you up, O Ephraim?
How surrender you, O Israel?
How can I make you like Admah,
Render you like Zeboiim?
I have had a change of heart,
All My tenderness is stirred.
I will not act on My wrath,
Will not turn to destroy Ephraim.
For I am God, not man,
The Holy One in your midst:
I will not come in fury.
The LORD will roar like a lion,
And they shall march behind Him;
When He roars, His children shall come
Fluttering out of the west.
They shall flutter from Egypt like sparrows,
From the land of Assyria like doves;
And I will settle them in their homes
                              —declares the LORD.

Hosea 11:1–11

כִּמְרִימֵי עֹל עַל לְחֵיהֶם
וְאַט אֵלָיו אוֹכִיל
לֹא
יָשׁוּב אֶל־אֶרֶץ מִצְרַיִם
וְאַשּׁוּר הוּא מַלְכּוֹ
כִּי מֵאֲנוּ לָשׁוּב
וְחָלָה חֶרֶב בְּעָרָיו
וְכִלְּתָה בַדָּיו
וְאָכָלָה מִמֹּעֲצוֹתֵיהֶם
וְעַמִּי תְלוּאִים
לִמְשׁוּבָתִי
וְאֶל־עַל יִקְרָאֻהוּ
יַחַד לֹא יְרוֹמֵם
אֵיךְ אֶתֶּנְךָ אֶפְרַיִם
אֲמַגֶּנְךָ יִשְׂרָאֵל

אֵיךְ אֶתֶּנְךָ כְאַדְמָה
אֲשִׂימְךָ כִּצְבֹאיִם
נֶהְפַּךְ עָלַי לִבִּי
יַחַד נִכְמְרוּ נִחוּמָי
לֹא אֶעֱשֶׂה חֲרוֹן אַפִּי
לֹא אָשׁוּב לְשַׁחֵת אֶפְרָיִם
כִּי אֵל אָנֹכִי וְלֹא־אִישׁ
בְּקִרְבְּךָ קָדוֹשׁ
וְלֹא אָבוֹא בְּעִיר
אַחֲרֵי יְהֹוָה יֵלְכוּ
כְּאַרְיֵה יִשְׁאָג
כִּי־הוּא יִשְׁאַג
וְיֶחֶרְדוּ בָנִים מִיָּם
יֶחֶרְדוּ כְצִפּוֹר מִמִּצְרַיִם
וּכְיוֹנָה מֵאֶרֶץ אַשּׁוּר
וְהוֹשַׁבְתִּים עַל־בָּתֵּיהֶם
נְאֻם־יְהֹוָה

Blow a Horn in Zion

Blow a horn in Zion,
Solemnize a fast,
Proclaim an assembly!
Gather the people,
Bid the congregation purify themselves.
Bring together the old,
Gather the babes
And the sucklings at the breast;
Let the bridegroom come out of his chamber,
The bride from her canopied couch.
Between the portico and the altar,
Let the priests, the LORD's ministers, weep
And say:
"Oh, spare Your people, LORD!
Let not Your possession become a mockery,
To be taunted by nations!
Let not the peoples say,
'Where is their God?'"
Then the LORD was roused
On behalf of His land
And had compassion
Upon His people.
In response to His people
The LORD declared:
"I will grant you the new grain,
The new wine, and the new oil,
And you shall have them in abundance.
Nevermore will I let you be
A mockery among the nations.
I will drive the northerner far from you,

תִּקְעוּ שׁוֹפָר בְּצִיּוֹן
קַדְּשׁוּ־צוֹם
קִרְאוּ עֲצָרָה
אִסְפוּ־עָם
קַדְּשׁוּ קָהָל
קִבְצוּ זְקֵנִים
אִסְפוּ עוֹלָלִים
וְיֹנְקֵי שָׁדָיִם
יֵצֵא חָתָן מֵחֶדְרוֹ
וְכַלָּה מֵחֻפָּתָהּ
בֵּין הָאוּלָם וְלַמִּזְבֵּחַ
יִבְכּוּ הַכֹּהֲנִים מְשָׁרְתֵי יְהוָה
וְיֹאמְרוּ
חוּסָה יְהוָה עַל־עַמֶּךָ
וְאַל־תִּתֵּן נַחֲלָתְךָ לְחֶרְפָּה
לִמְשָׁל־בָּם גּוֹיִם
לָמָּה יֹאמְרוּ בָעַמִּים
אַיֵּה אֱלֹהֵיהֶם
וַיְקַנֵּא יְהוָה
לְאַרְצוֹ
וַיַּחְמֹל
עַל־עַמּוֹ
וַיַּעַן יְהוָה
וַיֹּאמֶר לְעַמּוֹ
הִנְנִי שֹׁלֵחַ לָכֶם אֶת־הַדָּגָן
וְהַתִּירוֹשׁ וְהַיִּצְהָר
וּשְׂבַעְתֶּם אֹתוֹ
וְלֹא־אֶתֵּן אֶתְכֶם עוֹד
חֶרְפָּה בַּגּוֹיִם
וְאֶת־הַצְּפוֹנִי אַרְחִיק מֵעֲלֵיכֶם

195

I will thrust it into a parched and desolate
   land—
Its van to the Eastern Sea
And its rear to the Western Sea;
And the stench of it shall go up,
And the foul smell rise."
For the LORD shall work great deeds.
Fear not, O soil, rejoice and be glad;
For the LORD has wrought great deeds.
Fear not, O beasts of the field,
For the pastures in the wilderness
Are clothed with grass.
The trees have borne their fruit;
Fig tree and vine
Have yielded their strength.
O children of Zion, be glad,
Rejoice in the LORD your God.
For He has given you the early rain in His
   kindness,
Now He makes the rain fall as formerly—
The early rain and the late—
And threshing floors shall be piled with
   grain,
And vats shall overflow with new wine and
   oil.
"I will repay you for the years
Consumed by swarms and hoppers,
By grubs and locusts,
The great army I let loose against you.
And you shall eat your fill
And praise the name of the LORD your God
Who dealt so wondrously with you—
My people shall be shamed no more.
And you shall know

וְהִדַּחְתִּיו אֶל־אֶרֶץ צִיָּה וּשְׁמָמָה
אֶת־פָּנָיו אֶל־הַיָּם הַקַּדְמֹנִי
וְסֹפוֹ אֶל־הַיָּם הָאַחֲרוֹן
וְעָלָה בָאְשׁוֹ
וְתַעַל צַחֲנָתוֹ
כִּי הִגְדִּיל לַעֲשׂוֹת
אַל־תִּירְאִי אֲדָמָה גִּילִי וּשְׂמָחִי
כִּי־הִגְדִּיל יְהוָה לַעֲשׂוֹת
אַל־תִּירְאוּ בַּהֲמוֹת שָׂדַי
כִּי דָשְׁאוּ נְאוֹת מִדְבָּר
כִּי־עֵץ נָשָׂא פִרְיוֹ
תְּאֵנָה וָגֶפֶן
נָתְנוּ חֵילָם
וּבְנֵי צִיּוֹן גִּילוּ
וְשִׂמְחוּ בַּיהוָה אֱלֹהֵיכֶם
כִּי־נָתַן לָכֶם אֶת־הַמּוֹרֶה לִצְדָקָה
וַיּוֹרֶד לָכֶם גֶּשֶׁם
מוֹרֶה וּמַלְקוֹשׁ בָּרִאשׁוֹן
וּמָלְאוּ הַגֳּרָנוֹת בָּר
וְהֵשִׁיקוּ הַיְקָבִים תִּירוֹשׁ וְיִצְהָר
וְשִׁלַּמְתִּי לָכֶם אֶת־הַשָּׁנִים
אֲשֶׁר אָכַל הָאַרְבֶּה הַיֶּלֶק
וְהֶחָסִיל וְהַגָּזָם
חֵילִי הַגָּדוֹל אֲשֶׁר שִׁלַּחְתִּי בָּכֶם
וַאֲכַלְתֶּם אָכוֹל וְשָׂבוֹעַ
וְהִלַּלְתֶּם אֶת־שֵׁם יְהוָה אֱלֹהֵיכֶם
אֲשֶׁר־עָשָׂה עִמָּכֶם לְהַפְלִיא
וְלֹא־יֵבֹשׁוּ עַמִּי לְעוֹלָם
וִידַעְתֶּם

That I am in the midst of Israel:
That I the LORD am your God
And there is no other.
And My people shall be shamed no more."

Joel 2:15–27

Rise Again

Do not rejoice over me,
O my enemy!
Though I have fallen, I rise again;
Though I sit in darkness, the LORD is my
   light.
I must bear the anger of the LORD,
Since I have sinned against Him,
Until He champions my cause
And upholds my claim.
He will let me out into the light;
I will enjoy vindication by Him.
When my enemy sees it,
She shall be covered with shame,
She who taunts me with "Where is He,
The LORD your God?"
My eyes shall behold her downfall;
Lo, she shall be for trampling
Like mud in the streets.
A day for mending your walls—
That is a far-off day.
This is rather a day when to you
Tramplers will come streaming
From Assyria and the towns of Egypt—

כִּי בְקֶרֶב יִשְׂרָאֵל אָנִי
וַאֲנִי יְהוָה אֱלֹהֵיכֶם
וְאֵין עוֹד
וְלֹא־יֵבֹשׁוּ עַמִּי לְעוֹלָם

אַל־תִּשְׂמְחִי
אֹיַבְתִּי לִי
כִּי נָפַלְתִּי קָמְתִּי
כִּי־אֵשֵׁב בַּחֹשֶׁךְ יְהוָה אוֹר לִי
זַעַף יְהוָה אֶשָּׂא
כִּי חָטָאתִי לוֹ
עַד אֲשֶׁר יָרִיב רִיבִי
וְעָשָׂה מִשְׁפָּטִי
יוֹצִיאֵנִי לָאוֹר
אֶרְאֶה בְּצִדְקָתוֹ
וְתֵרֶא אֹיַבְתִּי
וּתְכַסֶּהָ בוּשָׁה
הָאֹמְרָה אֵלַי אַיּוֹ
יְהוָה אֱלֹהָיִךְ
עֵינַי תִּרְאֶינָּה בָּהּ
עַתָּה תִּהְיֶה לְמִרְמָס
כְּטִיט חוּצוֹת
יוֹם לִבְנוֹת גְּדֵרָיִךְ
יוֹם הַהוּא יִרְחַק־חֹק
יוֹם הוּא וְעָדֶיךָ
יָבוֹא
לְמִנִּי אַשּׁוּר וְעָרֵי מָצוֹר

From every land from Egypt to the
   Euphrates,
From sea to sea and from mountain to
   mountain—
And your land shall become a desolation—
Because of those who dwell in it—
As the fruit of their misdeeds.
Oh, shepherd Your people with Your staff,
Your very own flock.
May they who dwell isolated
In a woodland surrounded by farmland
Graze Bashan and Gilead
As in olden days.
I will show him wondrous deeds
As in the days when You sallied forth from
   the land of Egypt.
Let nations behold and be ashamed
Despite all their might;
Let them put hand to mouth;
Let their ears be deafened!
Let them lick dust like snakes,
Like crawling things on the ground!
Let them come trembling out of their
   strongholds
To the LORD our God;
Let them fear and dread You!
Who is a God like You,
Forgiving iniquity
And remitting transgression;
Who has not maintained His wrath forever
Against the remnant of His own people,
Because He loves graciousness!
He will take us back in love;
He will cover up our iniquities,

וּלְמִנִּי מָצוֹר וְעַד־נָהָר
וְיָם מִיָּם וְהַר הָהָר
וְהָיְתָה הָאָרֶץ לִשְׁמָמָה
עַל־יֹשְׁבֶיהָ
מִפְּרִי מַעַלְלֵיהֶם
רְעֵה עַמְּךָ בְשִׁבְטֶךָ
צֹאן נַחֲלָתֶךָ
שֹׁכְנִי לְבָדָד
יַעַר בְּתוֹךְ כַּרְמֶל
יִרְעוּ בָשָׁן וְגִלְעָד
כִּימֵי עוֹלָם
כִּימֵי צֵאתְךָ מֵאֶרֶץ מִצְרָיִם
אַרְאֶנּוּ נִפְלָאוֹת
יִרְאוּ גוֹיִם וְיֵבֹשׁוּ

מִכֹּל גְּבוּרָתָם
יָשִׂימוּ יָד עַל־פֶּה
אָזְנֵיהֶם תֶּחֱרַשְׁנָה
יְלַחֲכוּ עָפָר כַּנָּחָשׁ
כְּזֹחֲלֵי אֶרֶץ
יִרְגְּזוּ מִמִּסְגְּרֹתֵיהֶם
אֶל־יְהוָה אֱלֹהֵינוּ
יִפְחֲדוּ וְיִרְאוּ מִמֶּךָּ
מִי־אֵל כָּמוֹךָ
נֹשֵׂא עָוֹן
וְעֹבֵר עַל־פֶּשַׁע
לִשְׁאֵרִית נַחֲלָתוֹ
לֹא־הֶחֱזִיק לָעַד אַפּוֹ
כִּי־חָפֵץ חֶסֶד הוּא
יָשׁוּב יְרַחֲמֵנוּ
יִכְבֹּשׁ עֲוֹנֹתֵינוּ

You will hurl all our sins
Into the depths of the sea.
You will keep faith with Jacob,
Loyalty to Abraham,
As You promised on oath to our fathers
In days gone by.

Micah 7:8–20

Joy to Jerusalem

Shout for joy, Fair Zion,
Cry aloud, O Israel!
Rejoice and be glad with all your heart,
Fair Jerusalem!
The LORD has annulled the judgment against
    you,
He has swept away your foes.
Israel's Sovereign the LORD is within you;
You need fear misfortune no more.
In that day,
This shall be said to Jerusalem:
Have no fear, O Zion;
Let not your hands droop!
Your God the LORD is in your midst,
A warrior who brings triumph.
He will rejoice over you and be glad,
He will shout over you with jubilation.
He will soothe with His love
Those long disconsolate.
I will take away from you the woe
Over which you endured mockery.

וְתַשְׁלִיךְ בִּמְצֻלוֹת יָם
כָּל־חַטֹּאותָם
תִּתֵּן אֱמֶת לְיַעֲקֹב
חֶסֶד לְאַבְרָהָם
אֲשֶׁר־נִשְׁבַּעְתָּ לַאֲבֹתֵינוּ
מִימֵי קֶדֶם

רָנִּי בַּת־צִיּוֹן
הָרִיעוּ יִשְׂרָאֵל
שִׂמְחִי וְעָלְזִי בְּכָל־לֵב
בַּת יְרוּשָׁלָ͏ִם
הֵסִיר יְהוָה מִשְׁפָּטַיִךְ
פִּנָּה אֹיְבֵךְ
מֶלֶךְ יִשְׂרָאֵל יְהוָה בְּקִרְבֵּךְ
לֹא־תִירְאִי רָע עוֹד
בַּיּוֹם הַהוּא
יֵאָמֵר לִירוּשָׁלַ͏ִם
אַל־תִּירָאִי צִיּוֹן
אַל־יִרְפּוּ יָדָיִךְ
יְהוָה אֱלֹהַיִךְ בְּקִרְבֵּךְ
גִּבּוֹר יוֹשִׁיעַ
יָשִׂישׂ עָלַיִךְ בְּשִׂמְחָה
יַחֲרִישׁ בְּאַהֲבָתוֹ
יָגִיל עָלַיִךְ בְּרִנָּה
נוּגֵי מִמּוֹעֵד
אָסַפְתִּי מִמֵּךְ הָיוּ
מַשְׂאֵת עָלֶיהָ חֶרְפָּה

At that time I will make an end
Of all who afflicted you.
And I will rescue the lame sheep
And gather the strayed;
And I will exchange their disgrace
For fame and renown in all the earth.
At that time I will gather you,
And at that time I will bring you home;
For I will make you renowned and famous
Among all the peoples on earth,
When I restore your fortunes
Before their very eyes

—said the LORD.

Zephaniah 3:14–20

הִנְנִי עֹשֶׂה אֶת־כָּל־מְעַנַּיִךְ
בָּעֵת הַהִיא
וְהוֹשַׁעְתִּי אֶת־הַצֹּלֵעָה
וְהַנִּדָּחָה אֲקַבֵּץ
וְשַׂמְתִּים לִתְהִלָּה וּלְשֵׁם
בְּכָל־הָאָרֶץ בָּשְׁתָּם
בָּעֵת הַהִיא אָבִיא אֶתְכֶם
וּבָעֵת קַבְּצִי אֶתְכֶם
כִּי־אֶתֵּן אֶתְכֶם לְשֵׁם וְלִתְהִלָּה
בְּכֹל עַמֵּי הָאָרֶץ
בְּשׁוּבִי אֶת־שְׁבוּתֵיכֶם
לְעֵינֵיכֶם
אָמַר יְהוָה

WISDOM WRITINGS

Happy Is the Man

Recited at the unveiling of a tombstone

Happy is the man who has not followed the
    counsel of the wicked,
or taken the path of sinners,
or joined the company of the insolent;
rather, the teaching of the LORD is his
    delight,
and he studies that teaching day and night.
He is like a tree planted beside streams of
    water,
which yields its fruit in season,
whose foliage never fades,
and whatever it produces thrives.
Not so the wicked;
rather, they are like chaff that wind blows
    away.
Therefore the wicked will not survive
    judgment,
nor will sinners, in the assembly of the
    righteous.
For the LORD cherishes the way of the
    righteous,
but the way of the wicked is doomed.

Psalms 1:1–6

אַשְׁרֵי־הָאִישׁ אֲשֶׁר לֹא הָלַךְ
בַּעֲצַת רְשָׁעִים
וּבְדֶרֶךְ חַטָּאִים לֹא עָמָד
וּבְמוֹשַׁב לֵצִים לֹא יָשָׁב
כִּי אִם בְּתוֹרַת יְהוָה חֶפְצוֹ
וּבְתוֹרָתוֹ יֶהְגֶּה יוֹמָם וָלָיְלָה
וְהָיָה כְּעֵץ שָׁתוּל עַל־פַּלְגֵי מָיִם
אֲשֶׁר פִּרְיוֹ יִתֵּן בְּעִתּוֹ
וְעָלֵהוּ לֹא־יִבּוֹל
וְכֹל אֲשֶׁר־יַעֲשֶׂה יַצְלִיחַ
לֹא־כֵן הָרְשָׁעִים
כִּי אִם־כַּמֹּץ אֲשֶׁר־תִּדְּפֶנּוּ רוּחַ
עַל־כֵּן לֹא־יָקֻמוּ רְשָׁעִים
בַּמִּשְׁפָּט
וְחַטָּאִים בַּעֲדַת צַדִּיקִים
כִּי־יוֹדֵעַ יְהוָה דֶּרֶךְ צַדִּיקִים
וְדֶרֶךְ רְשָׁעִים תֹּאבֵד

In Praise of Wisdom

For learning wisdom and discipline;
For understanding words of discernment;
For acquiring the discipline for success,
Righteousness, justice, and equity;
For endowing the simple with shrewdness,
The young with knowledge and foresight.
—The wise man, hearing them, will gain
   more wisdom;
The discerning man will learn to be adroit;
For understanding proverb and epigram,
The words of the wise and their riddles.
The fear of the LORD is the beginning of
   knowledge;
Fools despise wisdom and discipline.

Proverbs 1:2–7

Listen to Your Father
and Mother

My son, heed the discipline of your father,
And do not forsake the instruction of your
   mother;
For they are a graceful wreath upon your
   head,
A necklace about your throat.

Proverbs 1:8–9

לָדַעַת חָכְמָה וּמוּסָר
לְהָבִין אִמְרֵי בִינָה
לָקַחַת מוּסַר הַשְׂכֵּל
צֶדֶק וּמִשְׁפָּט וּמֵישָׁרִים
לָתֵת לִפְתָאיִם עָרְמָה
לְנַעַר דַּעַת וּמְזִמָּה
יִשְׁמַע חָכָם וְיוֹסֶף לֶקַח
וְנָבוֹן תַּחְבֻּלוֹת יִקְנֶה
לְהָבִין מָשָׁל וּמְלִיצָה
דִּבְרֵי חֲכָמִים וְחִידֹתָם
יִרְאַת יְהוָה רֵאשִׁית דָּעַת
חָכְמָה וּמוּסָר אֱוִילִים בָּזוּ

שְׁמַע בְּנִי מוּסַר אָבִיךָ
וְאַל-תִּטֹּשׁ תּוֹרַת אִמֶּךָ
כִּי לִוְיַת חֵן הֵם לְרֹאשֶׁךָ
וַעֲנָקִים לְגַרְגְּרֹתֶיךָ

The Way of the Good

So follow the way of the good
And keep to the paths of the just.
For the upright will inhabit the earth,
The blameless will remain in it.
While the wicked will vanish from the land
And the treacherous will be rooted out of it.

Proverbs 2:20–22

Tree of Life

Happy is the man who finds wisdom,
The man who attains understanding.
Her value in trade is better than silver,
Her yield, greater than gold.
She is more precious than rubies;
All of your goods cannot equal her.
In her right hand is length of days,
In her left, riches and honor.
Her ways are pleasant ways,
And all her paths, peaceful.
She is a tree of life to those who grasp her,
And whoever holds on to her is happy.

Proverbs 3:13–18

לְמַעַן תֵּלֵךְ בְּדֶרֶךְ טוֹבִים
וְאָרְחוֹת צַדִּיקִים תִּשְׁמֹר
כִּי־יְשָׁרִים יִשְׁכְּנוּ־אָרֶץ
וּתְמִימִים יִוָּתְרוּ בָהּ
וּרְשָׁעִים מֵאֶרֶץ יִכָּרֵתוּ
וּבוֹגְדִים יִסְּחוּ מִמֶּנָּה

אַשְׁרֵי אָדָם מָצָא חָכְמָה
וְאָדָם יָפִיק תְּבוּנָה
כִּי טוֹב סַחְרָהּ מִסְּחַר־כָּסֶף
וּמֵחָרוּץ תְּבוּאָתָהּ
יְקָרָה הִיא מִפְּנִיִּים מִפְּנִינִים
וְכָל־חֲפָצֶיךָ לֹא יִשְׁווּ־בָהּ
אֹרֶךְ יָמִים בִּימִינָהּ
בִּשְׂמֹאולָהּ עֹשֶׁר וְכָבוֹד
דְּרָכֶיהָ דַרְכֵי־נֹעַם
וְכָל־נְתִיבוֹתֶיהָ שָׁלוֹם
עֵץ־חַיִּים הִיא לַמַּחֲזִיקִים בָּהּ
וְתֹמְכֶיהָ מְאֻשָּׁר

Do Not Fear

The LORD founded the earth by wisdom;
He established the heavens by understanding;
By His knowledge the depths burst apart,
And the skies distilled dew.
My son, do not lose sight of them;
Hold on to resourcefulness and foresight.
They will give life to your spirit
And grace to your throat.
Then you will go your way safely
And not injure your feet.
When you lie down you will be unafraid;
You will lie down and your sleep will be
    sweet.
You will not fear sudden terror
Or the disaster that comes upon the wicked,
For the LORD will be your trust;
He will keep your feet from being caught.

Proverbs 3:19–26

Acquire Wisdom

Acquire wisdom, acquire discernment;
Do not forget and do not swerve from my
    words.
Do not forsake her and she will guard you;
Love her and she will protect you.
The beginning of wisdom is – acquire
    wisdom;

יְהֹוָה בְּחָכְמָה יָסַד־אָרֶץ
כּוֹנֵן שָׁמַיִם בִּתְבוּנָה
בְּדַעְתּוֹ תְּהוֹמוֹת נִבְקָעוּ
וּשְׁחָקִים יִרְעֲפוּ־טָל
בְּנִי אַל־יָלֻזוּ מֵעֵינֶיךָ
נְצֹר תֻּשִׁיָּה וּמְזִמָּה
וְיִהְיוּ חַיִּים לְנַפְשֶׁךָ
וְחֵן לְגַרְגְּרֹתֶיךָ
אָז תֵּלֵךְ לָבֶטַח דַּרְכֶּךָ
וְרַגְלְךָ לֹא תִגּוֹף
אִם־תִּשְׁכַּב לֹא־תִפְחָד
וְשָׁכַבְתָּ וְעָרְבָה שְׁנָתֶךָ
אַל־תִּירָא מִפַּחַד פִּתְאֹם
וּמִשֹּׁאַת רְשָׁעִים כִּי תָבֹא
כִּי־יְהֹוָה יִהְיֶה בְכִסְלֶךָ
וְשָׁמַר רַגְלְךָ מִלָּכֶד

קְנֵה חָכְמָה קְנֵה בִינָה
אַל־תִּשְׁכַּח וְאַל־תֵּט מֵאִמְרֵי־פִי
אַל־תַּעַזְבֶהָ וְתִשְׁמְרֶךָּ
אֱהָבֶהָ וְתִצְּרֶךָּ
רֵאשִׁית חָכְמָה קְנֵה חָכְמָה

With all your acquisitions, acquire
    discernment.
Hug her to you and she will exalt you;
She will bring you honor if you embrace her.
She will adorn your head with a graceful
    wreath;
Crown you with a glorious diadem.

Proverbs 4:5–9

Woman of Valor

*Recited at
Sabbath dinner
by a husband to
his wife*

What a rare find is a capable wife!
Her worth is far beyond that of rubies.
Her husband puts his confidence in her,
And lacks no good thing.
She is good to him, never bad,
All the days of her life.
She looks for wool and flax,
And sets her hand to them with a will.
She is like a merchant fleet,
Bringing her food from afar.
She rises while it is still night,
And supplies provisions for her household,
The daily fare of her maids.
She sets her mind on an estate and acquires
    it;
She plants a vineyard by her own labors.
She girds herself with strength,
And performs her tasks with vigor.
She sees that her business thrives;
Her lamp never goes out at night.

וּבְכָל־קִנְיָנְךָ קְנֵה בִינָה
סַלְסְלֶהָ וּתְרוֹמְמֶךָּ
תְּכַבֵּדְךָ כִּי תְחַבְּקֶנָּה
תִּתֵּן לְרֹאשְׁךָ לִוְיַת־חֵן
עֲטֶרֶת תִּפְאֶרֶת תְּמַגְּנֶךָּ

אֵשֶׁת־חַיִל מִי יִמְצָא
וְרָחֹק מִפְּנִינִים מִכְרָהּ
בָּטַח בָּהּ לֵב בַּעְלָהּ
וְשָׁלָל לֹא יֶחְסָר
גְּמָלַתְהוּ טוֹב וְלֹא־רָע
כֹּל יְמֵי חַיֶּיהָ
דָּרְשָׁה צֶמֶר וּפִשְׁתִּים
וַתַּעַשׂ בְּחֵפֶץ כַּפֶּיהָ
הָיְתָה כָּאֳנִיּוֹת סוֹחֵר
מִמֶּרְחָק תָּבִיא לַחְמָהּ
וַתָּקָם בְּעוֹד לַיְלָה
וַתִּתֵּן טֶרֶף לְבֵיתָהּ
וְחֹק לְנַעֲרֹתֶיהָ
זָמְמָה שָׂדֶה וַתִּקָּחֵהוּ
מִפְּרִי כַפֶּיהָ נָטַע נָטְעָה כָּרֶם
חָגְרָה בְעוֹז מָתְנֶיהָ
וַתְּאַמֵּץ זְרֹעוֹתֶיהָ
טָעֲמָה כִּי־טוֹב סַחְרָהּ
לֹא־יִכְבֶּה בליל בַּלַּיְלָה נֵרָהּ

215

She sets her hand to the distaff;
Her fingers work the spindle.
She gives generously to the poor;
Her hands are stretched out to the needy.
She is not worried for her household because
    of snow,
For her whole household is dressed in
    crimson.
She makes covers for herself;
Her clothing is linen and purple.
Her husband is prominent in the gates,
As he sits among the elders of the land.
She makes cloth and sells it,
And offers a girdle to the merchant.
She is clothed with strength and splendor;
She looks to the future cheerfully.
Her mouth is full of wisdom,
Her tongue with kindly teaching.
She oversees the activities of her household
And never eats the bread of idleness.
Her children declare her happy;
Her husband praises her,
"Many women have done well,
But you surpass them all."
Grace is deceptive,
Beauty is illusory;
It is for her fear of the LORD
That a woman is to be praised.
Extol her for the fruit of her hand,
And let her works praise her in the gates.

Proverbs 31:10–31

יָדֶיהָ שִׁלְּחָה בַכִּישׁוֹר

וְכַפֶּיהָ תָּמְכוּ פָלֶךְ

כַּפָּהּ פָּרְשָׂה לֶעָנִי

וְיָדֶיהָ שִׁלְּחָה לָאֶבְיוֹן

לֹא־תִירָא לְבֵיתָהּ מִשָּׁלֶג

כִּי כָל־בֵּיתָהּ לָבֻשׁ שָׁנִים

מַרְבַדִּים עָשְׂתָה־לָּהּ

שֵׁשׁ וְאַרְגָּמָן לְבוּשָׁהּ

נוֹדָע בַּשְּׁעָרִים בַּעְלָהּ

בְּשִׁבְתּוֹ עִם־זִקְנֵי־אָרֶץ

סָדִין עָשְׂתָה וַתִּמְכֹּר

וַחֲגוֹר נָתְנָה לַכְּנַעֲנִי

עֹז־וְהָדָר לְבוּשָׁהּ

וַתִּשְׂחַק לְיוֹם אַחֲרוֹן

פִּיהָ פָּתְחָה בְחָכְמָה

וְתוֹרַת־חֶסֶד עַל־לְשׁוֹנָהּ

צוֹפִיָּה הֲלִיכוֹת בֵּיתָהּ

וְלֶחֶם עַצְלוּת לֹא תֹאכֵל

קָמוּ בָנֶיהָ וַיְאַשְּׁרוּהָ

בַּעְלָהּ וַיְהַלְלָהּ

רַבּוֹת בָּנוֹת עָשׂוּ חָיִל

וְאַתְּ עָלִית עַל־כֻּלָּנָה

שֶׁקֶר הַחֵן וְהֶבֶל הַיֹּפִי

אִשָּׁה יִרְאַת־יְהֹוָה הִיא תִתְהַלָּל

תְּנוּ־לָהּ מִפְּרִי יָדֶיהָ

וִיהַלְלוּהָ בַשְּׁעָרִים מַעֲשֶׂיהָ

217

On Wisdom

For as wisdom grows, vexation grows;
To increase learning is to increase heartache.

Ecclesiastes 1:18

Wisdom is superior to folly
As light is superior to darkness;
A wise man has his eyes in his head,
Whereas a fool walks in darkness.

Ecclesiastes 2:13–14

Observations

I realized, too, that whatever God has
    brought to pass will recur evermore:
Nothing can be added to it
And nothing taken from it—
    and God has brought to pass that men
    revere Him.
What is occurring occurred long since,
And what is to occur occurred long since:
    and God seeks the pursued.
And, indeed, I have observed under the sun:
Alongside justice there is wickedness,
Alongside righteousness there is wickedness.

Ecclesiastes 3:14–16

כִּי בְּרֹב חָכְמָה רָב־כָּעַס
וְיוֹסִיף דַּעַת יוֹסִיף מַכְאוֹב

שֶׁיֵּשׁ יִתְרוֹן לַחָכְמָה מִן־הַסִּכְלוּת
כִּיתְרוֹן הָאוֹר מִן־הַחֹשֶׁךְ
הֶחָכָם עֵינָיו בְּרֹאשׁוֹ
וְהַכְּסִיל בַּחֹשֶׁךְ הוֹלֵךְ

יָדַעְתִּי כִּי כָּל־אֲשֶׁר יַעֲשֶׂה הָאֱלֹהִים
הוּא יִהְיֶה לְעוֹלָם
עָלָיו אֵין לְהוֹסִיף
וּמִמֶּנּוּ אֵין לִגְרֹעַ
וְהָאֱלֹהִים עָשָׂה שֶׁיִּרְאוּ מִלְּפָנָיו
מַה־שֶּׁהָיָה כְּבָר הוּא
וַאֲשֶׁר לִהְיוֹת כְּבָר הָיָה
וְהָאֱלֹהִים יְבַקֵּשׁ אֶת־נִרְדָּף וְעוֹד
רָאִיתִי תַּחַת הַשָּׁמֶשׁ
מְקוֹם הַמִּשְׁפָּט שָׁמָּה הָרֶשַׁע
וּמְקוֹם הַצֶּדֶק שָׁמָּה הָרָשַׁע

The fool folds his hands together
And has to eat his own flesh.
[But no less truly],
Better is a handful of gratification
Than two fistfuls of labor which is pursuit of
    wind.

Ecclesiastes 4:5–6

I have further observed under the sun that
The race is not won by the swift,
Nor the battle by the valiant;
Nor is bread won by the wise,
Nor wealth by the intelligent,
Nor favor by the learned.

Ecclesiastes 9:11

Futility!

Utter futility!—said Koheleth—
Utter futility! All is futile!
What real value is there for a man
In all the gains he makes beneath the sun?
One generation goes, another comes,
But the earth remains the same forever.
The sun rises, and the sun sets—
And glides back to where it rises.
Southward blowing,
Turning northward,
Ever turning blows the wind;
On its rounds the wind returns.

הַכְּסִיל֙ חֹבֵ֣ק אֶת־יָדָ֔יו
וְאֹכֵ֖ל אֶת־בְּשָׂרֽוֹ
ט֕וֹב מְלֹ֥א כַ֖ף נָ֑חַת
מִמְּלֹ֥א חָפְנַ֛יִם עָמָ֖ל וּרְע֥וּת רֽוּחַ

11 שַׁ֣בְתִּי וְרָאֹ֣ה תַֽחַת־הַשֶּׁ֗מֶשׁ כִּ֣י
לֹא֩ לַקַּלִּ֨ים הַמֵּר֜וֹץ
וְלֹ֧א לַגִּבּוֹרִ֣ים הַמִּלְחָמָ֗ה
וְ֠גַם לֹ֣א לַחֲכָמִ֥ים לֶ֙חֶם֙
וְגַ֨ם לֹ֤א לַנְּבֹנִים֙ עֹ֔שֶׁר
וְגַ֛ם לֹ֥א לַיֹּדְעִ֖ים חֵ֑ן

הֲבֵ֤ל הֲבָלִים֙ אָמַ֣ר קֹהֶ֔לֶת
הֲבֵ֥ל הֲבָלִ֖ים הַכֹּ֥ל הָֽבֶל
מַה־יִּתְר֖וֹן לָֽאָדָ֑ם
בְּכָל־עֲמָל֔וֹ שֶֽׁיַּעֲמֹ֖ל תַּ֥חַת הַשָּֽׁמֶשׁ
דּ֤וֹר הֹלֵךְ֙ וְד֣וֹר בָּ֔א
וְהָאָ֖רֶץ לְעוֹלָ֥ם עֹמָֽדֶת
וְזָרַ֥ח הַשֶּׁ֖מֶשׁ וּבָ֣א הַשָּׁ֑מֶשׁ
וְאֶ֨ל־מְקוֹמ֔וֹ שׁוֹאֵ֛ף זוֹרֵ֥חַ ה֖וּא שָֽׁם
הוֹלֵךְ֙ אֶל־דָּר֔וֹם
וְסוֹבֵ֖ב אֶל־צָפ֑וֹן
סוֹבֵ֤ב ׀ סֹבֵב֙ הוֹלֵ֣ךְ הָר֔וּחַ
וְעַל־סְבִיבֹתָ֖יו שָׁ֥ב הָרֽוּחַ

221

All streams flow into the sea,
Yet the sea is never full;
To the place from which they flow
The streams flow back again.
All such things are wearisome:
No man can ever state them;
The eye never has enough of seeing,
Nor the ear enough of hearing.
Only that shall happen
Which has happened,
Only that occur
Which has occurred;
There is nothing new
Beneath the sun!

Ecclesiastes 1:2–9

There Is a Time

A season is set for everything, a time for
    every experience under heaven:
A time for being born and a time for dying,
A time for planting and a time for uprooting
    the planted;
A time for slaying and a time for healing,
A time for tearing down and a time for
    building up;
A time for weeping and a time for laughing,
A time for wailing and a time for dancing;
A time for throwing stones and a time for
    gathering stones,

כָּל־הַנְּחָלִים הֹלְכִים אֶל־הַיָּם
וְהַיָּם אֵינֶנּוּ מָלֵא
אֶל־מְקוֹם שֶׁהַנְּחָלִים הֹלְכִים
שָׁם הֵם שָׁבִים לָלָכֶת
כָּל־הַדְּבָרִים יְגֵעִים
לֹא־יוּכַל אִישׁ לְדַבֵּר
לֹא־תִשְׂבַּע עַיִן לִרְאוֹת
וְלֹא־תִמָּלֵא אֹזֶן מִשְּׁמֹעַ
מַה־שֶּׁהָיָה
הוּא שֶׁיִּהְיֶה
וּמַה־שֶּׁנַּעֲשָׂה
הוּא שֶׁיֵּעָשֶׂה
וְאֵין כָּל־חָדָשׁ
תַּחַת הַשָּׁמֶשׁ

לַכֹּל זְמָן וְעֵת לְכָל־חֵפֶץ תַּחַת
הַשָּׁמָיִם
עֵת לָלֶדֶת וְעֵת לָמוּת
עֵת לָטַעַת וְעֵת לַעֲקוֹר נָטוּעַ
עֵת לַהֲרוֹג וְעֵת לִרְפּוֹא
עֵת לִפְרוֹץ וְעֵת לִבְנוֹת
עֵת לִבְכּוֹת וְעֵת לִשְׂחוֹק
עֵת סְפוֹד וְעֵת רְקוֹד
עֵת לְהַשְׁלִיךְ אֲבָנִים וְעֵת כְּנוֹס אֲבָנִים

A time for embracing and a time for
   shunning embraces;
A time for seeking and a time for losing,
A time for keeping and a time for discarding;
A time for ripping and a time for sewing,
A time for silence and a time for speaking;
A time for loving and a time for hating;
A time for war and a time for peace.

Ecclesiastes 3:1–8

עֵת לַחֲבוֹק וְעֵת לִרְחֹק מֵחַבֵּק
עֵת לְבַקֵּשׁ וְעֵת לְאַבֵּד
עֵת לִשְׁמוֹר וְעֵת לְהַשְׁלִיךְ
עֵת לִקְרוֹעַ וְעֵת לִתְפּוֹר
עֵת לַחֲשׁוֹת וְעֵת לְדַבֵּר
עֵת לֶאֱהֹב וְעֵת לִשְׂנֹא
עֵת מִלְחָמָה וְעֵת שָׁלוֹם

LOVE SONGS

The Song of Songs
1

The Song of Songs, by Solomon.
Oh, give me of the kisses of your mouth,
For your love is more delightful than wine.
Your ointments yield a sweet fragrance,
Your name is like finest oil—
Therefore do maidens love you.
Draw me after you, let us run!
The king has brought me to his chambers.
Let us delight and rejoice in your love,
Savoring it more than wine—
Like new wine they love you!
I am dark, but comely,
O daughters of Jerusalem—
Like the tents of Kedar,
Like the pavilions of Solomon.
Don't stare at me because I am swarthy,
Because the sun has gazed upon me.
My mother's sons quarreled with me,
They made me guard the vineyards;
My own vineyard I did not guard.
Tell me, you whom I love so well;
Where do you pasture your sheep?
Where do you rest them at noon?
Let me not be as one who strays
Beside the flocks of your fellows.
If you do not know, O fairest of women,
Go follow the tracks of the sheep,

שִׁיר הַשִּׁירִים אֲשֶׁר לִשְׁלֹמֹה
יִשָּׁקֵנִי מִנְּשִׁיקוֹת פִּיהוּ
כִּי־טוֹבִים דֹּדֶיךָ מִיָּיִן
לְרֵיחַ שְׁמָנֶיךָ טוֹבִים
שֶׁמֶן תּוּרַק שְׁמֶךָ
עַל־כֵּן עֲלָמוֹת אֲהֵבוּךָ
מָשְׁכֵנִי אַחֲרֶיךָ נָּרוּצָה
הֱבִיאַנִי הַמֶּלֶךְ חֲדָרָיו
נָגִילָה וְנִשְׂמְחָה בָּךְ
נַזְכִּירָה דֹדֶיךָ
מִיַּיִן מֵישָׁרִים אֲהֵבוּךָ
שְׁחוֹרָה אֲנִי וְנָאוָה
בְּנוֹת יְרוּשָׁלָ͏ִם
כְּאָהֳלֵי קֵדָר
כִּירִיעוֹת שְׁלֹמֹה
אַל־תִּרְאוּנִי שֶׁאֲנִי שְׁחַרְחֹרֶת
שֶׁשֱּׁזָפַתְנִי הַשָּׁמֶשׁ
בְּנֵי אִמִּי נִחֲרוּ־בִי
שָׂמֻנִי נֹטֵרָה אֶת־הַכְּרָמִים
כַּרְמִי שֶׁלִּי לֹא נָטָרְתִּי
הַגִּידָה לִּי שֶׁאָהֲבָה נַפְשִׁי
אֵיכָה תִרְעֶה
אֵיכָה תַּרְבִּיץ בַּצָּהֳרָיִם
שַׁלָּמָה אֶהְיֶה כְּעֹטְיָה
עַל עֶדְרֵי חֲבֵרֶיךָ
אִם־לֹא תֵדְעִי לָךְ הַיָּפָה בַּנָּשִׁים
צְאִי־לָךְ בְּעִקְבֵי הַצֹּאן

And graze your kids
By the tents of the shepherds.
I have likened you, my darling,
To a mare in Pharaoh's chariots:
Your cheeks are comely with plaited wreaths,
Your neck with strings of jewels.
We will add wreaths of gold
To your spangles of silver.
While the king was on his couch,
My nard gave forth its fragrance.
My beloved to me is a bag of myrrh
Lodged between my breasts.
My beloved to me is a spray of henna
    blooms
From the vineyards of En-gedi.
Ah, you are fair, my darling,
Ah, you are fair,
With your dove-like eyes!
And you, my beloved, are handsome,
Beautiful indeed!
Our couch is in a bower;
Cedars are the beams of our house,
Cypresses the rafters.

2

I am a rose of Sharon,
A lily of the valleys.
Like a lily among thorns,
So is my darling among the maidens.
Like an apple tree among trees of the forest,
So is my beloved among the youths.
I delight to sit in his shade,

וּרְעִי אֶת־גְּדִיֹּתַיִךְ
עַל מִשְׁכְּנוֹת הָרֹעִים
לְסֻסָתִי בְּרִכְבֵי פַרְעֹה
דִּמִּיתִיךְ רַעְיָתִי
נָאווּ לְחָיַיִךְ בַּתֹּרִים
צַוָּארֵךְ בַּחֲרוּזִים
תּוֹרֵי זָהָב נַעֲשֶׂה־לָּךְ
עִם נְקֻדּוֹת הַכָּסֶף
עַד־שֶׁהַמֶּלֶךְ בִּמְסִבּוֹ
נִרְדִּי נָתַן רֵיחוֹ
צְרוֹר הַמֹּר דּוֹדִי לִי
בֵּין שָׁדַי יָלִין
אֶשְׁכֹּל הַכֹּפֶר דּוֹדִי לִי
בְּכַרְמֵי עֵין גֶּדִי
הִנָּךְ יָפָה רַעְיָתִי
הִנָּךְ יָפָה
עֵינַיִךְ יוֹנִים
הִנְּךָ יָפֶה דוֹדִי
אַף נָעִים
אַף־עַרְשֵׂנוּ רַעֲנָנָה
קֹרוֹת בָּתֵּינוּ אֲרָזִים
רחיטנו רַהִיטֵנוּ בְּרוֹתִים

אֲנִי חֲבַצֶּלֶת הַשָּׁרוֹן
שׁוֹשַׁנַּת הָעֲמָקִים
כְּשׁוֹשַׁנָּה בֵּין הַחוֹחִים
כֵּן רַעְיָתִי בֵּין הַבָּנוֹת
כְּתַפּוּחַ בַּעֲצֵי הַיַּעַר
כֵּן דּוֹדִי בֵּין הַבָּנִים

And his fruit is sweet to my mouth.
He brought me to the banquet room
And his banner of love was over me.
"Sustain me with raisin cakes,
Refresh me with apples,
For I am faint with love."
His left hand was under my head,
His right arm embraced me.
I adjure you, O maidens of Jerusalem,
By gazelles or by hinds of the field:
Do not wake or rouse
Love until it please!
Hark! My beloved!
There he comes,
Leaping over mountains,
Bounding over hills.
My beloved is like a gazelle
Or like a young stag.
There he stands behind our wall,
Gazing through the window,
Peering through the lattice.
My beloved spoke thus to me,
"Arise, my darling;
My fair one, come away!
For now the winter is past,
The rains are over and gone.
The blossoms have appeared in the land,
The time of pruning has come;
The song of the turtledove
Is heard in our land.
The green figs form on the fig tree,
The vines in blossom give off fragrance.
Arise, my darling;

בְּצִלּוֹ חִמַּדְתִּי וְיָשַׁבְתִּי
וּפִרְיוֹ מָתוֹק לְחִכִּי
הֱבִיאַנִי אֶל־בֵּית הַיָּיִן
וְדִגְלוֹ עָלַי אַהֲבָה
סַמְּכוּנִי בָּאֲשִׁישׁוֹת
רַפְּדוּנִי בַּתַּפּוּחִים
כִּי־חוֹלַת אַהֲבָה אָנִי
שְׂמֹאלוֹ תַּחַת לְרֹאשִׁי
וִימִינוֹ תְּחַבְּקֵנִי
הִשְׁבַּעְתִּי אֶתְכֶם בְּנוֹת יְרוּשָׁלַ͏ִם
בִּצְבָאוֹת אוֹ בְּאַיְלוֹת הַשָּׂדֶה
אִם־תָּעִירוּ וְאִם־תְּעוֹרְרוּ
אֶת־הָאַהֲבָה עַד שֶׁתֶּחְפָּץ
קוֹל דּוֹדִי
הִנֵּה־זֶה בָּא
מְדַלֵּג עַל־הֶהָרִים
מְקַפֵּץ עַל־הַגְּבָעוֹת
דּוֹמֶה דוֹדִי לִצְבִי
אוֹ לְעֹפֶר הָאַיָּלִים
הִנֵּה־זֶה עוֹמֵד אַחַר כָּתְלֵנוּ
מַשְׁגִּיחַ מִן־הַחַלֹּנוֹת
מֵצִיץ מִן־הַחֲרַכִּים
עָנָה דוֹדִי וְאָמַר לִי
קוּמִי לָךְ רַעְיָתִי
יָפָתִי וּלְכִי־לָךְ
כִּי־הִנֵּה הַסְּתָו עָבָר
הַגֶּשֶׁם חָלַף הָלַךְ לוֹ
הַנִּצָּנִים נִרְאוּ בָאָרֶץ
עֵת הַזָּמִיר הִגִּיעַ
וְקוֹל הַתּוֹר
נִשְׁמַע בְּאַרְצֵנוּ
הַתְּאֵנָה חָנְטָה פַגֶּיהָ
וְהַגְּפָנִים סְמָדַר נָתְנוּ רֵיחַ
קוּמִי לְכִי לָךְ רַעְיָתִי

My fair one, come away!
"O my dove, in the cranny of the rocks,
Hidden by the cliff,
Let me see your face,
Let me hear your voice;
For your voice is sweet
And your face is comely."
Catch us the foxes,
The little foxes
That ruin the vineyards—
For our vineyard is in blossom.
My beloved is mine
And I am his
Who browses among the lilies.
When the day blows gently
And the shadows flee,
Set out, my beloved,
Swift as a gazelle
Or a young stag,
For the hills of spices!

3

Upon my couch at night
I sought the one I love—
I sought, but found him not.
"I must rise and roam the town,
Through the streets and through the squares;
I must seek the one I love."
I sought but found him not.
I met the watchmen
Who patrol the town.

יָפָתִי וּלְכִי־לָךְ

יוֹנָתִי בְּחַגְוֵי הַסֶּלַע

בְּסֵתֶר הַמַּדְרֵגָה

הַרְאִינִי אֶת־מַרְאַיִךְ

הַשְׁמִיעִינִי אֶת־קוֹלֵךְ

כִּי־קוֹלֵךְ עָרֵב

וּמַרְאֵיךְ נָאוֶה

אֶחֱזוּ־לָנוּ שׁוּעָלִים

שׁוּעָלִים קְטַנִּים

מְחַבְּלִים כְּרָמִים

וּכְרָמֵינוּ סְמָדַר

דּוֹדִי לִי

וַאֲנִי לוֹ

הָרֹעֶה בַּשׁוֹשַׁנִּים

עַד שֶׁיָּפוּחַ הַיּוֹם

וְנָסוּ הַצְּלָלִים

סֹב דְּמֵה־לְךָ

דוֹדִי לִצְבִי

אוֹ לְעֹפֶר הָאַיָּלִים

עַל־הָרֵי בָתֶר

עַל־מִשְׁכָּבִי בַּלֵּילוֹת

בִּקַּשְׁתִּי אֵת שֶׁאָהֲבָה נַפְשִׁי

בִּקַּשְׁתִּיו וְלֹא מְצָאתִיו

אָקוּמָה נָּא וַאֲסוֹבְבָה בָעִיר

בַּשְּׁוָקִים וּבָרְחֹבוֹת

אֲבַקְשָׁה אֵת שֶׁאָהֲבָה נַפְשִׁי

בִּקַּשְׁתִּיו וְלֹא מְצָאתִיו

מְצָאוּנִי הַשֹּׁמְרִים

הַסֹּבְבִים בָּעִיר

233

"Have you seen the one I love?"
Scarcely had I passed them
When I found the one I love.
I held him fast, I would not let him go
Till I brought him to my mother's house,
To the chamber of her who conceived me.
I adjure you, O maidens of Jerusalem,
By gazelles or by hinds of the field:
Do not wake or rouse
Love until it please!
Who is she that comes up from the desert
Like columns of smoke,
In clouds of myrrh and frankincense,
Of all the powders of the merchant?
There is Solomon's couch,
Encircled by sixty warriors
Of the warriors of Israel,
All of them trained in warfare,
Skilled in battle,
Each with sword on thigh
Because of terror by night.
King Solomon made him a palanquin
Of wood from Lebanon.
He made its posts of silver,
Its back of gold,
Its seat of purple wool.
Within, it was decked with love
By the maidens of Jerusalem.
O maidens of Zion, go forth
And gaze upon King Solomon
Wearing the crown that his mother
Gave him on his wedding day,
On his day of bliss.

אֵת שֶׁאָהֲבָה נַפְשִׁי רְאִיתֶם
כִּמְעַט שֶׁעָבַרְתִּי מֵהֶם
עַד שֶׁמָּצָאתִי אֵת שֶׁאָהֲבָה נַפְשִׁי
אֲחַזְתִּיו וְלֹא אַרְפֶּנּוּ
עַד־שֶׁהֲבֵיאתִיו אֶל־בֵּית אִמִּי
וְאֶל־חֶדֶר הוֹרָתִי
הִשְׁבַּעְתִּי אֶתְכֶם בְּנוֹת יְרוּשָׁלַ͏ִם
בִּצְבָאוֹת אוֹ בְּאַיְלוֹת הַשָּׂדֶה
אִם־תָּעִירוּ וְאִם־תְּעוֹרְרוּ
אֶת־הָאַהֲבָה עַד שֶׁתֶּחְפָּץ
מִי זֹאת עֹלָה מִן־הַמִּדְבָּר
כְּתִימֲרוֹת עָשָׁן
מְקֻטֶּרֶת מוֹר וּלְבוֹנָה
מִכֹּל אַבְקַת רוֹכֵל
הִנֵּה מִטָּתוֹ שֶׁלִּשְׁלֹמֹה
שִׁשִּׁים גִּבֹּרִים סָבִיב לָהּ
מִגִּבֹּרֵי יִשְׂרָאֵל
כֻּלָּם אֲחֻזֵי חֶרֶב
מְלֻמְּדֵי מִלְחָמָה
אִישׁ חַרְבּוֹ עַל־יְרֵכוֹ
מִפַּחַד בַּלֵּילוֹת
אַפִּרְיוֹן עָשָׂה לוֹ הַמֶּלֶךְ שְׁלֹמֹה
מֵעֲצֵי הַלְּבָנוֹן
עַמּוּדָיו עָשָׂה כֶסֶף
רְפִידָתוֹ זָהָב
מֶרְכָּבוֹ אַרְגָּמָן
תּוֹכוֹ רָצוּף אַהֲבָה
מִבְּנוֹת יְרוּשָׁלָ͏ִם
צְאֶינָה וּרְאֶינָה בְּנוֹת צִיּוֹן
בַּמֶּלֶךְ שְׁלֹמֹה
בָּעֲטָרָה שֶׁעִטְּרָה־לּוֹ אִמּוֹ
בְּיוֹם חֲתֻנָּתוֹ
וּבְיוֹם שִׂמְחַת לִבּוֹ

4

Ah, you are fair, my darling,
Ah, you are fair.
Your eyes are like doves
Behind your veil.
Your hair is like a flock of goats
Streaming down Mount Gilead.
Your teeth are like a flock of ewes
Climbing up from the washing pool;
All of them bear twins,
And not one loses her young.
Your lips are like a crimson thread,
Your mouth is lovely.
Your brow behind your veil
Gleams like a pomegranate split open.
Your neck is like the Tower of David,
Built to hold weapons,
Hung with a thousand shields—
All the quivers of warriors.
Your breasts are like two fawns,
Twins of a gazelle,
Browsing among the lilies.
When the day blows gently
And the shadows flee,
I will betake me to the mount of myrrh,
To the hill of frankincense.
Every part of you is fair, my darling,
There is no blemish in you.
From Lebanon come with me;
From Lebanon, my bride, with me!
Trip down from Amana's peak,
From the peak of Senir and Hermon,
From the dens of lions,

הִנָּךְ יָפָה רַעְיָתִי
הִנָּךְ יָפָה
עֵינַיִךְ יוֹנִים
מִבַּעַד לְצַמָּתֵךְ
שַׂעְרֵךְ כְּעֵדֶר הָעִזִּים
שֶׁגָּלְשׁוּ מֵהַר גִּלְעָד
שִׁנַּיִךְ כְּעֵדֶר הַקְּצוּבוֹת
שֶׁעָלוּ מִן־הָרַחְצָה
שֶׁכֻּלָּם מַתְאִימוֹת
וְשַׁכֻּלָה אֵין בָּהֶם
כְּחוּט הַשָּׁנִי שִׂפְתֹתַיִךְ
וּמִדְבָּרֵיךְ נָאוֶה
כְּפֶלַח הָרִמּוֹן
רַקָּתֵךְ מִבַּעַד לְצַמָּתֵךְ
כְּמִגְדַּל דָּוִיד צַוָּארֵךְ
בָּנוּי לְתַלְפִּיּוֹת
אֶלֶף הַמָּגֵן תָּלוּי עָלָיו
כֹּל שִׁלְטֵי הַגִּבּוֹרִים
שְׁנֵי שָׁדַיִךְ כִּשְׁנֵי עֳפָרִים
תְּאוֹמֵי צְבִיָּה
הָרוֹעִים בַּשּׁוֹשַׁנִּים
עַד שֶׁיָּפוּחַ הַיּוֹם
וְנָסוּ הַצְּלָלִים
אֵלֶךְ לִי אֶל־הַר הַמּוֹר
וְאֶל־גִּבְעַת הַלְּבוֹנָה
כֻּלָּךְ יָפָה רַעְיָתִי
וּמוּם אֵין בָּךְ
אִתִּי מִלְּבָנוֹן כַּלָּה
אִתִּי מִלְּבָנוֹן תָּבוֹאִי
תָּשׁוּרִי מֵרֹאשׁ אֲמָנָה
מֵרֹאשׁ שְׂנִיר וְחֶרְמוֹן

From the hills of leopards.
You have captured my heart,
My own, my bride,
You have captured my heart
With one glance of your eyes,
With one coil of your necklace.
How sweet is your love,
My own, my bride!
How much more delightful your love than
   wine,
Your ointments more fragrant
Than any spice!
Sweetness drops
From your lips, O bride;
Honey and milk
Are under your tongue;
And the scent of your robes
Is like the scent of Lebanon.
A garden locked
Is my own, my bride,
A fountain locked,
A sealed-up spring.
Your limbs are an orchard of pomegranates
And of all luscious fruits,
Of henna and of nard—
Nard and saffron,
Fragrant reed and cinnamon,
With all aromatic woods,
Myrrh and aloes—
All the choice perfumes.
You are a garden spring,
A well of fresh water,
A rill of Lebanon.
Awake, O north wind,

מִמְּעֹנוֹת אֲרָיוֹת
מֵהַרְרֵי נְמֵרִים
לִבַּבְתִּנִי
אֲחֹתִי כַלָּה
לִבַּבְתִּינִי
בְּאַחַד בְּאַחַת מֵעֵינַיִךְ
בְּאַחַד עֲנָק מִצַּוְּרֹנָיִךְ
מַה־יָּפוּ דֹדַיִךְ
אֲחֹתִי כַלָּה
מַה־טֹּבוּ דֹדַיִךְ מִיַּיִן
וְרֵיחַ שְׁמָנַיִךְ
מִכָּל־בְּשָׂמִים
נֹפֶת תִּטֹּפְנָה
שִׂפְתוֹתַיִךְ כַּלָּה
דְּבַשׁ וְחָלָב
תַּחַת לְשׁוֹנֵךְ
וְרֵיחַ שַׂלְמֹתַיִךְ
כְּרֵיחַ לְבָנוֹן
גַּן נָעוּל
אֲחֹתִי כַלָּה
גַּל נָעוּל
מַעְיָן חָתוּם
שְׁלָחַיִךְ פַּרְדֵּס רִמּוֹנִים
עִם פְּרִי מְגָדִים
כְּפָרִים עִם־נְרָדִים
נֵרְדְּ וְכַרְכֹּם
קָנֶה וְקִנָּמוֹן
עִם כָּל־עֲצֵי לְבוֹנָה
מֹר וַאֲהָלוֹת
עִם כָּל־רָאשֵׁי בְשָׂמִים
מַעְיַן גַּנִּים
בְּאֵר מַיִם חַיִּים
וְנֹזְלִים מִן־לְבָנוֹן
עוּרִי צָפוֹן

Come, O south wind!
Blow upon my garden,
That its perfume may spread.
Let my beloved come to his garden
And enjoy its luscious fruits!

5

I have come to my garden,
My own, my bride;
I have plucked my myrrh and spice,
Eaten my honey and honeycomb,
Drunk my wine and my milk.
Eat, lovers, and drink:
Drink deep of love!
I was asleep,
But my heart was wakeful.
Hark, my beloved knocks!
"Let me in, my own,
My darling, my faultless dove!
For my head is drenched with dew,
My locks with the damp of night."
I had taken off my robe—
Was I to don it again?
I had bathed my feet—
Was I to soil them again?
My beloved took his hand off the latch,
And my heart was stirred for him.
I rose to let in my beloved;
My hands dripped myrrh—
My fingers, flowing myrrh—
Upon the handles of the bolt.
I opened the door for my beloved,

וּבוֹאִי תֵימָן
הָפִיחִי גַנִּי
יִזְּלוּ בְשָׂמָיו
יָבֹא דוֹדִי לְגַנּוֹ
וְיֹאכַל פְּרִי מְגָדָיו

בָּאתִי לְגַנִּי
אֲחֹתִי כַלָּה
אָרִיתִי מוֹרִי עִם־בְּשָׂמִי
אָכַלְתִּי יַעְרִי עִם־דִּבְשִׁי
שָׁתִיתִי יֵינִי עִם־חֲלָבִי
אִכְלוּ רֵעִים שְׁתוּ
וְשִׁכְרוּ דּוֹדִים
אֲנִי יְשֵׁנָה
וְלִבִּי עֵר
קוֹל דּוֹדִי דוֹפֵק
פִּתְחִי־לִּי אֲחֹתִי
רַעְיָתִי יוֹנָתִי תַמָּתִי
שֶׁרֹאשִׁי נִמְלָא־טָל
קְוֻצּוֹתַי רְסִיסֵי לָיְלָה
פָּשַׁטְתִּי אֶת־כֻּתָּנְתִּי
אֵיכָכָה אֶלְבָּשֶׁנָּה
רָחַצְתִּי אֶת־רַגְלַי
אֵיכָכָה אֲטַנְּפֵם
דּוֹדִי שָׁלַח יָדוֹ מִן־הַחֹר
וּמֵעַי הָמוּ עָלָיו
קַמְתִּי אֲנִי לִפְתֹּחַ לְדוֹדִי
וְיָדַי נָטְפוּ־מוֹר
וְאֶצְבְּעֹתַי מוֹר עֹבֵר
עַל כַּפּוֹת הַמַּנְעוּל

241

But my beloved had turned and gone.
I was faint because of what he said.
I sought, but found him not;
I called, but he did not answer.
I met the watchmen
Who patrol the town;
They struck me, they bruised me.
The guards of the walls
Stripped me of my mantle.
I adjure you, O maidens of Jerusalem!
If you meet my beloved, tell him this:
That I am faint with love.
How is your beloved better than another,
O fairest of women?
How is your beloved better than another
That you adjure us so?
My beloved is clear-skinned and ruddy,
Preeminent among ten thousand.
His head is finest gold,
His locks are curled
And black as a raven.
His eyes are like doves
By watercourses,
Bathed in milk,
Set by a brimming pool.
His cheeks are like beds of spices,
Banks of perfume
His lips are like lilies;
They drip flowing myrrh.
His hands are rods of gold,
Studded with beryl;
His belly a tablet of ivory,
Adorned with sapphires.
His legs are like marble pillars

פָּתַחְתִּי אֲנִי לְדוֹדִי
וְדוֹדִי חָמַק עָבָר
נַפְשִׁי יָצְאָה בְדַבְּרוֹ
בִּקַּשְׁתִּיהוּ וְלֹא מְצָאתִיהוּ
קְרָאתִיו וְלֹא עָנָנִי
מְצָאֻנִי הַשֹּׁמְרִים
הַסֹּבְבִים בָּעִיר
הִכּוּנִי פְצָעוּנִי
נָשְׂאוּ אֶת־רְדִידִי מֵעָלַי
שֹׁמְרֵי הַחֹמוֹת
הִשְׁבַּעְתִּי אֶתְכֶם בְּנוֹת יְרוּשָׁלָם
אִם־תִּמְצְאוּ אֶת־דּוֹדִי מַה־תַּגִּידוּ לוֹ
שֶׁחוֹלַת אַהֲבָה אָנִי
מַה־דּוֹדֵךְ מִדּוֹד
הַיָּפָה בַּנָּשִׁים
מַה־דּוֹדֵךְ מִדּוֹד
שֶׁכָּכָה הִשְׁבַּעְתָּנוּ
דּוֹדִי צַח וְאָדוֹם
דָּגוּל מֵרְבָבָה
רֹאשׁוֹ כֶּתֶם פָּז
קְוֻצּוֹתָיו תַּלְתַּלִּים
שְׁחֹרוֹת כָּעוֹרֵב
עֵינָיו כְּיוֹנִים
עַל־אֲפִיקֵי מָיִם
רֹחֲצוֹת בֶּחָלָב
יֹשְׁבוֹת עַל־מִלֵּאת
לְחָיָו כַּעֲרוּגַת הַבֹּשֶׂם
מִגְדְּלוֹת מֶרְקָחִים
שִׂפְתוֹתָיו שׁוֹשַׁנִּים
נֹטְפוֹת מוֹר עֹבֵר
יָדָיו גְּלִילֵי זָהָב
מְמֻלָּאִים בַּתַּרְשִׁישׁ
מֵעָיו עֶשֶׁת שֵׁן
מְעֻלֶּפֶת סַפִּירִים

Set in sockets of fine gold.
He is majestic as Lebanon,
Stately as the cedars.
His mouth is delicious
And all of him is delightful.
Such is my beloved,
Such is my darling,
O maidens of Jerusalem!

6

"Whither has your beloved gone,
O fairest of women?
Whither has your beloved turned?
Let us seek him with you."
My beloved has gone down to his garden,
To the beds of spices,
To browse in the gardens
And to pick lilies.
I am my beloved's
And my beloved is mine;
He browses among the lilies.
You are beautiful, my darling, as Tirzah,
Comely as Jerusalem,
Awesome as bannered hosts.
Turn your eyes away from me,
For they overwhelm me!
Your hair is like a flock of goats
Streaming down from Gilead.
Your teeth are like a flock of ewes
Climbing up from the washing pool;
All of them bear twins,
And not one loses her young.

שׁוֹקָיו עַמּוּדֵי שֵׁשׁ
מְיֻסָּדִים עַל־אַדְנֵי־פָז
מַרְאֵהוּ כַּלְּבָנוֹן
בָּחוּר כָּאֲרָזִים
חִכּוֹ מַמְתַקִּים
וְכֻלּוֹ מַחֲמַדִּים
זֶה דוֹדִי
וְזֶה רֵעִי
בְּנוֹת יְרוּשָׁלָם

אָנָה הָלַךְ דּוֹדֵךְ
הַיָּפָה בַּנָּשִׁים
אָנָה פָּנָה דוֹדֵךְ
וּנְבַקְשֶׁנּוּ עִמָּךְ
דּוֹדִי יָרַד לְגַנּוֹ
לַעֲרוּגוֹת הַבֹּשֶׂם
לִרְעוֹת בַּגַּנִּים
וְלִלְקֹט שׁוֹשַׁנִּים
אֲנִי לְדוֹדִי
וְדוֹדִי לִי
הָרֹעֶה בַּשּׁוֹשַׁנִּים
יָפָה אַתְּ רַעְיָתִי כְּתִרְצָה
נָאוָה כִּירוּשָׁלָם
אֲיֻמָּה כַּנִּדְגָּלוֹת
הָסֵבִּי עֵינַיִךְ מִנֶּגְדִּי
שֶׁהֵם הִרְהִיבֻנִי
שַׂעְרֵךְ כְּעֵדֶר הָעִזִּים
שֶׁגָּלְשׁוּ מִן־הַגִּלְעָד
שִׁנַּיִךְ כְּעֵדֶר הָרְחֵלִים
שֶׁעָלוּ מִן־הָרַחְצָה
שֶׁכֻּלָּם מַתְאִימוֹת

Your brow behind your veil
Gleams like a pomegranate split open.
There are sixty queens,
And eighty concubines,
And damsels without number.
Only one is my dove,
My perfect one,
The only one of her mother,
The delight of her who bore her.
Maidens see and acclaim her;
Queens and concubines, and praise her.
Who is she that shines through like the dawn,
Beautiful as the moon,
Radiant as the sun
Awesome as bannered hosts?
I went down to the nut grove
To see the budding of the vale;
To see if the vines had blossomed,
If the pomegranates were in bloom.
Before I knew it,
My desire set me
Mid the chariots of Ammi-nadib.

7

Turn back, turn back,
O maid of Shulem!
Turn back, turn back,
That we may gaze upon you.
"Why will you gaze at the Shulammite
In the Mahanaim dance?"
How lovely are your feet in sandals,
O daughter of nobles!

וְשַׁכֻּלָה אֵין בָּהֶם
כְּפֶלַח הָרִמּוֹן
רַקָּתֵךְ מִבַּעַד לְצַמָּתֵךְ
שִׁשִּׁים הֵמָּה מְלָכוֹת
וּשְׁמֹנִים פִּילַגְשִׁים
וַעֲלָמוֹת אֵין מִסְפָּר
אַחַת הִיא יוֹנָתִי
תַמָּתִי
אַחַת הִיא לְאִמָּהּ
בָּרָה הִיא לְיוֹלַדְתָּהּ
רָאוּהָ בָנוֹת וַיְאַשְּׁרוּהָ
מְלָכוֹת וּפִילַגְשִׁים וַיְהַלְלוּהָ
מִי־זֹאת הַנִּשְׁקָפָה כְּמוֹ־שָׁחַר
יָפָה כַלְּבָנָה
בָּרָה כַּחַמָּה
אֲיֻמָּה כַּנִּדְגָּלוֹת
אֶל־גִּנַּת אֱגוֹז יָרַדְתִּי
לִרְאוֹת בְּאִבֵּי הַנָּחַל
לִרְאוֹת הֲפָרְחָה הַגֶּפֶן
הֵנֵצוּ הָרִמֹּנִים
לֹא יָדַעְתִּי
נַפְשִׁי שָׂמַתְנִי
מַרְכְּבוֹת עַמִּי־נָדִיב

שׁוּבִי שׁוּבִי
הַשּׁוּלַמִּית
שׁוּבִי שׁוּבִי
וְנֶחֱזֶה־בָּךְ
מַה־תֶּחֱזוּ בַּשּׁוּלַמִּית
כִּמְחֹלַת הַמַּחֲנָיִם
מַה־יָּפוּ פְעָמַיִךְ בַּנְּעָלִים
בַּת־נָדִיב
חַמּוּקֵי יְרֵכַיִךְ כְּמוֹ חֲלָאִים

247

Your rounded thighs are like jewels,
The work of a master's hand.
Your navel is like a round goblet—
Let mixed wine not be lacking!—
Your belly like a heap of wheat
Hedged about with lilies.
Your breasts are like two fawns,
Twins of a gazelle.
Your neck is like a tower of ivory,
Your eyes like pools in Heshbon
By the gate of Bath-rabbim,
Your nose like the Lebanon tower
That faces toward Damascus.
The head upon you is like crimson wool,
The locks of your head are like purple—
A king is held captive in the tresses.
How fair you are, how beautiful!
O Love, with all its rapture!
Your stately form is like the palm,
Your breasts are like clusters.
I say: Let me climb the palm,
Let me take hold of its branches;
Let your breasts be like clusters of grapes,
Your breath like the fragrance of apples,
And your mouth like choicest wine.
"Let it flow to my beloved as new wine
Gliding over the lips of sleepers."
I am my beloved's,
And his desire is for me.
Come, my beloved,
Let us go into the open;
Let us lodge among the henna shrubs.
Let us go early to the vineyards;
Let us see if the vine has flowered,
If its blossoms have opened,

מַעֲשֵׂה יְדֵי אָמָּן

שָׁרְרֵךְ אַגַּן הַסַּהַר

אַל-יֶחְסַר הַמָּזֶג

בִּטְנֵךְ עֲרֵמַת חִטִּים

סוּגָה בַּשּׁוֹשַׁנִּים

שְׁנֵי שָׁדַיִךְ כִּשְׁנֵי עֳפָרִים

תָּאֳמֵי צְבִיָּה

צַוָּארֵךְ כְּמִגְדַּל הַשֵּׁן

עֵינַיִךְ בְּרֵכוֹת בְּחֶשְׁבּוֹן

עַל-שַׁעַר בַּת-רַבִּים

אַפֵּךְ כְּמִגְדַּל הַלְּבָנוֹן

צוֹפֶה פְּנֵי דַמָּשֶׂק

רֹאשֵׁךְ עָלַיִךְ כַּכַּרְמֶל

וְדַלַּת רֹאשֵׁךְ כָּאַרְגָּמָן

מֶלֶךְ אָסוּר בָּרְהָטִים

מַה-יָּפִית וּמַה-נָּעַמְתְּ

אַהֲבָה בַּתַּעֲנוּגִים

זֹאת קוֹמָתֵךְ דָּמְתָה לְתָמָר

וְשָׁדַיִךְ לְאַשְׁכֹּלוֹת

אָמַרְתִּי אֶעֱלֶה בְתָמָר

אֹחֲזָה בְּסַנְסִנָּיו

וְיִהְיוּ-נָא שָׁדַיִךְ כְּאֶשְׁכְּלוֹת הַגֶּפֶן

וְרֵיחַ אַפֵּךְ כַּתַּפּוּחִים

וְחִכֵּךְ כְּיֵין הַטּוֹב

הוֹלֵךְ לְדוֹדִי לְמֵישָׁרִים

דּוֹבֵב שִׂפְתֵי יְשֵׁנִים

אֲנִי לְדוֹדִי

וְעָלַי תְּשׁוּקָתוֹ

לְכָה דוֹדִי

נֵצֵא הַשָּׂדֶה

נָלִינָה בַּכְּפָרִים

נַשְׁכִּימָה לַכְּרָמִים

נִרְאֶה אִם-פָּרְחָה הַגֶּפֶן

פִּתַּח הַסְּמָדַר

If the pomegranates are in bloom.
There I will give my love to you.
The mandrakes yield their fragrance,
At our doors are all choice fruits;
Both freshly picked and long-stored
Have I kept, my beloved, for you.

8

If only it could be as with a brother,
As if you had nursed at my mother's breast:
Then I could kiss you
When I met you in the street,
And no one would despise me.
I would lead you, I would bring you
To the house of my mother,
Of her who taught me—
I would let you drink of the spiced wine,
Of my pomegranate juice.
His left hand was under my head,
His right hand caressed me.
I adjure you, O maidens of Jerusalem:
Do not wake or rouse
Love until it please!
Who is she that comes up from the desert,
Leaning upon her beloved?
Under the apple tree I roused you;
It was there your mother conceived you,
There she who bore you conceived you.
Let me be a seal upon your heart,
Like the seal upon your hand.
For love is fierce as death,
Passion is mighty as Sheol;

הֵנֵצוּ הָרִמּוֹנִים
שָׁם אֶתֵּן אֶת־דֹּדַי לָךְ
הַדּוּדָאִים נָתְנוּ־רֵיחַ
וְעַל־פְּתָחֵינוּ כָּל־מְגָדִים
חֲדָשִׁים גַּם־יְשָׁנִים
דּוֹדִי צָפַנְתִּי לָךְ

מִי יִתֶּנְךָ כְּאָח לִי
יוֹנֵק שְׁדֵי אִמִּי
אֶמְצָאֲךָ בַחוּץ
אֶשָׁקְךָ
גַּם לֹא־יָבֻזוּ לִי
אֶנְהָגֲךָ אֲבִיאֲךָ
אֶל־בֵּית אִמִּי
תְּלַמְּדֵנִי
אַשְׁקְךָ מִיַּיִן הָרֶקַח
מֵעֲסִיס רִמֹּנִי
שְׂמֹאלוֹ תַּחַת רֹאשִׁי
וִימִינוֹ תְּחַבְּקֵנִי
הִשְׁבַּעְתִּי אֶתְכֶם בְּנוֹת יְרוּשָׁלַָם
מַה־תָּעִירוּ וּמַה־תְּעֹרְרוּ
אֶת־הָאַהֲבָה עַד שֶׁתֶּחְפָּץ
מִי זֹאת עֹלָה מִן־הַמִּדְבָּר
מִתְרַפֶּקֶת עַל־דּוֹדָהּ
תַּחַת הַתַּפּוּחַ עוֹרַרְתִּיךָ
שָׁמָּה חִבְּלַתְךָ אִמֶּךָ
שָׁמָּה חִבְּלָה יְלָדַתְךָ
שִׂימֵנִי כַחוֹתָם עַל־לִבֶּךָ
כַּחוֹתָם עַל־זְרוֹעֶךָ
כִּי־עַזָּה כַמָּוֶת אַהֲבָה
קָשָׁה כִשְׁאוֹל קִנְאָה

Its darts are darts of fire,
A blazing flame.
Vast floods cannot quench love,
Nor rivers drown it.
If a man offered all his wealth for love,
He would be laughed to scorn.
"We have a little sister,
Whose breasts are not yet formed.
What shall we do for our sister
When she is spoken for?
If she be a wall,
We will build upon it a silver battlement;
If she be a door,
We will panel it in cedar."
I am a wall,
My breasts are like towers.
So I became in his eyes
As one who finds favor.
Solomon had a vineyard
In Baal-hamon.
He had to post guards in the vineyard:
A man would give for its fruit
A thousand pieces of silver.
I have my very own vineyard:
You may have the thousand, O Solomon,
And the guards of the fruit two hundred!
O you who linger in the garden,
A lover is listening;
Let me hear your voice.
"Hurry, my beloved,
Swift as a gazelle or a young stag,
To the hills of spices!"

– The Song of Songs 1:1 – 8: 14

רְשָׁפֶּיהָ רִשְׁפֵּי אֵשׁ
שַׁלְהֶבֶתְיָה
מַיִם רַבִּים לֹא יוּכְלוּ לְכַבּוֹת אֶת־
הָאַהֲבָה
וּנְהָרוֹת לֹא יִשְׁטְפוּהָ
אִם־יִתֵּן אִישׁ אֶת־כָּל־הוֹן בֵּיתוֹ בָּאַהֲבָה
בּוֹז יָבוּזוּ לוֹ
אָחוֹת לָנוּ קְטַנָּה
וְשָׁדַיִם אֵין לָהּ
מַה־נַּעֲשֶׂה לַאֲחֹתֵנוּ
בַּיּוֹם שֶׁיְּדֻבַּר־בָּהּ
אִם־חוֹמָה הִיא
נִבְנֶה עָלֶיהָ טִירַת כָּסֶף
וְאִם־דֶּלֶת הִיא
נָצוּר עָלֶיהָ לוּחַ אָרֶז
אֲנִי חוֹמָה
וְשָׁדַי כַּמִּגְדָּלוֹת
אָז הָיִיתִי בְעֵינָיו
כְּמוֹצְאֵת שָׁלוֹם
כֶּרֶם הָיָה לִשְׁלֹמֹה
בְּבַעַל הָמוֹן
נָתַן אֶת־הַכֶּרֶם לַנֹּטְרִים
אִישׁ יָבִא בְּפִרְיוֹ
אֶלֶף כָּסֶף:
כַּרְמִי שֶׁלִּי לְפָנָי
הָאֶלֶף לְךָ שְׁלֹמֹה
וּמָאתַיִם לְנֹטְרִים אֶת־פִּרְיוֹ
הַיּוֹשֶׁבֶת בַּגַּנִּים
חֲבֵרִים מַקְשִׁיבִים
לְקוֹלֵךְ הַשְׁמִיעִינִי
בְּרַח דּוֹדִי
וּדְמֵה־לְךָ לִצְבִי אוֹ לְעֹפֶר הָאַיָּלִים
עַל הָרֵי בְשָׂמִים

INDEX OF SCRIPTURAL PASSAGES